The Ragged Rebel

Gallaway, B. P.

The ragged rebel.

$10.95

DATE			
		APR 8 1993	

David Carey Nance, taken about 1866

THE RAGGED REBEL

*A Common Soldier in
W. H. Parsons' Texas Cavalry,
1861–1865*

by B. P. Gallaway

University of Texas Press, Austin

Copyright © 1988 by the University of Texas Press
All rights reserved
Printed in the United States of America

Second Paperback Printing, 1991

Requests for permission to reproduce material from this
work should be sent to
Permissions
University of Texas Press
Box 7819
Austin, Texas 78713-7819

♾ The paper used in this publication meets the minimum
requirements of American National Standard for
Information Sciences—Permanence of Paper for Printed
Library Materials, ANSI Z39.48-1984.

Library of Congress Cataloging-in-Publication Data

Gallaway, B. P.
   The ragged rebel: a common soldier in W. H.
Parsons' Texas Cavalry, 1861–1865 / by B. P.
Gallaway.
      p.   cm.
   Bibliography: p.
   Includes index.
   ISBN 0-292-77047-2 pbk.
   1. Nance, David Carey.   2. Confederate States of
America. Army. Texas Cavalry Regiment, 12th—
Biography.   3. Texas—History—Civil
War, 1861–1865—Campaigns.   4. United States—
History—Civil War, 1861–1865—Campaigns.
5. Soldiers—Texas—Biography.   I. Title.
E580.6 12th.N36G34 1988
973.7′ 464—dc19   87-28826
                                                  CIP

*This book is dedicated to the memory of
Don Heath Morris*

Renowned educator, university administrator,
Bible scholar, community leader, and
grandson of the Ragged Rebel

Contents

Preface

This study, written after fourteen years of preparation, is designed to accomplish several purposes. First, it should provide insight into the personal life of a young North Texas farmer, David Carey Nance. Enlisting in the Confederate cavalry against his father's will, he initially longed for the camaraderie of military service and the storybook adventures it seemed to promise. But, as happened with thousands of his comrades in arms, his romantic concepts of war quickly were replaced by the grim realities of suffering, hardship, and horror. As a disproportionate number of his comrades died of disease or fell mortally wounded around him, he somehow managed to stay alive, and his personal quest for an explanation for his survival constitutes a fascinating aspect of his story. Second, with the exception of Stephen Oates' *Confederate Cavalry West of the River*, little has been written about the role of mounted troops in the western Confederacy, and this study is intended to help fill that gap. And, finally, it is hoped that this book may shed new light on one of the most famous mounted units in the service of the Confederacy, William H. Parsons' Texas Cavalry Brigade.

A word of explanation concerning the narrative is in order. Because of gaps in the Nance papers, I have been forced to weave together segments of Nance's story from information taken from a multitude of other sources. Nevertheless, some holes remained. Although inference and guesswork were necessary to plug them, the segments in question are believed to be accurate in essential details. Though authority for every statement has not been cited, footnotes document each chapter, notations give the sources of all direct quotations, and a general bibliography lists all works consulted.

Dave Nance's War for Southern Independence began on September 11, 1861, in Rocket Springs, Texas, as he watched the organization of William H. Parsons' regiment of cavalry, which the next year became the core unit in the formation of Parsons' Brigade. It was a stirring ceremony, and at that time he decided to join his friends in enlisting in one of the companies of the new regiment. After defending the Trans-Mississippi in Arkansas and Louisiana, Parsons' Brigade was sent back to Texas, where Dave's war ended on May 20, 1865, in Robertson County as his regiment broke camp for the last time. The optimism and high spirits so evident in 1861 had declined rapidly the last two years as shortages of men and matériel caused battles to be lost and morale to plummet.

Just as the battle of Shiloh served notice to residents of the Confederate Trans-Mississippi that the Civil War would be no holiday excursion, so the fall of Vicksburg signaled the region's continued economic decline and impending military defeat. Living on a wild and sparsely settled frontier laced with rivers connecting with the enemy-owned Mississippi, they suddenly found themselves isolated, vulnerable, almost defenseless, and ripe for Federal conquest. During the months that followed, these hardy pioneers witnessed enemy occupation of additional segments of their territory, suffered tragically from shortages of everything, and cursed the effectiveness of the Union blockade and their own industrial insufficiency. Trapped in a web of hopelessness and despair, they braced themselves for total defeat.

Nowhere were the western Confederacy's declining fortunes more clearly evident than in the appearance of its fighting men. Lieutenant Colonel A. J. L. Fremantle, whose diary perhaps is the best single source on the subject, noted that James Duff's cavalry wore flannel shirts and black hats; the Third Texas Infantry was decked out in a strange assortment of French kepis, "wide-awakes," and Mexican sombreros; Charles Pyron's regiment had "every variety of costume"; John Liddell's Arkansas Brigade was in shirt-sleeves; and John Walker's Infantry Division in Louisiana was dressed in ragged civilian clothes. By 1864 the only common feature in their apparel was its steadily increasing need for repair. As the end drew near, their ranks thinned, and their clothes became more soiled, threadbare, makeshift, and unsightly. These conditions prevailed in every corner of the Trans-Mississippi—in the sunbaked deserts of West Texas and along the Rio Bravo, in the dank backwoods of western Louisiana and southern Arkansas, and in the swamps of the Red River and the East Texas piney woods.

Bearded, sick, hungry, dirty, and terrible, these spindle-shanked, hollow-eyed, and shabbily clad soldiers looked more like corpses in their grave clothes than living men. But they somehow continued the struggle until disarmed by the western Confederacy's total collapse.

The narrative which follows is the story of one of those gallant warriors. Although a Northern-born Yankee who disliked slavery, he saw the war as a great adventure, a fight for sectional self-determination, and a rebellion against tyranny. He served his country as a frontier patriot, a citizen-soldier, and a Southern rebel. And since his clothing, like those of his comrades, became increasingly threadbare, tattered, and torn, he indeed was . . . . . . a ragged rebel!

Acknowledgments

No writer can ever hope to acknowledge all of the assistance and courtesies received in pursuit of a project, and so I can merely mention some of the persons and institutions to whom I feel most indebted.

Obviously this book never could have been written had it not been for the cooperation and support of the descendants of David Carey Nance. Jackie Morris Warmsley, Nance's great-granddaughter, generously granted access to the family archives containing the old soldier's private papers, articles of his clothing, several military documents, dozens of photographs, and various personal keepsakes. (These items currently are in the possession of Nance's great-great-grandson, Jimmy Lawson, of the Boston law firm Oteri, Weinberg, and Lawson.) Abilene Christian University's first chancellor, Don H. Morris, and its former athletic director, A. B. Morris, graciously provided advice, personal recollections of Nance, business documents, and a rare privately printed family history. Before his death in 1974, Chancellor Morris spent countless hours with me in regularly scheduled conferences discussing his grandfather and determining the accuracy of the first three chapters of the manuscript.

I am equally grateful to other good friends—many distinguished historians—who have taken time to read portions of the manuscript and make suggestions: Alwyn Barr of Texas Tech University; Robert C. Cotner, University of Texas at Austin; Thomas Olbricht, Abilene Christian University; Marla Eden, Southwestern College, Waxahachie; Jim Eison, Museum of Science and Natural History, Little Rock; T. R. Fehrenbach, San Antonio; President Emeritus Jim Dan Hill, Wisconsin State University at Superior; Margaret Ross, *Arkansas Gazette;* Mildred Padon, Ann Bailey, and Danny Sessums, Layland Museum, Cleburne; Colonel Harold B. Simpson, Confederate Research Center, Hillsboro; President Frank E. Vandiver and Allan Ashcraft, Texas A&M University; George Werner, Railway Historical Society, Houston; Bell I.

Wiley, Agnes Scott College, Decatur, Georgia; and Charles P. Roland, U.S. Army Military History Institute, Carlisle Barracks, Pennsylvania.

I also wish to express appreciation to Floyd Dunn and R. L. Roberts of Abilene Christian University, whose encouragement and assistance have been invaluable and to the Cullen Foundation and the University's Research and Academic councils for granting generous financial support and course reductions. This assistance made possible several fact-finding tours to obscure battlesites, military campgrounds, and distant research centers, where I discovered vital and exciting new material.

And I especially want to thank the staff members of the following libraries and repositories: the Archives, University of Texas Library; Layland Museum, Cleburne; Sims Library, Waxahachie; Little Rock Public Library; the R. C. Crane Collection, Richardson Research Center for the Southwest, Hardin-Simmons Library; Texas Confederate Research Center, Hillsboro; the Jay-Rollins Library, McMurry College; Houston Public Library; the Mansfield Battle Park Museum in Louisiana; the Archives of the Brown Library and the Special Collections of the Center for Restoration Studies, Abilene Christian University; the National Archives, Washington, D.C.; the Texas State Archives, Texas State Library; the Houston Railway Historical Society Museum; the Museum of Science and Natural History, Little Rock; and the Special Collections, Northwestern State University of Louisiana Library, Nachitoches, Louisiana.

I owe a particular debt of gratitude to Mrs. L. L. McNair, who owns the old Nance farm in DeSoto; Mrs. Norman Capps, whose DeSoto property contains the Nance family cemetery; Ann E. Cerney of Wichita Falls, whose great-great-grandfather, William H. Parsons, commanded both the regiment and the brigade of which David C. Nance was a member; Mrs. A. L. Miles, who lives on Sims Bayou at the site of old Camp Parsons; and Ira S. Couvillon, whose lifetime study of the Yellow Bayou battlefield was invaluable. I likewise am grateful to Delno Roberts and Marsha Harper for devoting endless hours to correcting the manuscript. And I am indebted to my two sons, Steve and Brad, who supplied the title and made a number of helpful suggestions. But, above all, I want to thank my wife, Betty, for sustaining me during the throes of composition, and my daughter, Lori, for putting up with it all.

CHAPTER 1

Frontier Origins

*I*n the beginning nature was kind to David Carey Nance. He was blessed with the makings of a powerful physique, gregarious temperament, splendid tenor voice, and insatiable curiosity. His childhood was happy, filled with endless youthful explorations and dynamic new discoveries, and throughout his life he clung with more than ordinary fondness to his early memories.

Dave was born on February 2, 1843, "on the top of the highest hill in Middle Creek Prairie in Cass County, Illinois, . . . near the little village of Newmanville." His paternal great-grandparents, Zachariah and Susanna Nance, had been early residents of Jamestown, Virginia. His paternal grandfather, also named Zachariah, had served in the American Revolution and was present when General Cornwallis surrendered at Yorktown in 1781. His parents, Allen Quilla ("Quill") and Elizabeth Dearing Nance, were born in Kentucky but immigrated to Illinois. In his recollections, Dave wrote:

> My father was Allen Q. Nance and my mother was Elizabeth Dearing. Both were born in Green County, Kentucky, their post office being Campbellsville. At the age of nineteen my father went with his father to Illinois in 1832 when that country was a wilderness. When Mother was six years of age, her mother died and she went to live with her older sister, Sallie Nance, wife of my father's brother, Otwa Bird Nance. Uncle Otwa and Grandfather Dearing were at that time still living in Kentucky, but in 1839 Uncle Otwa also moved to Illinois and bought a farm adjoining father's farm on the north. Here Father and Mother met and were married January 11, 1841.[1]

Dave, their firstborn, spent his first nine years in Illinois, during which time Elizabeth gave birth to two daughters (Mary and Ellen) and another son (Gustavus Adolphus).[2]

But if Dave was a Southerner by ancestry and a Midwesterner by birth, he became a Texan by happenstance in the winter of 1852 when his parents decided to move to Texas. Uncle Otwa had gone to Texas the year before, purchased a half section of grazing land along Pleasant Run River (a tributary of the Trinity known today as Ten Mile Creek), and sent word back to Quill that good sheep range was available adjoining his place at four dollars an acre.[3]

So in the winter of 1852 Quill sold his Illinois property and loaded the family possessions into a large, four-horse wagon. Then he placed his wife and four children in a two-horse carriage and began a thousand-mile trek to Texas. Mary, Ellen, and Gus, ranging in age from seven years to six months, required the constant vigil of their mother; so Dave, although less than ten years old and ill with chills and fever much of the way, took turns with his father driving the two vehicles. Dave explained in his recollections that the little caravan "crossed the Illinois River at Meredosia, . . . the Mississippi at Quincy, the Missouri at Boonville, the Arkansas at Van Buren, and the Red River at Preston, six miles from Denison, Texas." Undeterred by hardships and dangers such as high water, bad weather, horse thieves, sickness, difficult river crossings, and the loss of a carriage horse to lameness, the six hardy souls finally arrived at their destination. "On the night of December 9th," Dave wrote, "we camped on White Rock Creek north of Dallas and the next day, the 10th, got to Uncle Otwa's, three months to the day on the road."[4]

Although most of the land along the Upper Trinity was unpatented and Quill received no deeds until later, he purchased 160 acres of land adjoining Uncle Otwa's farm and a few days later added 80 acres from "the northeast quarter of the John Kiser Section." Then in 1854 he acquired another 30 acres from a neighbor, Jeremiah Heath, whose grandson later married Dave's only daughter. By the time the Civil War began, Quill's farm embraced about 500 acres of choice prairie and timberland interspersed with artesian springs and streams that meandered among rocky crags and jumbled stands of Osage orange, oak, cottonwood, hickory, redbud, and pecan.[5]

The year following Quill's arrival in Texas, he bought a prairie plow, and Uncle Otwa purchased several yokes of oxen, and the two brothers began cultivating their feed crops together. But to reduce chances of spreading disease among their livestock, from the beginning they ran their sheep in separate pastures. Rail fences were constructed from red cedar logs hauled from a mountain near Cedar Hill, and the combined farms blossomed into a neat checkerboard of green pastures, cultivated fields, hog and cow lots, orchards, and vegetable gardens. Both farms were dotted with wild berries and fruit trees, but the most beautiful and productive orchard, affectionately called "the garden," occupied about twenty acres east of Quill's main house, which was situated on a hilltop almost exactly fifteen miles due south of the Dallas courthouse. Two sparkling artesian streams marked the northern and southern extremities of the garden and merged at the foot of the hill directly in front of the house to form a larger stream known as Heath Branch. As a consequence Quill's farm came to be known as "the Heath Branch Farm."[6]

Quill's house on the hilltop, enlarged almost every year to accommodate his steadily growing family, soon had a large semicircular gallery overlooking the garden, which served as a site for family gatherings on summer evenings. The view from the gallery was breathtaking, a panoramic vista of "tall oaks, sparkling springs, and rolling hills." Dave evidently loved this old house and later built another one much like it at the foot of the hill, but it was the old one—the one constructed on the hilltop—that received so much attention in his recollections. In describing its construction, he explained that a three-room cabin below Heath Branch was moved to the top of the hill to become the first section of the structure that gradually became the large, rambling, hilltop home with the semicircular gallery. Dave wrote: "In the spring, after the moving, Father pried up a little old house and put wheels under it, and borrowed Uncle Otwa's ox teams and hands. Then they hitched twenty oxen to the house in two teams and hauled it across the branch at the crossing near the field gate in the pasture west and around to the top of the hill between the branches which till then had always been a wilderness with high grass and buffalo trails."[7]

Once Quill had provided shelter for his family, he turned his attention to his fields and livestock. Hard work was necessary, but the Trinity watershed abounded in small game and natural resources. The development of the farm promised a bright future, and a measure of prosperity was not long in coming. Fertile bottomlands for raising corn, good pastures for livestock, and abundant water enabled Quill to purchase two milk cows, several yokes of oxen, some chickens, and increase the size of his flock of sheep. And here in this picture book setting, Dave's father "herded sheep, penned the cows, drove the oxen, . . . plowed the fields, . . . and hauled the red cedar rails and fenced the farm with great ox teams." Heath Branch provided abundant water for household use, livestock, irrigation, and—after the war—a huge waterwheel that powered a gristmill.[8]

And Dave's role in the farm's operations, though perhaps meager in the beginning, nevertheless was vital. In an autobiographical sketch written after the war, he recalled some of his early duties:

> Of course one of my tender years could not help much but I did what
> I could and was always busy. In the winter of 1853–54, when I was

ten past, my daily morning task was to shuck and shell a large water
bucket full of corn, and feed the sheep. . . . This I did day by day with
my own bare little hands, and then turned out the flock, and with my
little lunch, I took the flock out on the open prairie to graze and kept
them till time to bring them home in the evening. This we had to do to
save the sheep from the wolves, and even then they would kill a few.[9]

Nor were wolves the only problem. Dave wrote that Heath Branch
was "the snakiest place one ever saw, so that the first year or two, . . .
[we] killed snakes by day and by night—the foxes barked, the wolves
howled, and coons and opossums and snakes caught the chickens." [10]

But despite the dangers and hardships of frontier living, Dave ma-
tured and gradually became more involved in the farm's daily operations. Soon he was doing almost all of the plowing and planting as well
as most of the shearing of the sheep and the marketing of the wool.
Quill taught Dave that time must never be wasted, and this lesson,
along with Dave's desire to further his education, resulted in a rather
lucrative auxiliary enterprise. "Then by the time I was fifteen years of
age," Dave wrote in his recollections, "I had learned the cooper's
trade, and during rainy days and odd times I made cedar churns, pails,
tubs, and water barrels, well buckets and so on and sold them to our
neighbors. In that way I obtained a few dollars with which I bought
mostly books [and] . . . attended a few [tuition] summer schools near
home," conducted by itinerant teachers.[11]

As Dave worked among the "sparkling springs and the rolling hills"
of the farm, the size of the family residing in the "old, old, sweet
home" on the hill increased dramatically. During the nine years following the Nances' arrival in Texas, Dave's mother gave birth to four
more children, two girls and two boys. But the second son, born July 4,
1860, died the same day and became the first to be buried in a family
cemetery about a quarter mile from the house and plainly visible from
the front gallery.[12]

By this time, the house on the hilltop provided accommodations for
Dave, his parents, a teenager, an eleven-year-old, and three younger
children under ten, each with his or her own personality, interests, and position in the family hierarchy. Forty-six-year-old Quill, of
course, was the patriarch, and Elizabeth, Dave's thirty-four-year-old
mother, was Quill's mainstay and unflagging helpmate. Under Quill
and Elizabeth's gentle supervision were Mary, their fifteen-year-old
daughter, who performed most of the domestic chores; Gustavus
("Little Gus") Adolphus, their eleven-year-old son whose boundless
energy had turned the farm into a huge playground; Ellen, their
eight-year-old daughter, who served as the self-designated "mother"

of the younger children; Ann Lee, Mary's chief assistant in the kitchen; and the baby, two-year-old Sara. Another son, Charles Palmer, was born the following summer, about eight weeks before Dave rode off to war.[13]

An ardent believer in education, Quill worked diligently to see that every member of his family learned to read the Bible as early as possible and that all his children attended private "pay" schools when available. Most of Quill's education was self-acquired, but he supported the concept of public education and despaired that Texas was so far behind Illinois in that regard.[14]

An astute student of history and geography as well as the Bible, Quill considered the pursuit of knowledge a lifelong endeavor. He had convinced Dave that humanity's only hope of understanding the mysteries of the universe and the reasons for human existence lay hidden in the Holy Scriptures. Quill therefore spent several hours each night fervently studying his Bible, a practice he sought to pass on to his children. Dave wrote: "Aside from his home building ability, Allen Q. Nance was a great student also, and this is what made him great. In his latter days he read incessantly. His geographical knowledge was wonderful, but one thing stood above all the rest—he was a student of the Hebrew prophets. This was his delight, and days upon days he read and thought and talked on this wonderful theme."[15]

Dave, with similar interests enhanced by a probing intellectual curiosity, was his father's favorite, and father and son spent many late evening hours studying the Bible together. As Dave indicated, the Hebrew prophets fascinated them, and they read everything they could find concerning Jewish origins and history. Both longed to study the Hebrew language so they could read the Old Testament "in the original" and perhaps better understand the meaning of God's cryptic messages to His people and therefore to all humanity. When Lincoln's election and the secession of South Carolina made armed conflict seem possible, Dave and his father grimly pondered the words "With a great army . . . the king of the North shall come . . . and take the most fenced cities; and the arms of the south shall not withstand."[16]

Quill's abiding belief in the Bible as God's revelation to man was reflected by his serious demeanor, reverential bearing, and unobtrusive face, etched with deep lines and furrows. He was a large man who weighed almost two hundred pounds and "wore a number eight hat." He had broad shoulders, a square jaw, thinning hair, soft eyes, a contagious smile, and a pleasant disposition. His favorite spot for study and discussion, especially after the war when his health began to fail, was the shaded gallery overlooking the garden. During his latter years he spent most of his time on the gallery, smoking his corncob pipe, studying his Bible, and watching the sheep grazing in the east pasture. Dave's papers contain frequent references to his father's failing health, but nowhere do they reveal the nature of his illness. After Quill's death in 1873, Dave liked to study his Bible sitting in the same spot on the gallery that his father had occupied.[17]

Dave evidently was not as close to his mother as he was to his father. Neither was he as challenged by her intellectually, although her education was superior to that of most frontier women. Elizabeth was a small, quiet, smartly groomed woman, but perhaps because of her earlier hardships and sorrow, she looked older than her thirty-four years. Having lost both parents by the time she was six, she married Quill at fifteen, bore her first son—Dave—at seventeen, and by twenty-one had experienced the loss of her first child in infancy. Elizabeth bore other children, one almost every year, but her new life in Texas was somewhat easier, happier, and more abundant. She delighted in her husband and children, and since Mary did most of the housework during these years, Elizabeth had time to read, visit with neighbors, sew and weave, and care for her ailing husband.[18]

Something of a storybook romantic, Elizabeth loved fiction and read with delight the novels of Sir Walter Scott. As the war approached, her love for individual freedom and self-determination transformed her into a flaming secessionist. In her mind the war was a fight for Southern honor and independence and against Northern tyranny and oppression. Confident that the soldiers of the western Confederacy, like the heroes in Scott's novels, were braver and more gallant than the men of the North, she was convinced that Texas boys would never permit their state to be conquered. Elizabeth also believed, in the beginning at least, that the war would be short and filled with romance and adventure. Like many Southern women, she thrilled to see neighbor boys in colorful uniforms parade on prancing horses and therefore did nothing to discourage Dave's enlistment. During the war she became a member of several patriotic organizations, such as the Lancaster Ladies' Aid Society, and devoted much time to making gaily colored dresses into banners and flags, knitting socks, and making underwear for the men of local regiments. As the war wore on and shortages of materials curtailed her operations, she restricted her patriotic endeavors to knitting socks for Dave and his messmates.[19]

Although Dave later entered the war with some of his mother's romantic notions, he had not acquired them from reading fiction. He preferred studying philosophy, geography, history, theology, and various other so-called true sciences which his father recommended. "I loved . . . good books," he wrote, but "I never read fiction. I read good books or none, and the Bible was one I loved to read."[20]

Dave's papers contain occasional references to his brothers and sisters, but the name of his oldest sister, Mary, appears most often. She evidently spent much of her time spinning, weaving, and sewing and kept Dave and the rest of the family supplied with clothing. She was always busy making coats, jeans, flannel and lindsey shirts, winter drawers, woolen mittens, bed comforters, and blankets. Mary later sent many of these to Dave after his enlistment, and he cherished this demonstration of her love for the rest of his life. "During the Civil War, she was the mainstay in her father's house, doing most of the labor, clothing the family in homespun," Dave wrote after the war. "To her the writer, her brother, is due many thanks for the warm clothes which her own hands furnished during those four terrible years of privation."[21]

Mary's energetic domestic activities, when coupled with Dave's hard work in the fields, help explain the farm's unparalleled productivity and self-sufficiency by 1860. In addition to yielding significant quantities of wool for sale and home consumption, the farm produced an abundance of grain, vegetables, honey, meat, milk, butter, and eggs. Even lye soap and leather shoes, two of the scarcest items of the war years, were produced regularly during the hardest of times. Soap was made in a great iron pot in the backyard at least twice a year, and shoes and boots were fashioned from tanned cowhides by an old, itinerant shoemaker who visited the farm each spring.[22]

Despite the heavy work schedule at Heath Branch, the Nances surprisingly found time to open their doors to a steady stream of visitors, many of whom spent the night. Well known for their hospitality, Quill and Elizabeth welcomed prominent military and government officials, itinerant teachers and preachers, wealthy businessmen and tradesmen, and strangers seeking food and lodging. These overnight guests broke the monotony of the day-to-day farm routines and brought the latest news on state and national events, economic conditions elsewhere, and recent developments in distant places. Since newspapers were scarce in the backcountry, this method of obtaining news was both pleasant and effective. When overnight visitors were in the house, everyone looked forward to after supper get-togethers around the fireplace when current events would be explained, analyzed, and evaluated.[23]

A favorite topic for after supper analysis during the winter of 1859–60 was John Brown's raid on a Federal arsenal in Harpers Ferry, Virginia. Brown's plans are obscure, but apparently he intended to distribute guns from the arsenal to slaves, who, he assumed, would flock to his banner to wage guerrilla warfare against Virginia slaveholders. Although no slave insurrection occurred and Brown was

hanged for treason, the fear of abolitionist subversion and slave insurrections made slaveholders everywhere jittery. Slaveholders in the
Heath Branch neighborhood, like those all across the Lone Star State,
refused to consider the incident an isolated act by a fanatic but instead
concluded that a Northern conspiracy was under way to instigate insurrections among their slaves. This topic must have stimulated some
heated discussions around the Nance fireplace, for Dave wrote that
the "Harpers Ferry insurrection was fresh in the minds of all." [24]

Although the Nances disliked slavery and Dave's father initially opposed secession, both Dave and Quill agreed with the secessionists
that the states of the South should be permitted to decide for themselves whether or not to permit slavery within their own borders. Evidently both became convinced that secession, although a drastic alternative, would be preferable to an abolitionist maneuver to free all
slaves by force. Quill came to see secession as a nonviolent means of
halting abolitionist subversion in Texas, convinced that the North
would not fight to keep the Federal Union intact. His opposition to
violence and war, of course, sprang from God's admonition to the
Israelites that they should not kill. [25]

Most of Quill's North Texas neighbors were proslavery secessionists,
but a substantial number of Unionist families from the Old Northwest
lived along Red River north of Dallas and in a tier of counties extend-
ing from Young to Collin. These Texas Unionists, frightened by the
hysterical frenzy stirred up by John Brown's raid, found it safer to
keep their antislavery and Unionist sentiments to themselves. [26]

Just as the furor over the raid began to fade and North Texas
seemed to be returning to normal, a series of mysterious fires broke
out in Dallas and neighboring towns. Again an atmosphere of fear
and suspicion gripped the Heath Branch neighborhood and the
northeastern part of the state. Surely this was the beginning of another abolitionist conspiracy to overthrow the white race and drench
Texas in the blood of massive slave insurrections. Almost everyone in
North Texas, including Quill and even some of his Unionist neighbors
northwest of Dallas, concluded that an "abolitionist plot" was responsible for the unexplained fires. There came to be widespread agree-
ment among peace-loving Texans, slaveholding secessionists and
Unionists alike, that the perpetrators of these acts of arson should be
ferreted out and driven from the state. Dave, only seventeen at the
time, evidently joined his father and friends in advocating the estab-
lishment of vigilance committees to preserve order, defend local institutions against abolitionist subversion, and "investigate persons of
suspicious quality," both black and white. "All this stirred the people,

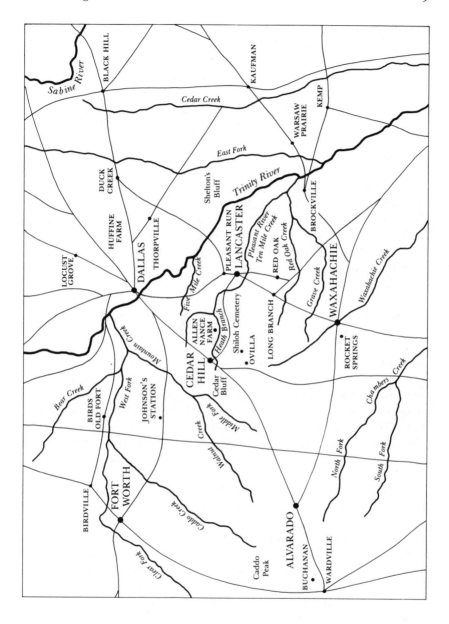

Map. 1.   The Trinity River Region of North Texas, 1861–1865

me with the rest," he wrote in his recollections after the war, but "I was only a boy, and like other boys, thought the old folks knew best."[27]

Although persuaded that the slaveholders' fear was justified, neither Dave nor Quill was prepared for the campaign of terror the quickly organized vigilance committees unleashed. Three local blacks were convicted of arson largely on hearsay evidence and hanged, and three preachers from the North were beaten mercilessly and driven from the country. Hundreds of helpless slaves were rounded up "like cattle" by "slaveholders, [traders], and their dupes" and whipped "without mercy." Dave and his father evidently witnessed one of these brutal displays and stood in horror as scores of blacks were almost beaten to death. Fearing for their lives, Dave and Quill made no effort to interfere, but Dave later wrote that neither he nor his father took part in the whipping and that the sight of it "made his blood run cold."[28]

Attempting to give the reasons behind the brutal beating, Dave explained: "The object of this whipping was twofold: first on the part of the traders, to bring down the price of slaves in North Texas; second to discourage betimes any possible . . . insurrection in case of war. But . . . this whipping hastened the war and the war brought down the price of slaves everywhere."[29]

Quill, who had agreed to serve on one of the vigilance committees, promptly resigned, thus arousing suspicion in some quarters that he was in league with abolitionists. His refusal to use slaves on his farm, plus his resistance to the purging of local blacks, gave rise to a rumor that one of the committees had charged Quill and Uncle Otwa with complicity with abolitionist conspirators. There also was a rumor circulated that a warrant had been issued for Quill's arrest, but since no action was ever taken, it seems likely that both rumors were without foundation.

During the months that followed, five states of the Deep South followed South Carolina's example and passed secession ordinances. Texas became the seventh in February and March, 1861, when a secession convention in Austin drew up an ordinance of secession and submitted it to the people for ratification. The state's electorate approved the ordinance overwhelmingly with more than a fourth of the votes cast against secession coming from the Unionist counties north of Dallas. Quill and Uncle Otwa, troubled by the brewing storm of secession and possible war, did not vote at all, but this also precipitated controversy, since it was becoming increasingly impossible to take a neutral stand on any question.[30]

These circumstances took some of the pleasure out of the after supper get-togethers around the Nance fireplace, but Quill and Elizabeth refused to close their doors to anyone. The fall of Fort Sumter in South Carolina served notice that fighting already had begun between the United States and the newly organized Confederate States of America, of which Texas now was a part. But although the flow of visitors to Heath Branch diminished somewhat during the weeks that followed, the Nance hospitality continued and both Unionists and Confederates received the same courteous welcome.[31]

But the Nances faced a perplexing question: Would Dave, who had become eighteen in February, serve in the Confederate army if the fighting continued? This question, first raised in a whimsical way by Elizabeth without realizing its terrible implications, would have to be answered by Dave himself.

CHAPTER 2

Man on a Dark Morgan

*T*he Civil War brought the end of an era in the life of David C. Nance. Other eras would follow, some equally glorious and happy, but there was no other period that he remembered more fondly than his childhood. For the rest of his life he liked to recall those carefree days before the war when Dallas County was a "wild waste" and when he worked the farm under the supervision of his father, studied geography and theology by candlelight, fished and swam in nearby rivers and creeks, and hunted "bear, panthers, wildcats, foxes, and so on" in the occasional forests and on the rolling prairies.[1]

Because of Dave's expanding role in the daily operations of the farm, hunting and fishing excursions were possible only during certain seasons of the year, but they were carefully planned, happily anticipated, and delightfully fulfilled. As a rule, Dave did not go alone. Occasionally Quill or Uncle Otwa went with him, but his usual companions were two young prairie farmers named "Lonesome John" M. Sullivan and William T. "Little Will" Stuart. Lonesome John was from Red Oak, a village six miles south of Lancaster, and Little Will lived with his parents on a farm near Long Branch, a small community nine miles north of Waxahachie.[2]

Lonesome John was a giant of a man, largely illiterate, droll, entertaining, and profane to the point of ingenuity. He was only eighteen years old when the war started, but he was a fervent secessionist and delighted in verbal abuse of abolitionists and their suspected Negro "agents." Subject to fits of melancholy, he was high tempered, easily provoked, possessed with great strength, quick to use his fists, and an expert marksman. Dave and his father liked to take John with them on hunts to reduce the wolf population, for John always brought down more than his share of the sheep-killing predators.[3]

Little Will, on the other hand, was a mild-mannered, freckle-faced young man of twenty-two whose intellectual curiosity matched Dave's.

He had accompanied his parents to North Texas from White County, Tennessee, arriving almost exactly one year before the Nances arrived from Illinois. Handsome despite his freckles and slight frame, he was an avid reader who loved all types of books. He and Dave enjoyed discussing history, philosophy, literature, and religion, and both displayed considerable insight into such works as Caesar's *Commentaries,* Homer's *Iliad,* and the Holy Bible. Will also had an intense interest in military science and tactics, and while fighting for the Confederacy in Louisiana in 1864, he took a copy of General W. J. Hardee's *Rifle and Infantry Tactics* off the body of a Union officer near Marksville. This battered little manual became Little Will's most cherished memento, and he enjoyed showing it after the war at his unit's annual reunions.[4]

It was Little Will's interest in the military that led to the enlistment of all three boyhood friends. Will's eagerness to join a local cavalry company became almost uncontrollable in July and August 1861, when William H. Parsons, a former lawyer and newspaper editor, came through North Texas seeking volunteers for a mounted regiment Governor Edward Clark had authorized for service on the Indian frontier of West Texas. Three Ellis County companies—named the Grays, Blues, and Rangers—were formed, and their captains happily consented to their becoming part of Parsons' new regiment. Since Captain John C. Brown of Milford, the commander of the Grays, was a personal friend of the Stuart family, Little Will enlisted in Brown's company on September 10 and encouraged Dave and Lonesome John to do likewise.[5]

Neither rushed to the colors without considerable thought. Lonesome John agreed to join the Grays if Dave would, but Dave, encouraged to enlist by his mother, found his father "bitterly opposed" on religious grounds. At the time, Dave appreciated his mother's support of his enlistment, but he later repudiated her action, calling it "a good illustration of the evil influence of bad advice. Perhaps if Mother had added her influence to that of my father, I would have . . . escaped the horrors that befell me later."[6]

Dave's papers and those of other members of Parsons' original regiment (first known as the Fourth Texas Mounted Dragoons) paint a vivid picture of the unit's formal organization ceremonies conducted on September 11, 1861, at Rocket Springs, a village not far from Waxahachie. Lonesome John, who had not yet decided to enlist, could not attend the ceremonies because he was busy hauling fence rails from Cedar Hill, but Dave, eager to see the proceedings, accompanied the exuberant Little Will, whose company was to become part of the new regiment. "I went down," Dave wrote, "[just] to prospect . . .

for myself and John M. Sullivan, for we were neighbor boys who had grown up together." [7]

As Dave and Little Will guided their horses into Rocket Springs on the morning of the ceremonies, they were surprised to see the roads leading into town ribboned with humanity on the move. Horsedrawn vehicles of every description were joined by hundreds of men on horseback and on foot eager to witness the organization of the regiment. By ten o'clock the little town was filled to overflowing. Little Will, thrilled to be a part of the occasion, proudly found his place in the ranks of the Grays, leaving Dave to join the press of spectators, many standing in wagons or on tiptoe, waiting for the great historic event about to unfold before them. [8]

Writing after the war, several former members of the regiment recalled the major events that constituted their unit's formal organization:

> At the hour of ten a.m., the bugle sounded and ten companies, comprising about twelve hundred men, formed a "hollow square" in order to better perform the work at hand; this done, the marshal of the day (whose name is forgotten) demanded to know the nominations:—
> First, for Colonel. . . . [When] the name of Parsons was called by many voices, . . . a proud form on as proud an animal glided into the open space and made a brief address to the volunteers around him, after which the marshall called for a vote and W. H. Parsons was unanimously elected. John W. Mullins was elected Lieutenant Colonel; E. W. Rogers, Major; John Hogan was then appointed Surgeon; D. Embree, Assistant Surgeon; T. G. A. Willis, quartermaster; Frank Ayers, Commissary; A. Bell Burleson, Adjutant; these with the appointment of Reverend J. Fred Cox to the Chaplaincy, completed the organization of one of the best regiments that ever went into the service of any country. [9]

The emotion of the moment, heightened by martial music, thundering drum rolls, and colorful banners, had its effect on Dave. It seems to have been here at Rocket Springs that he made his decision to spurn his father's advice and become a soldier. After conferring with Lonesome John to make certain that he would enlist with him, Dave announced to his parents that he had decided to join the Ellis County Grays. Quill, having said all he could to prevent Dave from enlisting, evidently had nothing to say in response to the announcement. [10]

So less than a week later, Dave and Lonesome John packed their personal belongings, said their good-byes, and rode north out of Dallas looking for the Fourth Dragoons. Dave wrote: "[The] regiment moved up into Collin County and while camped near the old Huffines farm, John and I overtook it and enlisted. It was a cavalry regiment of State troops, and so we were now Texas Rangers. We were well mounted and fairly well armed, having our own horses and arms."[11]

Dave, however, did not stay long with his unit. Chills and fever, which had troubled him all summer, struck again. Early in October, while his company was bivouacked at Camp Tarrant in western Ellis County, he obtained a sick leave and returned home.[12]

While Dave recuperated at his parents' farm, the ten companies of the Fourth Dragoons scattered across the northern and central portions of the state collecting recruits and supplies, finally rendezvousing at Camp Hébert near Hempstead. On October 28, after two weeks of intensive drill and training, the regiment was transferred from state to Confederate service, and the Fourth Texas Mounted Dragoons became the Twelfth Texas Cavalry, Army of the Confederate States of America. Since Dave was not present when the transfer occurred, his name was dropped from his company's muster rolls, and several days later he received a discharge by mail. Dave was sorely disappointed and determined to enlist a second time as soon as his health permitted.[13]

Dave did not have to wait long. The low-grade fever which had bothered him for weeks finally vanished, and he began preparations to return to his regiment. "So I kept the discharge a secret," he wrote, "so as not to be opposed when I should start again. I did this because my father was bitterly opposed to my enlistment, but mother favored it."[14]

On the morning of November 13, 1861, Dave lashed his provisions and equipment on the back of his dark Morgan stallion, mounted, and set out in search of his unit. This time he rode south. As he jogged along, he must have impressed observers along the way with his military bearing, although dressed in civilian clothes. He was a ramrod-straight six footer, eighteen years old, with a wiry, angular frame. He sat on his horse in a stiff, dignified manner, as if he were riding in a formal dress parade. A battered hat pulled down over his wide-set eyes partly concealed a bronzed face, a perfectly shaped chin, and a black mustache. His splendid black-stockinged Morgan reflected a regal bearing not unlike that of his master.[15]

The young horseman was well equipped for his great adventure. Various cooking utensils and a grub bag—containing oven-baked bread, a cured ham, pickled cucumbers, honey, and other items— swung lazily from his saddle. A double-breasted stormcoat, spare clothing, bedding, and various toilet articles—rolled tightly inside a black oilcloth poncho—rode snugly behind him. A glistening new Whitney pistol rested comfortably in its holster on his right hip, and a double-barreled shotgun rode easily in its saddlesocket under his left knee.[16]

The beginning of his journey was pleasant enough. The Trinity River region of North Texas basked in the warm sunshine of an Indian summer, and the landscape shimmered with the subdued colors of late autumn. During the first four days on the road, Dave traveled at a leisurely pace, made camp early each evening, prepared his meals over cheery campfires, and slept peacefully under star-studded heavens.

Then things began to go wrong. At dawn on the fifth day, while camped on a tributary of the Navasota, Dave awakened under a gray, overcast sky. By midafternoon it had begun to rain—a sullen, persistent drizzle that looked as if it might go on for days. When darkness fell that evening, so did the temperature, and an icy wind caused Dave to seek the warmth and protection of his stormcoat.

Although the drizzle had stopped by the next morning, dreary, gray skies remained. Then that afternoon a starving pack of wolves and wild dogs began following him. That night, as Dave made camp "in a timbered country with few settlements," the wolves closed in, their eyes gleaming like fiery coals in the darkness beyond the campfire. He tossed a couple of shots into the pack, keeping it at bay, but sleep did not come that night. Toward dawn, as Dave's campfire burned low, the wolves again pressed forward, forcing him to use both his pistol and his shotgun to protect himself and his Morgan. "The wolves kept up a terrific howling around me for an hour or two," he wrote in his recollections, but not wishing to appear cowardly, he added, "but I was not frightened." [17]

Another heart-stopping incident occurred three days later south of Hempstead, this time as a result of Dave's own carelessness. He wrote: "I dismounted to shoot a wild goose. The goose flew before I shot and as I remounted my coat hung on the hammer of the gun, but it snapped. I looked down and the muzzle of the gun was against my instep. If it had fired it would have blown my foot off, and I didn't see why it didn't fire." [18]

Having learned at Camp Hébert that his regiment had moved south, Dave rode into Houston. In answer to his inquiries, he learned that the Twelfth Cavalry had "marched through the city in platoons of eights" that morning, having "performed admirably" as Parsons' boys had taken the road to Galveston. This meant, Dave reasoned, that his regiment could not be far away. [19]

Dave found the bayou country south of Houston hauntingly beautiful. An eerie light filtered through low-hanging clouds. Belts of timber decorated with streamers of Spanish moss stood deathly still in a dank, vacuumlike atmosphere. The arrow-straight railroad to Galveston, which sliced through the forest to connect with the coastal marshland to the south, seemed fanciful and unreal, as if it existed in a dream, and the muddy highway that paralleled the railroad lay devoid of any living thing.

Suddenly it began to rain. Dave had to dismount to don his poncho, and by the time he got it on, he was soaked to the skin. Remounting but blinded by the heavy downpour, Dave wondered whether God intended for him to find his unit. If the fury of the storm continued to increase, he realized that he would have to abandon his search and seek shelter. With visibility drastically curtailed, Dave easily could ride past his unit's bivouac without seeing it, especially if it was situated some distance from the road. With a heavy heart, he considered returning to Houston to seek shelter.

But as abruptly as it had begun, the downpour ended. The dark clouds rolled inland, and the eerie light returned, revealing a landscape of mud and standing water. A cold, soaking drizzle continued but at least the young horseman could see a considerable distance in all directions.[20]

Then as Dave topped a gentle hill, he reined in his Morgan as his weariness turned to exhilaration. Scattered out before him at the foot of the hill lay the bivouac of the Twelfth Texas Cavalry, lining the north bank of Sims Bayou and filling a crescent-shaped plateau that skirted the winding stream. Dave sat motionless for several moments, savoring his feeling of relief mingled with excitement. The sprawling military community before him, almost buried in a sea of mud and water, represented the end of the trail and his new home!

The bivouac, apparently erected in great haste, had a jumbled, cluttered appearance. Several Sibley tents, large conical structures ordinarily used by infantry rather than cavalry, were scattered across the plateau. Several hundred smaller tents of various shape and design also were in evidence, but tents of all types were vastly outnumbered by a veritable forest of crude shelters constructed from wagon sheets, sections of oilcloth, pine boughs, and other makeshift materials. The occupants of the camp probably had intended to arrange these structures in neat, orderly patterns, but the rows of shelters and their accompanying streets were irregular, intermittent, crooked, and unsightly.[21]

There was little movement in camp, and the entire plateau, soaked by earlier rains and the current drizzle, had a foreboding dreariness about it. Piles of partly packed boxes of goods and equipment, dozens of mule- and horse-drawn wagons, and stacks of freshly cut timber cluttered the campsite. The center of the bivouac and the roads that connected with the highway—churned by countless animals, carts, and wagons—were lakes of mud. Horses, mules, and oxen, either tethered to tightly strung lariats or enclosed in rough log corrals, stood motionless in the icy, gray mist. And little knots of rain-soaked rangers, dressed in every conceivable gear, huddled around camp fires drinking boiled coffee.

Touching his spurs to the flanks of his Morgan, Dave guided the little stallion down a slippery slope and entered the mud-choked camp. There was no sentry to challenge him, so he turned up one of the irregular, slushy streets. Dave walked his horse slowly, scanning the tents and makeshift shelters. After several minutes he spotted the banners and standards of the Ellis County Grays, now designated Company E. As he dismounted, a cry of recognition, probably the voice of Lonesome John, came from one of the shelters, and several members of Dave's mess splashed out into the mud to greet him. The boisterous display of camaraderie that followed convinced Dave that the hardships of the last several days had been worthwhile.[22]

Dave wasted no time in seeking out the Sibley tent that housed the commander of the Ellis County Grays. Proudly, he once again informed Captain John C. Brown that he wanted to be a member of his company. It was November 23, but evidently Dave's name was not officially added to the muster rolls until four weeks later. The date of Dave's second enlistment in the Grays, as recorded in his military records, was December 21, 1861. The reason for the discrepancy between the date of his arrival and the date recorded in his records is unknown.[23]

According to the Nance papers, the Twelfth Texas Cavalry at this time contained 1,160 men, not counting regimental officers, and although there was considerable reorganization and turnover during the war, the three Ellis County companies retained the same letter designations and essentially the same membership. Captain Brown's Grays continued to be called Company E; the Blues, commanded by Captain William Stokes of Waxahachie, retained the designation Company H; and the Ellis County Rangers, also known as the Methodist Bulls and commanded by Captain William G. Veal of Red Oak, continued to carry the designation of Company F.[24]

In addition to the three Ellis County companies, there was one each from Hill, Johnson, Kaufman, Limestone, Williamson, Freestone, and Bastrop counties. Each of these also was given a letter designation: the Hill County Volunteers became Company A; the Johnson County Slashers, Company C; the Kaufman County Guards, Company G; the Limestone County Mounted Rifles, Company K; the Williamson County Bowies, Company I; the Freestone County Rangers, Company B; and the Bastrop County Rawhides, Company D.[25]

Having reported to Captain Brown, Dave quickly stowed away his gear in one of the shelters and turned his attention to his horse. Lonesome John and Little Will led the way through the waterlogged camp to a muddy slope where the Company E livestock was tethered. Here the three friends prepared accommodations for Dave's Morgan.[26]

Dave, more concerned with his horse's health than his own, urged his companions to work rapidly before the animal became chilled. With rivulets of water rolling down their ponchos and streaming from the brims of their hats, they suspended a section of wagon sheet from low-hanging branches, erected a crude stall supplied with fodder, and threw a blanket over the well-brushed little stallion.[27]

Unlike Union cavalry, Confederate cavalrymen furnished their own mounts and most of their firearms. If a horse or weapon was lost or destroyed, the soldier usually received a sixty-day furlough to try to replace his loss. These personal possessions were carefully evaluated by Confederate appraisers with the expectation that the Confederate government would reimburse its soldiers after the war for the use of their property. Since the South lost the war, of course no reimbursements were ever made.[28]

Confederate appraisers, who usually valued horses at somewhere between $75 and $100, set the value of Dave's Morgan at $225. A gift from his father on his fifteenth birthday, the beautiful Morgan evidently became the envy of every man in the regiment. "[In] the army everybody wanted him," Dave wrote, "but he was mine."[29]

Unfortunately, the Morgan was killed six months later in Arkansas during the battle of Cache River. Dave's love for his horse and his continuing grief over its death are reflected in the following tribute written in 1913: "This was the finest horse I ever owned, a Morgan horse, a dark bay with black feet, mane, and tail. He was four years old, round and fat, a real beautiful horse, broad between the eyes, and gentle. He had a little white spot between his eyes the size of a thumb nail. I called him 'Morgan.' . . . This was the horse killed in battle [in July 1862]. . . . And I know if I had not been so nearly killed, too, I should have cried bitterly at his death at the time."[30]

A bone-chilling darkness had descended upon the camp on Sims Bayou by the time Dave's Morgan was settled in for the night. Hundreds of sputtering fires across the plateau illuminated small patches of soggy ground where cold, miserable rangers prepared their evening meal.[31]

The three friends fell into line, splashed back to their company area, and joined their messmates in rekindling their own faltering fire. Within the hour they were enjoying the magnificent fare young Dave had brought from home.

CHAPTER 3

Storm Clouds over Sims Bayou

*D*ave found the first weeks in the Sims Bayou encampment filled with happiness, thrills, and excitement. Even digging drainage ditches was fun when done in the company of happy and prank-loving comrades. His pride in soldiering increased as days passed, and he looked forward to meeting the enemy so that he could prove his bravery. His only fear was that the war might end before he got the chance.

Dave was impressed with Colonel William H. Parsons, his regimental commander. Although Parsons and his officers spent a great deal of time in Houston with wives or girl friends, Dave had opportunities to observe his colonel in the performance of his duty and to listen to his famous speeches delivered from horseback. It was said that no commander west of the Mississippi could deliver more fiery, colorful, and enthusiastic speeches from the saddle. There was no doubt in Dave's mind that Colonel Parsons would emerge from the war a national hero. Dave, in turn, determined to conduct himself in such a way as to deserve the honor of serving under him.[1]

Certainly the commander of the Twelfth Texas Cavalry looked and acted like the western Confederacy's answer to Napoleon Bonaparte. He possessed a contagious confidence and swashbuckling presence that thrilled those around him. Having served as a state supreme court judge, an officer in the Texas Senate, and the publisher of the Tyler *Telegraph*, he had both the bearing and the experience of a born leader. To look at Parsons, decked out in his brass buttons and black hat with white plume, one could see marvelously uniformed soldiers marching into battle amid brilliantly colored flags to the accompaniment of drum rolls and bugle calls.[2]

To see Parsons, therefore, was to see his regiment. His men trusted him, responded eagerly to his every command, and sought to acquire for themselves his grace and martial bearing. "My boys," he liked to say, as if they were his personal possessions. And somehow this pleased the men of the Twelfth. Since almost every one of them glorified in being a member of his command, it was not only appropriate but largely accurate.[3]

When Parsons was in camp, he frequently called the regiment together to listen to his colorful and informal pep talks. He enjoyed this, but these lighthearted orations also bolstered the morale of his men and kept them aware of the important role they would be expected to play in the event of enemy landings on the Texas coast.[4]

Prompted by his inquisitive nature and drawing from information provided by Parsons and stories told by his comrades, Dave learned how the Twelfth came to be camped on Sims Bayou. Late in October 1861, Brigadier General Paul O. Hébert, the new Confederate commander of Texas, had ordered Parsons into the bayou country to establish a "permanent winter encampment . . . halfway between . . . [Houston] and Galveston." Parsons had selected the Sims Bayou site, just a few miles north of sites chosen by Matthew F. Locke and William Young, commanders of the Tenth and Eleventh, who had received similar orders. Once situated, Parsons was directed to instruct his troops in "military science . . . and regimental drill," always "standing ready" in the event of enemy landings on the coast. Supplementary orders had emphasized the "absolute necessity of defending the major avenues of communication with Galveston Island,"—that is, the Galveston, Houston, and Henderson Railroad; the Galveston highway; and the telegraph line that linked Galveston Island with the interior.[5]

But Parsons, Locke, and Young were not the only commanders with troops in the region. Major Robert B. (Sackfield) Maclin, acting chief of quartermaster and interim commander of the Sub-Department of the Gulf, reported on October 19 that he had ten thousand troops in the vicinity of Galveston. He revealed their deployment as follows: five thousand at Galveston and Virginia Point; two thousand "at Magnolia, Clear Creek, and near the railroad"; two thousand at Spring Creek near Millican; and one thousand stationed in a state camp near Harrisburg.[6]

Parsons' Sims Bayou site, selected with consummate care, gave the men of the Twelfth a central position from which to move in any direction in the event of an invasion. The camp itself was situated on a rolling plateau on the north bank of Sims Bayou, east of the railroad and highway bridges, and approximately halfway between Houston and Galveston. Four miles to the northwest, Sims Bayou emptied into a larger stream, Buffalo Bayou, a major artery of maritime commerce that connected with Galveston Bay near Lynchburg. Harrisburg, a "depot for subsistence, supplies, . . . [and] forage for the quartermaster's department," was six miles west of the junction, and Houston, with its housetops and steeples rising above the trees, lay only three miles farther upstream. To the south, the forest fanned out on a rolling coastal plain, washed by the shallow blue-green waters of the bay, whose sweeping vistas were interrupted only by occasional salt domes, bottomless inland marshes, and sluggish backwater streams.[7]

Although hampered by early morning fogs, frequent rainstorms, and oceans of mud, Dave and the men of the Twelfth probed the forests, patrolled the highway, and guarded the telegraph line. Parsons established his chief line of defense along Clear Creek, a winding bayou that circled to within five miles of camp, extended south along the railroad for about nine miles, and then drifted through a large swamp that served as a drainage sump for several smaller streams. Parsons reasoned that if invaders sought access to the interior, the Clear Creek swamp with its impassable bogs would effectively shorten his battle lines and permit the strengthening of strategic positions at each end.

Duty rosters were prepared weekly by company commanders on a rotating basis, and Dave soon learned which days he would be in the saddle. Like most of Parsons' boys, he vastly preferred the mounted patrols to camp duty or to manning stationary posts. Each mounted patrol consisted of two commissioned officers, ten to twelve non-commissioned officers, and about one hundred enlisted men. These scouting operations carried Dave into every part of the bayou country between Galveston and Houston, and his familiarity with the region became a source of great satisfaction. If called upon to repel an invasion, Dave and his comrades would enjoy the advantage of having intimate knowledge of the terrain.[8]

Despite long periods of wet weather, the Sims Bayou camp grew rapidly. The mushrooming tent city—dubbed "Camp Parsons" in honor of the colonel—exploded into long lines of Sibley and wagon sheet tents, sutlers' shanties, supply cribs, service sheds, commissary and equipment houses, livestock corrals, and log barracks. Bulletin boards appeared at various intersections displaying announcements of special events and notices of scouting schedules, guard duty, and fatigue details. Crudely lettered signs appeared in profusion, proclaiming company accomplishments, mess names, company boundaries, and traffic regulations. Soon the thriving community occupied all of the plateau east of the road and both banks of the bayou for a thousand yards on each side of the railroad bridge.

Dave's first few weeks in camp were busy ones. Except for days when drenching rain or deep mud curtailed operations, the encampment was a beehive of activity. Dave not only served on guard and fatigue details but participated in training programs that included mounted maneuvers, tent inspection, infantry drill, and dress parades.

But as weeks passed, training programs became more intermittent, and as a result Dave and his comrades found more time to write letters, lark from one tent to another, sing "jocular songs," compete in shooting and riding contests, and participate in various kinds of organized sports. Their leisure sprang from widespread work reductions due to illness and to the growing tendency of commanding officers to spend extended periods in Houston and Harrisburg. Company commanders "like to put on their fine brass button coats," wrote one soldier, "and spree about entirely too much."[9]

Parsons' boys enjoyed various kinds of sports, but perhaps the most popular was a game called "town ball." On December 21 a member of Veal's company wrote: "Within the last two weeks, the health has generally improved, and the boys are cheerful and gay. They have several ways of amusing themselves; the most popular one at present is town ball. Each company has some two or three Indian [India] rubber balls, and they choose about ten or fifteen on each side. Such knocking, running, and shouting you never heard. The captains and lieutenants sometimes take a hand. Lieutenant [W. P.] Payne is hard to beat."[10]

Although town ball was not the only organized sport, it without doubt was the most popular. It also served to galvanize squads, companies, and especially messes into close knit units. There was a growing camaraderie among members of the same mess, usually composed of from six to twelve members, and messmates almost always played on the same team. Eventually these teams invented their own names and fighting insignias. Victories and championships were much heralded, and team members took pride in their team's accomplishments.[11]

Since the Confederate government could not begin to supply all the needs of its troops, the mess system was basic to the army's existence. Born of necessity, it was by far the most intimate and cohesive informal subdivision of the Confederate military organization. It usually consisted of close friends or former neighbors in civilian life who enjoyed sharing their forage, rations, cooking utensils, and meals. Each mess usually elected a "captain" for a specified term who was responsible for the preparation of meals. Although the captain sometimes enlisted the aid of other members, he did most of the cooking and cleaned up after meals, although each soldier usually washed his own eating utensils. Occasionally there were arguments and differences of opinion among members of a mess, but these usually involved only good-natured horseplay and seldom resulted in angry exchanges or lasting hostility.

If listed at all on the company rosters, messes were designated by number, but most also devised for themselves colorful names similar to those used by ball teams. Dave and his messmates dubbed their mess "the Long Branch" in honor of Little Will's hometown in Ellis County. The name was neither flamboyant nor especially unique, but it at least could be mentioned in polite society. Many mess names could not.[12]

At this time the Long Branch consisted of Dave, Lonesome John, Little Will, B. K. ("Howdy") Bingham, Billy Parsons (not related to the regimental commander), and "Sor'ful Sam" E. Patton. Two other rangers joined the mess at different times during the war, but only one, Robert Couch, retained membership for the duration. The other, Bill Malone, served only intermittently because of a crippling injury and missed the extreme hardships of the last days.[13]

Not much is known of Bingham, Couch, and Malone, but Dave's papers provide glimpses into the lives and character of the others, especially Little Will, Lonesome John, and Sor'ful Sam Patton. Patton, the oldest member of the mess, was a native of North Texas but had no close friends, spent most of his time by himself, and from the beginning ignored all rules of personal hygiene. Even when clothing was plentiful early in the war, Patton dressed like a scarecrow, seldom bathed, and provided residence for "graybacks and other creeping things." Round-shouldered, sad-eyed, and sporting a bushy mustache usually matted with dried tobacco juice, he wore the same clothes (a homespun coat with oversized britches held in place by homemade, knit galluses) until they literally fell apart and had to be replaced.[14]

His disposition matched his appearance. Quick to flash a glare of contempt, Patton left no doubt that he wanted to be left alone. He frequently disappeared for days, seldom did his share of the work, and on at least one occasion was left behind when his regiment moved out unexpectedly. After the war Patton never attended regimental or brigade reunions, and when Dave and Little Will made inquiries, they could find no trace of him.[15]

But except for Patton, the friendship of the men of the Long Branch never faded. In the summer of 1912, a sixty-nine-year-old Dave wrote:

> These six [excluding Billy Parsons but including Couch and Malone] with myself constituted the mess, and from the time they enlisted till the war closed they remained together as one mess, one family—and they were a family indeed. They were always friends, and rude actions were never known among us, not even a quarrel occurred among us,

not even an insult. When the war closed in 1865, no seven men were more warmly attached to each other than we; and to this day, I love them as my own brothers. Sullivan and Couch live in Ellis County near Rocket and Red Oak, Stuart at last account was in Old Mexico. Bingham is dead as perhaps the others too. All of us are near three score and ten, except Patton, who, if alive, is nearer eighty. May God bless their memories, for they were friends indeed and everyone was brave. Indeed I have never known any other six men truer to an obligation if we omit Patton.[16]

While at Camp Parsons, Dave and the men of the Twelfth enjoyed an endless parade of supplies and "good things to eat." Commodities of all kinds, shipped by rail from Harrisburg, Houston, or Hempstead, included several types of meat, molasses, fruit, vegetables, cornmeal, and flour. One of Dave's comrades, writing to his mother, boasted that his company had received "seventy pounds of firm [fine?] dried apples, one pint of molasses to the man, some pickles and candles." The only commodity that from the beginning was in short supply was soap. The same soldier wrote, "It seems impossible for us to get soap enough; we only get a little occasionally; consequently we can't keep clean."[17]

Another ranger describing life in the camps mentioned that his company's weekly rations consisted of "meal, flour, beef, and pork," along with "sugar, molasses, potatoes, pumpkins, and salt." Even the horses looked fine, he concluded, since each ranger also drew hay for his mount.[18]

In addition to provisions acquired through military channels, Parsons' boys had access to private donations and the commodities in sutlers' stores. But the sutlers' exorbitant prices, high interest for credit, and limited inventory persuaded many soldiers to shop elsewhere. A Camp Parsons soldier wrote, "I prefer going to Houston when I want anything and 'look around.'"[19]

Houston, overrun by refugees from the coast and filled with saloons and ladies of the evening, was much preferred to Galveston. One of Dave's comrades described Houston as "very pleasantly situated on the west side of Buffalo Bayou" with "many neat and some elegant buildings. Its sidewalks are adorned by trees" and "its gardens and yards decorated by shrubs and flowers." Galveston, on the other hand, was the scene of massive military buildup where hundreds of slaves worked in gangs constructing barricades, gun emplacements, and bombproofs. Since Galveston was considered indefensible, Confederate officials had ordered all civilians to evacuate the island, and this they did in large numbers. "Every train leaving [Galveston]," one of Parsons' rangers reported, "is loaded with women and children, their plunder and goods."[20]

A few days before Christmas, Dave experienced his first real thrill as a member of the "glory boys" (a derisive label given mounted troops by foot soldiers). He rode for the first time in a formal dress parade through the streets of Houston for the benefit of civilian spectators. Dave and his messmates were keenly aware of the scores of young ladies with brightly colored parasols lining the sidewalks, so they displayed rare good humor, each convinced that all eyes were on him. Dave sat rigidly erect in his saddle, his head held high, giving his spirited Morgan free rein to prance down the crowded thoroughfare. With furrowed brow, he looked neither to the right nor to the left, assuming the demeanor of a courageous warrior with serious business on his mind.[21]

Dave, Little Will, Bingham, and Sullivan rode stirrup to stirrup by company in a column of fours sporting their best civilian attire bedecked with jingling equipment and military trappings intended to bedazzle all who beheld them. Their horses seemed to sense the splendor of the occasion and walked with special quickness as if they shared their owners' pride and patriotic zeal.

Toward the end of the parade intermittent rain thinned the lines of spectators, and Dave and his messmates discovered that their exhilaration decreased in direct proportion to the size of their audience. A final downpour drenched the resplendent horsemen, but they stuck to their designated route and pretended not to notice the rain. One soldier labeled the parade a "magnificent display," but most were inclined to believe that "rain interposing" had turned the whole affair into "a sublime failure."[22]

A few days later Parsons and his boys celebrated Christmas "far out on the tented field" on the banks of Sims Bayou. Since only a handful of rangers had received furloughs, most members of the regiment were on hand to participate in the festivities.[23]

Dave wrote that on Christmas Eve he heard his first cannon fire "when one of the 'Twin Sisters' . . . [was] fired" to mark the beginning of the celebration. "The 'Twin Sisters'", he explained, "were two . . . howitzers used by the Texas army under General Sam Houston at the battle of San Jacinto—brass howitzers."[24]

Christmas Day was filled with horse races, shooting matches, singing contests, and patriotic speeches. Plenty of "busthead" was on hand for those who wanted it, and as a result, at least two of Parsons' boys became highly intoxicated. A soldier in Company F wrote:

Christmas in camps. Before Aurora had dawned, the campfire was burning brightly and before "Sol" had smiled upon the encampment, the Fourth Cavalry was seen with their shiny caps in hand marching up or grouped around the "center of attraction" impatiently awaiting to slake their thirst at the "sparkling bowl." The Colonel's fire served to elicit the largest crowd, but few refused to participate in drinking toasts. Most everybody was more or less merry and some became "groggy." However, it only got the upper hand of two of the Rangers and exerted a very lively influence over them the greater portion of the day.[25]

But December 1861 was not noted merely for its merrymaking. It was the month that marked the beginning of a "bayou fever" (pneumonia and typhoid) epidemic that eventually claimed the lives of more than four dozen soldiers. The first fatality occurred about four days after Christmas, and during the weeks that followed, a long line of Parsons' boys succumbed to the epidemic. One soldier explained how sick call worked at Camp Parsons: "This is the way they ascertain: every morning at six o'clock the orderly goes around to all the tents, and if a person is a little unwell he has to give him his name, and he goes to the hospital in order for the doctors to prescribe for him; if he does not, he gets no medicine. If the person sick is unable to go, he is visited at his tent by a physician."[26]

As time passed and the number of deaths mounted, the more seriously ill were transferred to the county hospital in Houston. But the epidemic continued unabated. The bodies of some of the rangers were returned to their families, but others were buried on the banks of the bayou. "During the last weeks a great deal of fatal sickness occurred in camp," Dave wrote in 1912 in his recollections, "and over south of the camp on the side of a small ravine are about forty graves."[27]

Convinced that inclement weather was the cause of the prevailing sickness, Parsons took steps to protect his soldiers. First he arranged with railroad officials to transport guard details to and from some of their stationary posts by rail. Then he obtained permission from the state's commanding general, Paul O. Hébert, to shorten the mounted patrol routes, especially along Clear Creek. "We are truly glad the guard has been narrowed down," a soldier wrote, "for we believe the exposure attending this has been the chief cause of sickness among us."[28]

This belief was widely held. One soldier explained that one "cause of sickness here is the dampness of the atmosphere or fogs in the latter part of the nights and mornings, but this is the case all over the Gulf country." Although no evidence exists to indicate that Parsons ever considered moving his winter quarters, there was "talk of the regiment moving above Houston . . . to find a more healthy location." [29]

Rains and frigid temperatures in late January compounded the suffering of Dave and his comrades. "A very heavy rain fell last week which has almost covered this country with water," a resident of Camp Parsons wrote, "[but we] kept our things dry though the water ran in some of the tents." On this occasion, the soldier continued, the camp was paralyzed by "the coldest spell we have had." Tons of soggy firewood were hauled into camp by railcar to keep "good fires" going. [30]

During the last week in January, Camp Parsons received a special visitor. General Hébert, on his way to inspect Galveston defenses, spent several hours conferring with Parsons and visiting sick soldiers. The general cut a striking figure as he moved from tent to tent, sporting a greased rat-tail mustache and wearing an ornate, broad-brimmed hat, brass-buttoned coat, and shiny, red-topped boots. A stickler for ceremony and protocol, he and Parsons moved about camp in the company of a "suite of waiters" and aides, admonishing ailing soldiers to get well while collecting information concerning their needs. After promising additional medicines and blankets, Hébert mounted his private railroad car and was off for Galveston. [31]

Hébert must have enjoyed his short stay at Camp Parsons because he stopped again several days later while en route to Austin. This time he spent most of the afternoon. The weather for a change was good, and Parsons prevailed upon the commanding general to witness "a demonstration of equestrian skill" staged in his honor. Since the parade ground was in poor condition, the demonstration took place on an open space between the camp and the highway. Dave and his comrades began by passing in review and then executed a series of intricate cavalry movements. Then they "wound up charging, first by platoons, then by divisions, and thirdly by squadrons." Evidently delighted with the show, Hébert complimented "the men of the troop" in a long-winded speech delivered in his curiously high-pitched voice. "He appeared highly pleased with us," one of Parsons' rangers wrote, "and the regiment . . . also appeared pleased with him." [32]

During the weeks that followed, Dave and the men of Camp Parsons added still another malady to their growing list of ailments—black depression. Additional deaths, continued bad weather, and fading prospects of moving their bivouac made life in the camps increasingly intolerable. In their dejected state, they questioned their presence in the bayou country, concluding that they served no worthwhile purpose by being there. Either the War Department had forgotten them or was indifferent to their welfare.

In the beginning Dave and his comrades had expected the Federals to attack Galveston early in the war, but when enemy landings failed to materialize, they decided that the enemy had no interest in Texas. The only evidence to the contrary was the presence of a Federal blockader, the *Santee,* that hovered off the coast, guarding the approaches to Galveston harbor. From time to time other enemy vessels were spotted in Galveston waters, but they usually were gone in a few days.[33]

On February 9, however, Dave and the men of the Twelfth were shaken from their melancholy by the report of an enemy fleet off the coast. A ranger in Company F described the excitement that swept through Camp Parsons:

> There was quite a sensation with some here this morning. The report first came that about fifteen vessels were off Galveston Bay this morning. The next that the *Niagara* and four others besides the *Santee* and the brig *Sam Houston* [had appeared]. Some of our regiment who came up this morning say they saw four or five. Colonel Parsons and some others are smartly excited, and the cry over camp is, "Fight in a few days," and expecting at any hour to receive orders to march there. Others pronounce it a sensation and care little for it. It has not shocked me at all yet, though if it is not a recruiting or sounding expedition I think it probable there will be fighting soon.[34]

Yet only four days later, the same soldier expressed the disappointment felt by all when he wrote that the Federal vessels had sailed away leaving only the *Santee.* Once again boredom and despair gripped the camp.[35]

And to make matters worse, a new siege of pneumonia and typhoid broke out. During the next two weeks another four rangers died in the Houston hospital, two in the same afternoon. One was Dave's messmate, Billy Parsons.[36]

Captain Brown, commander of Company E, asked Dave and the men of the Long Branch to serve as a special honor guard to accompany Billy's body back to Ellis County for burial. All eagerly consented and immediately began preparations for the journey.[37]

But the next day another startling report arrived in camp, this time delivered by Colonel Parsons himself. Having spent most of the morning conferring with members of Hébert's staff in Houston, Parsons and his adjutant galloped into camp "bearing the important message" that the Twelfth was "destined for Missouri or Kentucky service."[38]

Rejoicing this time was restrained, since the men feared another disappointment, but the enthusiasm of the Twelfth was stirred by one of Parsons' unique horseback orations in which he carefully outlined the regiment's route. The substance of the speech was revealed in a letter written the next day by one of his men:

> Have received orders to march towards Missouri at the earliest prac-
> ticable moment. Arrangements are being made for conveyance or
> transportation. The regiment will first go to Hempstead and sojourn
> there until all things are ready. Some of the company will start from
> that point in a few days. The regiment is to report itself to General
> Albert Pike at Fort Smith, though the route designated is to cross the
> Trinity at Cincinnati (which is below Crockett) and Red River at Fulton,
> though I think there is a probability of it being changed.[39]

Dave and his messmates shared the excitement and anticipation of their comrades, but they realized that the transportation of Billy Parsons' body back to Ellis County must come first. Captain Brown instructed them to deliver the body, attend the funeral, and rejoin their company as soon as possible wherever it happened to be at the time. So the next day Dave and the men of the Long Branch, escorting the ambulance bearing the body of their messmate, rode out of Camp Parsons for the last time.[40]

The camp they left behind was a beehive of excitement as the men of the Twelfth prepared for their unit's departure. About four o'clock on February 27, Parsons conducted another dress parade on the Galveston Road, ending the affair with another speech from his saddle delivered "in his usually warm, impulsive style." He informed his troops that he had decided to "permit the companies to march by their respective homes and rendezvous at Fulton on Red River." Parsons' boys were surprised and pleased, for earlier the colonel had stated that "no furloughs to go by way of home would be granted under any consideration." Therefore, the men of the Twelfth whooped it up for their commander. As one soldier put it, "The boys fairly made the 'welkin ring' in applauding Parsons for granting them this priviledge."[41]

The next day, February 28, Parsons announced the manner of his regiment's departure. Five of his ten companies would move out first and proceed to a point "some five miles above Houston" where they would wait for the other five companies prior to the men's scattering to return to their homes. To set the whole affair in motion, company representatives drew straws to determine which five companies would move out first.[42]

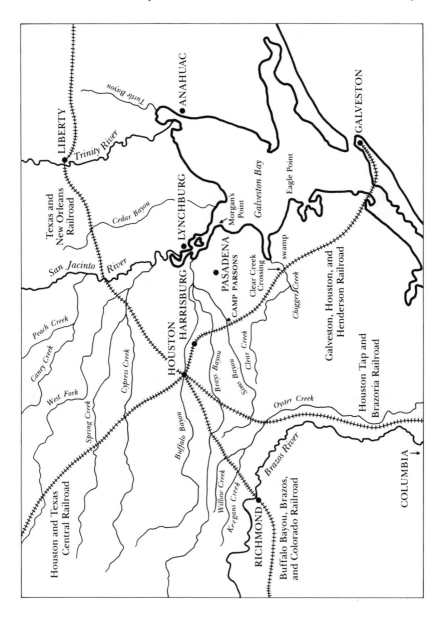

Map 2. The Texas Bayou Country, 1861–1862

On March 1 the first detachment made its grand departure. A soldier in Company F, part of the detachment, described the prevailing excitement:

> The sun soon shone out beautifully and the Gulf breeze swept with a solemn murmuring through the heavy, fine woodland that skirted the roadside. Presently I heard the shrill notes of Bugler [Henry] Brown, warning the Fourth Cavalry to make ready for their departure. I soon reached camps and found all awake to their interests. Tents were being pulled down, bed clothing being rolled up, and everyone seemed to be in a bustle. The camp equipage was soon arranged in the wagons, horses saddled, and all arranged; and with light, merry hearts the Rangers mounted their chargers and rent the air with the acclamations of "Goodbye, Camp Parsons!"[43]

As the Twelfth Cavalry (formerly the Fourth Texas Mounted Dragoons) took its leave of Camp Parsons, Dave and the surviving members of the Long Branch delivered Billy Parsons' body to his parents in Ellis County. Since their regiment was en route to the front, they would have preferred remaining with their unit. But for a brief interlude Dave and his messmates had to forget the war to bury one of its victims.

Billy Parsons' funeral services were conducted with military honors in a brush arbor south of Cedar Hill with the burial in a nearby graveyard that Dave identified as "the Shiloh Cemetery near Ovilla." Their messmate buried, Dave and the men of the Long Branch rushed to rejoin their regiment.[44]

CHAPTER 4

The Road to Cache River

*D*ave and the men of the Long Branch returned to duty after the funeral of Billy Parsons and joined their regiment at Camp Burleson, near Hempstead, on March 5, 1862. The next day, however, the regiment scattered in all directions as Parsons' boys went to spend a few days with their families. Dave and his messmates had no choice but to turn around and return to their homes. Though happy to have additional days to spend with their families, they resented having made the long trip to Hempstead for nothing.[1]

Dave spent the next two weeks at Heath Branch; but when time came for him and his messmates to rendezvous with their company, he was too ill to do so. "[We] started to the front, coming by home again," Dave wrote in his recollections, "and again I was sick, this time with pneumonia."[2]

But by staying at Heath Branch, Dave missed the frustrations experienced by his comrades, who found their rendezvous sites and destination changed repeatedly. Confederate reverses in western Tennessee and northwestern Arkansas panicked Trans-Mississippi officials and resulted in a flurry of conflicting orders, which complicated Parsons' consolidation and caused his men to wander aimlessly through three states and Indian Territory. After a tiresome trek to the Mississippi River, where at least part of the regiment spent almost three weeks, Parsons finally got word to his scattered companies through townspeople and travelers on the roads that Little Rock would be their ultimate destination and that consolidation would take place there.[3]

By this time Dave had recovered from his illness and was preparing to rejoin his unit. Having learned of the Little Rock rendezvous and of the bloody fighting in the northern reaches of the Trans-Mississippi, he knew he must not postpone his departure another day. But for the first time he realized that deep in his heart he did not relish the prospects of fighting. In all probability news of the decisive Confederate defeat at Pea Ridge in Northwest Arkansas and the recent bloodbath at Shiloh in western Tennessee had convinced him that if he left Heath Branch this time he might never return. Somehow that had not occurred to him before. Dave became moody and melancholy, given to long introspections about death and his reason for being. His papers are filled with allusions to the transitory nature of human life and to himself as merely a passing moment in the river of time.[4]

As Dave took his leave of his home and family early in May 1862, he left behind a poem which captured some of his private fears and thoughts:

Pleasant home I hate to leave you,
 My support, my seeming life.
My proudest spot and my only pleasure,
 For you I'll fight the bloody strife.

If life should leave me while in battle,
 Then Oh—Friends you need not weep.
Peace will be my future nature,
 As it is with those that sleep.

Weep not for me sweet Mother,
 Then I'll have a home afar.
Then you will have a son in peace,
 And not, as now, a son in war.[5]

But as Dave set out for Little Rock in search of his unit, the beauty of the landscape must have helped him forget the foreboding nature of his destination. From Dallas he followed the Greenville Road through a rolling blackland prairie, as pleasant to see in the springtime as anything east of the Western Cross Timbers. The countryside changed fifteen or twenty miles east of Greenville, and the prairie became spotted with post oak and blackjack interspersed with elm and redbud. Between Mount Pleasant and Boston, Nance crossed the Sulphur Fork of the Red and entered a "poor piny country" that supported a few small, drab, isolated communities whose advanced age was indicated by their widespread dilapidation. At Fulton, Dave and his Morgan mounted a creaking ferry and crossed the Red, about eighty yards wide at that point, and took the road to Little Rock. Except for frequent stands of loblolly pine, the country changed but little after that, still sprinkled with drab villages and isolated farms. "This is one of the poorest counties I ever saw," a soldier southwest of Little Rock wrote. "Corn is almost as high as your finger and some is just coming up."[6]

Dave found the traffic on the road heavier as he approached Little Rock, and for the first time he realized that a cloudbank on the horizon was smoke caused by burning cotton. Torched by its owners to prevent its falling into enemy hands, it produced heavy clouds of dense smoke that clung to the treetops, climbed high into the sky, and darkened the horizon. "Most every farm was seen smoking with burning cotton," wrote one of Parsons' rangers in Little Rock. "More than 50,000,000 dollars worth has been burned along the Arkansas and Mississippi rivers during the last month."[7]

As Dave walked his Morgan down the main street of Little Rock, he noted the sights and sounds of the city. Beautifully situated on the south bank of the Arkansas, Little Rock was "built after the fashion of other towns in the Southwest," although it had a "very dilapidated appearance." Birds sang in the trees that lined the thoroughfare, and the clatter of carts and horses' hooves was everywhere. The normally beautiful walks and drives, shaded with flowers, shrubs, and creeping vines, were cluttered with the foreboding equipage of war. All business was "suspended . . . except that done in a military line." Most of the city's magnificent buildings—the state house, arsenal, penitentiary, St. John's College, and the gas works—were occupied by troops or otherwise adapted to military use. "[The] 'places where gentlemen most do congregate' are closed," one Texas soldier lamented, "and it is only by display of the most extraordinary talent that . . . privates can obtain . . . anything like spiritous or vinous liquors."[8]

The civilian and military personnel who crowded the streets moved with a briskness born of desperation, aware that Federal troops might descend upon their city at any hour. U.S. General Samuel R. Curtis, operating from a base camp near the Pea Ridge battlefield, had mounted an offensive down the White River and now threatened Batesville, only ninety miles away, while off to the east heavy fighting was reported around Corinth. If Federal troops occupied Corinth and Memphis, they could use the lower White and Arkansas rivers to strike into the heart of Arkansas from the southeast. Then if Curtis drove down the White from Batesville, the residents of Little Rock would be caught in a pincers movement that could doom their city and lead to enemy conquest of the entire state.[9]

South of town Dave encountered some Texas boys at a campground called "Camp Texas" and learned from them that Parsons' regiment was bivouacked across the river. Crossing the Arkansas on the town ferry, Dave entered a dense woodland that lay along the north bank. At the end of a heavily furrowed road, Dave found the camp of the Twelfth Cavalry, its regimental banners fluttering in the breeze.[10]

The camp was a jumble of "dog" tents, makeshift shelters, rows of

Sibleys, parked wagons, and tethered livestock. Only about two hundred soldiers were in camp, many with measles, while the remainder either were on scout or en route from Memphis to Little Rock by boat. Parsons, though absent when Dave arrived, appeared the next day with the news that the regiment would not be sent to Corinth as he had expected. Then the following morning a three-company squadron commanded by Major E. W. Rogers returned, riding jauntily into camp with several wounded men, having fought a small but bloody engagement on a lane near Searcy on May 17, the day of Dave's arrival.[11]

This was Dave's first sight of wounded soldiers, and he discovered that he envied them. Their bravery under fire was established, and their wounds proclaimed to the world that they were real soldiers. As veterans of the regiment's first firefight, a successful Confederate ambush, they enjoyed telling stories of the battle, explaining in loving detail how they behaved under fire while taking pride in the swiftness and totality of their victory.[12]

Perhaps the most fascinating story told by Searcy Lane veterans was about a mysterious wild boy, too young for military service, who had tried to enlist in Rogers' squadron. When this was denied him, he tagged along on foot and was present when Rogers' boys pounced on the Federal patrol. During the battle that followed, the tattered urchin crawled among the wounded Federals and cut their throats with a large Bowie knife, killing "all the wounded [Yankees] he could find." When Rogers and his rangers withdrew, the apparently kill-crazed boy was left standing in the road, splashed with the blood of his helpless victims.[13]

Dave, impressed with the lighthearted manner with which Rogers' boys told their stories, put his unspoken fears behind him and tried to look forward to the day when he would face the enemy. Although not certain how he would act in the presence of hostile guns, he nevertheless determined to die if necessary rather than show cowardice or even the slightest hesitation. If he must die, he reasoned, he must do so in such a way as to enable those around him to report that he had shown no fear.

It seems probable that the Searcy Lane veterans embellished their stories, but this seems never to have occurred to Dave. When writing about their skirmish, he always praised them as heroes, expert in the art of bloodletting. "In all the annals of modern warfare," he wrote, "I have never known a conflict so bloody."[14]

Dave's messmates were part of another scouting detachment commanded by W. H. Getzendaner, and their whereabouts were unknown. Therefore, he cooked and ate alone the next several days until the wayward squadron returned. Finally on the sixth day after his arrival, the patrol containing the men of the Long Branch rode into camp, having reconnoitered as far north as Chickasaw Crossing without seeing any Federals.

In regimental elections held the next day, Dave and his messmates voted for officers as prescribed by reorganization procedures in the new conscription law of April 16, 1862. Fearing that twelve-month volunteers might leave military service and weaken Southern armies, the Confederate Congress had incorporated into the law enticements for reenlistment, including new company elections. Dave wrote that the men of his company reelected Captain John C. Brown of Milford company commander, W. N. Kenner of Corsicana first lieutenant, W. H. Getzendaner of Waxahachie second lieutenant, and Tom Cureton third lieutenant. "Cureton [later] was killed in the [entire regiment's] first battle on July 7th at Cache River," Dave added, "as was also many others." [15]

About noon on Friday, May 30, Parsons ordered his boys to leave all nonessential gear and prepare for a forced march to an unknown destination. Except for tents and nondescript materials used for shelter, the rangers did not have much equipment anyway. Most did not have—nor did they want—knapsacks, preferring to carry their toilet articles and extra clothing in their blanket rolls. Oilcloth ponchos usually were wrapped around their blanket rolls for protection against the elements. Other essential items either were tied to their saddles or crammed into saddlebags. Some of this equipment—which included shotguns, sabers, and cooking utensils—often was lashed to their saddle rigging and accounted for the jingling that accompanied the movement of mounted troops. Dave and his comrades, forming a column of about seven hundred horsemen, moved into the forest heading in a northeastern direction.

That night Parsons' boys bedded down on a public campground in Lonoke County near the little town of Austin, but early the next morning they were back in their saddles, this time traveling due north. They spent the next night at a site called Stony Point, and the next evening camped by a small stream about seven miles south of Searcy. The next two days were spent scouting the region between Prospect Bluff and Chickasaw Crossing. Then Parsons moved his camp to a more desirable site on the Little Red near Searcy about "one and one-half miles west of town." This site, which was to be occupied indefinitely, was dubbed Camp Searcy. [16]

Camp Searcy became a link in a northern defense line guarding the northern approaches to Little Rock. Mounted troops in Arkansas were under the command of General Albert Rust, a crafty and experienced officer who regularly conferred with his commanders and

frequently visited their campsites. Other mounted units that were assigned positions along Rust's northern perimeter or were otherwise
stationed in or near Little Rock were William Fitzhugh's Sixteenth;
James R. Taylor's Seventeenth; Nicholas H. Darnell's Eighteenth;
George W. Sweet's Fifteenth; and C. L. Morgan's so-called battalion,
which consisted of only five companies. Several widely scattered infantry units, including Allison Nelson's Tenth Texas, also were on
hand to join Rust's cavalry in contesting any move by Curtis toward
Little Rock. Less than a week after Parsons' arrival on the Little Red,
DeWitt Giddings, commanding part of George W. Carter's Twenty-
first Texas Cavalry, rode into Camp Searcy from Shreveport, but after
a few days moved to a site on Cache River about a mile below the
ferry.[17]

The overall picture of the war in Arkansas during these weeks is
difficult to define because of changes in the upper echelons of command and repeated troop transfers. Shortly after the battle of Pea
Ridge, Generals Earl Van Dorn and Sterling Price and more than
twenty thousand men were ordered east of the Mississippi River, leaving only a handful of undersized, poorly armed units to defend Arkansas. General John S. Roane, the Confederate commander of the state,
and Henry Rector, the Arkansas governor, complained loudly to the
War Department about the massive transfers, and the Richmond government sent General Thomas Hindman to Arkansas under orders to
use whatever means necessary to preserve Confederate authority and
defend the state. Upon his arrival Hindman immediately declared
martial law, formulated a policy to encourage the local manufacture
of war matériel, commissioned guerrillas to operate behind enemy
lines, ordered deserters hunted down and shot, launched a vigorous
recruitment program that pressed beardless boys and old men into
military service, and harangued officials in neighboring states to send
all available reinforcements. Hindman's methods were often questioned, and the charge was made that he actually abducted several
Texas regiments which were crossing Arkansas en route to battlefields
on the other side of the river. Nevertheless, within an amazingly short
period of time, Hindman converted a meager force of unarmed ragamuffins into an eighteen-thousand-man army which, although still
poorly equipped, had a good chance of defending the state. His disposition of these fighting men across northern and central Arkansas
explains Parsons' presence at Camp Searcy.[18]

But Hindman's defense preparations did not end there. Anticipat-
ing the fall of Memphis and Helena, which would open the lower
White and Arkansas rivers to Federal gunboats, he set to work trying
to block three probable avenues of Federal approach: down the White

from Batesville, up the White via St. Charles, and across the L'Anguille from Helena. First he secured civilian volunteers for the erection of "permanent obstructions" along the lower Arkansas and White and scuttled some out-of-date warships at strategic narrows above St. Charles. Next he dispatched a steamer armed with an eight-inch Columbiad to Clarendon and created man-made logjams in the White and Arkansas rivers. Then he personally supervised the delivery of rifles and shotguns to some "high-spirited" troops at Des Arc and strengthened artillery emplacements and infantry garrisons at St. Charles and DeVall's Bluff, where Federal forces by the middle of June were "making serious demonstrations by land and water daily." [19]

Dave and the men of the Twelfth were at Camp Searcy only a few days when news arrived that Memphis had fallen. This meant that the Mississippi River as far south as Vicksburg was Federal water, and for the first time Union gunboats and troop carriers enjoyed uncontested access to the lower Arkansas and White rivers. In less than two weeks a Federal flotilla of ironclad gunboats and troop transports carrying more than one thousand men entered the lower White and laid siege to St. Charles. "This is discouraging and sorrowful news," one of Dave's comrades in Camp Searcy wrote, but he and his fellow Texans found comfort in the fact that at least they were "between the enemy and Texas." [20]

Two days later Dave and the men of Camp Searcy were surprised by a visit from General Hindman, who was on a whirlwind inspection of Rust's northern perimeter. He evidently was pleased by what he found, for he wrote several days later that he did not believe the enemy could descend on Little Rock from the north or west "without meeting formidable opposition." [21]

Parsons' boys at Camp Searcy described Hindman as a small man, only about five feet tall, with blue eyes, a fair complexion, and a commanding presence. Since one leg was shorter than the other, he seldom dismounted, preferring instead to review the men of the Twelfth from the back of a big gray stallion. On those rare occasions when he did dismount, he walked with a decided limp, caused in part by a specially constructed boot with a high heel to compensate for his handicap. Nevertheless, the general had an imposing presence, and Dave and his comrades were impressed with his importance and flattered by his attention. [22]

Except for a minor clash with some "Hessian" (Pennsylvania Dutch) troops that ventured into their territory, Dave and the men of the Twelfth had no serious conflict with Federal raiding parties during June. This largely was because Federal squadrons intentionally avoided Confederate patrols while waging a relentless war on resources. Some of Parsons' boys got the wrong impression from this, incorrectly concluding that "the Yankees are as afraid as death of the Texans." Actually Federal patrols were merely following Curtis' orders to destroy or carry away everything that could provide sustenance for Rust's cavalry. More provisions were necessary for mounted troops than for infantry, since cavalry horses also had to be fed, and Dave and the men of Camp Searcy were not long in feeling the effects of Federal raids. One of Parsons' boys admitted: "We are now sending twenty miles after forage—it is very scarce."[23]

Curtis' raiders, moving with the stealth and cunning of blue-clad phantoms, struck quickly and disappeared into the shadows of the nearby forests. They cleaned out supply depots, burned wagon trains, looted smokehouses, shot livestock in the fields, and destroyed or carted off everything that might aid the Confederates. "The Feds came in last week and laid hands on everything they chose," one of Dave's companions wrote on June 6. "They have taken all the bread-stuffs in the immediate neighborhood, and at some places they de-stroyed almost everything and carried off the most of the Negroes." Three days later the same soldier observed that "the enemy has drained the country of forage and provisions wherever they have trav-eled and reduced some families to poverty and almost starvation."[24]

In retaliation Confederate cavalry combed the countryside, stalking an enemy that defied detection, one indeed that seemed to exist only in their imagination. Dave and his messmates participated in these scouts, operating from both the Stony Point and Searcy campgrounds, but they spotted the enemy only occasionally and even less frequently got him to fight.[25]

As the month of June drew to a close, the complexion of the war in Arkansas continued to change. Curtis, although convinced that he faced a larger force than he actually did, consolidated his approxi-mately ten thousand troops around Elkhorn (Pea Ridge), moved down the east bank of the upper White, entered Batesville, and set out to link up with Federal forces in the vicinity of St. Charles.[26]

Believing that Curtis was bound for Little Rock, Hindman sent three wooden steamers up the White to bombard Federal troop con-centrations and instructed Rust to dispatch all available cavalry to con-test Curtis' movement down the river. Hindman's anxiety and desper-ation can be seen in his orders that called for civilians, guerrillas, and regular troops to oppose the Federal advance "to the last extremity, blocking roads, burning bridges, destroying all supplies," including crops in the fields, and polluting rivers "by killing cattle, ripping the carcasses open, and throwing them in."[27]

In response to these and other orders, Parsons' boys abandoned

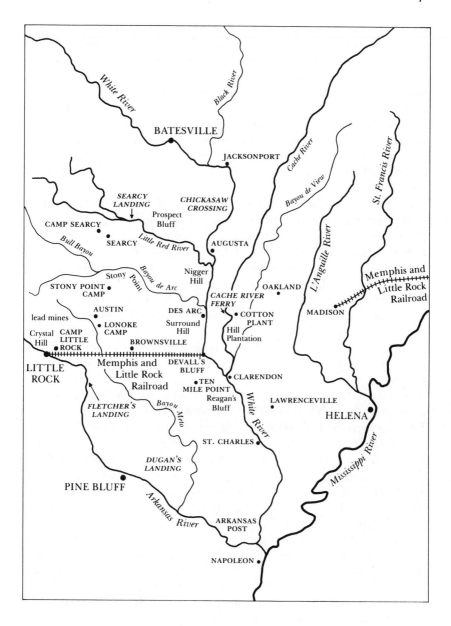

Map 3. Confederate Arkansas, 1862

Camp Searcy on June 29 and temporarily joined other troops at Stony Point, by this time a minor staging area for Confederate cavalry. Dave and his messmates were happy to leave Camp Searcy, since it no longer was fit for human habitation. After weeks of occupation, the site stank horribly. The heat and humidity were oppressive, and mosquitoes and flies seemed worse here than anywhere else. Pits dug for refuse were not adequate; seepage from latrines was an abomination, and in recent weeks there had arisen a serious question about the quality of the water in the river. "We all have derangement of the bowels," a camp resident complained, "which we attribute to this red-sandy river water." [28]

Dave and the men of the Twelfth spent only one day at Stony Point while Parsons conferred with other cavalry commanders. The overall plan, evidently formulated largely by Rust, called for Sweet's Fifteenth to move up the west bank of the White, cross the river above Batesville, and strike Curtis in the rear in a daring surprise attack. This almost suicidal maneuver was intended to hold Curtis temporarily in Batesville while Parsons and Fitzhugh challenged Federal patrols reported near DeVall's Bluff and Rust moved his main force into position for a grand confrontation. [29]

So while Rust consolidated his troops and Sweet began his forced march up the White, Parsons (followed the next day by Fitzhugh) set out on a seek-and-destroy sortie. One of Dave's comrades in the Twelfth described the movements of Parsons' troops during the first six days in July: "The command left Stony Point the first of July on a forced march for DeVall's Bluff and arrived there the third. Upon our arrival there, we learned there was no Federal force near, but that they were some thirty miles northeast of Cash [Cache] River. So on Saturday, the fifth, our cavalry force started on a scout. We crossed White River at Des Arc fifteen or eighteen miles above in the evening and night and Sunday morning went on and crossed Cash [Cache] River late in the evening." [30]

The marshland on the east bank of the Cache seemed even more inhospitable than that on the west. During part of the year, lower elevations of the forest became part of the river, and driftwood and other debris infested the lower branches of the trees, marking the high water level of the stream's annual overflow. More than once Dave and his comrades had to dismount and lead their horses through boggy recesses that threatened to envelop them.

As Dave and the men of the Twelfth pitched camp that evening, scouts reported Fitzhugh's column across the river and the presence of an enemy force on the east bank only four miles upstream. Without doubt this meant "fighting on the morrow." [31]

But sleep did not come easily to Parsons' boys that night. It was hot and humid, and they were attacked by swarms of swamp mosquitoes "as big as humming birds." Although wet with perspiration, Dave and his messmates covered their bodies with scratchy wool blankets and placed handkerchiefs over their hands which in turn were placed "over . . . [their] faces to mitigate the torments of the mosquitoes." For almost an hour Dave and Little Will lay awake discussing the likelihood that at least one of them probably would not survive the next day's fighting. Although conversation was difficult because of their antimosquito measures, they made a "life or death" pact, each pledging that he would not forsake the other in battle. Whatever the circumstances, the two friends promised to be "true in the hour of need."[32]

Perhaps comforted by their pact, Dave and Little Will then drifted off into fitful slumber, the unwilling victims of stifling heat, high humidity, and bloodthirsty mosquitoes. The discordant, rasping croaks of bullfrogs echoed through the dark forest.

CHAPTER 5

Dried Blood and Swamp Water

On Monday, July 7, 1862, mess captains and their assistants at Parsons' Cache River encampment arose early, went up the road for water, and began preparing breakfast. Suddenly a distant shot echoed down the river, and bleary-eyed rangers grabbed their weapons and peered into the dark forest with its "almost impenetrable swamps." When there was no more commotion, they disregarded the shot, supposing that some early forager had slipped out of camp to fetch an Arkansas pig for his mess.

Breakfast was under way when a small scouting party composed mostly of the Freestone County boys rode into camp with news that the enemy, whose camp was spotted the evening before, had vacated its campsite and was nowhere to be seen. The scouts had no new information on Fitzhugh's regiment, reported across the river the day before, thereby smashing Parsons' hope of consolidating the two Confederate regiments before confronting the enemy. Now he had no choice but to proceed alone.[1]

Shortly after seven o'clock Parsons again dispatched scouts and ordered the rest of the regiment to saddle up. Dave tossed his saddle across the back of his Morgan, shoved his shotgun into his concha socket, and swung aboard. Instinctively he checked his Whitney pistol, returned it to his holster, and guided his horse into line.

A formation, such as it was, took shape quickly as Parsons' boys crowded around him. Parsons called for "seven volunteers from each of the ten companies" to form an advance guard. Dave and Little Will were among the seven responding from Company E. As a further precaution against a surprise attack, Parsons then requested twenty volunteers from the advance guard for a skirmish line to spearhead the entire column. Dave and Little Will "answered again in this second request" and assumed positions in a great semicircle at the head of the column. Then two "points" were selected from the skirmishers. They guided their horses "out in advance of all" and entered the forest followed by Dave, Little Will, the other skirmishers, the fifty rangers now constituting the advance guard, and the rest of the regiment.[2]

Parsons assumed a position at the head of the main contingent near the middle of the column with the intention of determining the speed of march, but the men of the advance guard and skirmish line stepped out prematurely, and he became hard pressed to stay within sight of them. Thus the segmented column plunged into the shadowy depths of the woodland, battling scratchy branches, dense undergrowth, spiraling creepers, clouds of black mosquitoes, and treacherous stretches of marshland.[3]

Although the Hill Plantation was known to be in the vicinity and the town of Cotton Plant was somewhere off to the east, there was no sign of human habitation. The distant cry of a great bird mingled with other strange and mysterious sounds that seemed to come from the dark recesses of hades. The dark and eerie environment reminded Dave of the dawn of creation where primeval forests were inhabited by strange beasts and flying things.

As Dave and his comrades laboriously picked their way through this seemingly supernatural world of mystery and wonder, the column became more segmented and strung out as minutes passed. Dave wrote: "The two [point men] went forward, then fifty yards behind came the other eighteen, two hundred yards still to the rear came the fifty, and then the regiment perhaps a half mile farther back. Thus we marched in silence through a dense forest to the battle."[4]

Although little distance was covered, considerable time passed, and the heat and humidity in the forest became almost unbearable. Dave and Little Will were situated in the center of the skirmish line, but they now found movement relatively easy as long as they could follow the dim outlines of a trail.

Parsons knew that the enemy was somewhere in the forest, but the question was where. The Federal troops seemed to have disappeared from the face of the earth. The situation was especially tense, since Parsons' boys knew their disadvantage if ambushed by infantry in this dense woodland.

Time passed slowly. Sometimes the two point men, about fifty yards in front of Dave, Little Will, and the rest of the skirmishers, disappeared into the underbrush only to reappear several seconds later still picking their way through the green jungle hell. "The two men were instructed not to fire but to keep a close watch," Dave wrote, "and when the enemy should be discovered, to fall back and take their places quietly with the twenty."[5]

Just as the skirmish line emerged from a large cypress swamp, Little Will suddenly yanked his horse to a stop, and Dave quickly did likewise. The reason was apparent: the two point riders had frozen in their tracks. Then as the point men began a slow, cautious retreat, Union cavalry was sighted ahead among the trees on both sides of the road. Dave wrote: "Just as we had passed through a quagmire in which mud was knee deep to our horses, the two fell back, and then the twenty formed in line across the road—my place was in the road, and Stuart was the second man to my right. Immediately the Federal advance came up, they were mounted too, and halted not to exceed forty yards in front."[6]

Dave and his comrades, facing the advance guard of a Federal force of about two thousand men, were hopelessly outnumbered. Units constituting the enemy force included a small squadron of Missouri cavalry; remnants of infantry regiments from Missouri, Wisconsin, and Illinois; and a handful of Indiana cavalrymen with a small cannon. Although Dave and the rest of the skirmishers did not know it at the time, Fitzhugh's regiment was only a short distance away and would join the fight. Together Parsons' and Fitzhugh's regiments numbered in excess of sixteen hundred men. But the Federal troops initially were better positioned for combat, and Parsons' and Fitzhugh's boys found movement difficult in the timbered marshland. The advantages enjoyed by the Federals, however, were more than offset near the end of the battle when Rust appeared with more than two thousand Confederate reinforcements. This gave the Southerners almost a two-to-one numerical advantage, but Rust, perhaps unfortunately, elected to break off the engagement.[7]

But when Dave and the rest of Parsons' skirmishers first became aware of the Federal presence, they were well out in front of their advance guard, and neither Fitzhugh's nor Rust's forces were on the scene. The closest Confederate reinforcements were those of Parsons' advance guard, at least two hundred yards back down the road. Parsons and the rest of his regiment, about six hundred men, were more than a quarter mile farther behind, separated from their advance guard by dense forest and intermittent swamp. This left Dave and the nineteen Confederate skirmishers, now including the two point men, to face the Federal advance guard alone until the rest of Parsons' boys could move up.[8]

Since Dave occupied the center of the skirmish line, he was squarely in the road, a position certain to draw most of the enemy fire. He felt exposed, cornered, betrayed, and helpless. For several moments neither side made any attempt to fire. Separated by a mere forty yards, the two opposing forces simply stared. Time seemed to stand still.

The standoff ended abruptly as the Federal horsemen nearest Dave opened fire. Dave's head snapped back in a violent, convulsive motion as a one-ounce ball found its mark. He reeled giddily in his saddle, instinctively retaining his seat on his plunging Morgan, which also was hit.[9]

The firing continued as both sides scattered. Almost immediately, Dave was hit again. "I don't know much . . . about the battle," Dave wrote in his recollections, "for at the very first volley, a one-ounce ball hit my left cheek, coming out the back of my neck. The man on my right went down," he explained in another account, "and then the one on my left. And at about the same time another ball hit the right side of my neck," Dave continued in his recollections, "though I have no recollections of that event." The young ranger slumped so low in his saddle that his face was almost down to the horn. "I only know the [second] wound was there a few minutes later, . . . with two streams of blood flowing fast."[10]

Of course Dave knew when the firing started, but for several moments he was not aware of what happened. There was a blinding flash, a fleeting moment of semiconsciousness, and then inky darkness. As his senses returned, he became aware of his horse pitching under him. He heard musketry around him, muffled at first but soon swelling into an ear-splitting staccato.

As the Federals and Confederates exchanged volleys at close range, the distance between them slowly widened, the rear ranks on both sides moved up, and the swamp became a cyclone of plunging horses, flying spray, blood-curdling screams, flashing sabers, and tumbling bodies. The air resounded with the shrill ping of miniés, the dull drone of old-fashioned musket balls, and the deadly spit of buckshot. Parsons' boys, armed largely with shotguns, took a heavy toll on the enemy when the Federals were within range. One of Dave's comrades wrote that "the destructive double-barrels of the Twelfth . . . threw the elite of the St. Louis regiments into dismay."[11]

The Federal cavalry fell back among the trees, dismounted, and assumed positions among their infantry, forming a battle line in the timber at the edge of the swamp. A desperate charge by Parsons' horsemen ended in failure, driven back by the withering fire of Wisconsin and Missouri sharpshooters.

About this time Fitzhugh's regiment arrived and engaged Federal positions on Parsons' right, enabling Parsons' troops to launch two more attacks. As they again were forced back, General Rust arrived with remnants of three regiments including James R. Taylor's Seventeenth. A soldier in a squadron of the Seventeenth, dispatched by Rust to circle the Federals and "attack them from the rear," wrote that Parsons and his troops made at least three charges upon enemy lines but were repulsed every time with "considerable loss[es]."[12]

With the arrival of Rust, the Confederates had a good chance of defeating the Federals, and Parsons urged Rust to launch an all-out attack. But Rust, believing that he faced a large Federal force and seeing that Parsons' boys seemed to be getting the worst of it, ordered a retreat. Evidently the battle ended with both sides running in opposite directions, for a soldier in Taylor's regiment wrote that "it is said the Yankeys put out one way and us the other." [13]

Meanwhile, the badly injured Nance concentrated on staying alive. When he regained consciousness after the first volley, he slipped from the back of his mortally wounded Morgan only to discover that his rubbery legs would not support him. Falling on his hands and knees in the murky waters of the swamp, Dave realized that another lapse of consciousness meant drowning. He also feared "being trampled underfoot" by the plunging horsemen around him.

In an effort to escape these dangers, Dave crawled under a large tree, evidently knocked over by lightning, where mud was several inches deep. Except for the Whitney in his holster and over a hundred dollars in his jeans, he had lost all of his earthly possessions. "My . . . [shotgun] and hat were gone as also my horse and saddle and all my clothes save the ones I wore," he wrote, "and I was in my shirt sleeves." [14]

Dave must have been a ghastly sight. He was covered with mud and blood from head to foot, and his face was a swollen, discolored, shapeless mass. His normally handsome features were distorted and frightful. Swelling practically closed his throat and reduced his breathing to painful, gurgling gasps. In an effort to stop the bleeding, Dave ripped a strip of homespun from the right sleeve of his shirt and wrapped it around his neck. Little could be done, however, to stem the flow gushing from the gaping hole where the first ball had exited.

Nance did not know how long he lay under the fallen tree. Part of the time he was only semiconscious, vaguely aware of the battle raging around him. He wrote: "Then came a cavalry charge, on, on, through the roar of guns, the rattle of balls against the trees, mingled with the cries of men. The storm was on—dreadful and yet sublime. It swept the earth of men and passed. They spiked the cannons, and stopped their hellish mouths, and then the roar abated some. But the enemy rallied and drove them back; but I was in the rear of friends. [15]

Finally the sounds of battle faded. Except for the cries of the wounded and an occasional sputter of distant gunfire by the river, the forest became strangely still and silent. Birds had disappeared, rabbits had run away, and squirrels and chipmunks had vanished into the next county.

Realizing that he could be captured, Dave hid his pistol and money in the soggy leaves and mud beneath the fallen tree. Then he waited, hoping that Confederate rather than Federal soldiers would appear.[16]

Dave was unprepared for what happened next. First there was movement in the bushes off to his left. Then a sharp, searing pain shot through his right shoulder accompanied by the sound of a musket fired at close range. Dave explained in his recollections that another one-ounce ball had passed through his right shoulder, "severing the deltoid muscle."[17]

The impact of the one-ounce ball had slammed Dave into the muddy ground beneath the fallen tree, and he remained perfectly still hoping the "brute" who had fired the ball would not shoot him again. "A little later," Dave wrote in another account, "a ruffian from my native state [of] Illinois discovered me, and said: 'Get up you Reb, or I'll shoot you!'" Seeing Dave's holster and gunbelt buckled around his waist, the Illinois soldier demanded Dave's handgun. "In the rush of events I had forgotten to dispose of the scabbard," Dave explained, "and so I failed to save my pistol, a new Whitney."[18]

When Dave reluctantly produced the pistol, his blue-clad persecutor grabbed the weapon, placed its muzzle squarely between Nance's eyes, pulled back the hammer, and "threatened to shoot." Tormented and terrified, Dave was certain that his time had come. Helpless and pitiful, he frantically called upon someone for protection.[19]

But the Illinois soldier was restrained, perhaps at the last moment. Dave wrote, "Fortunately his captain was at hand, and was not a beast, and when I called for help he gave it readily (may God bless his memory). Tenderly he took me by the hand and assured me of his care." Dave, however, became a prisoner of war, "the very thing," he wrote in the *Nance Family Memorial,* that he "dreaded most."[20]

Dave was lifted from the bloody mire in which he had fallen and carried a short distance from the swamp. Although he had no conception of time, he was aware of renewed fighting down by the river and the frantic work of Federal litter bearers rushing back and forth from the front.

Shortly before the fighting ended by the river, two litter bearers collecting the "mangled bodies" of the dead and wounded stopped by to inspect the bloody heap that was Dave Nance. Seeing that Dave still lived, one of the bearers poked him with the toe of his boot and said, "Get up and go with us!" But the other Federal soldier, believing Dave was breathing his last, responded, "Let him alone, it will soon be all day with him."[21]

Soon thereafter Dave again was lifted from his "whirlpool of blood" and carried to a grassy knoll near the road where scores of dead and critically wounded soldiers lay. After "being a prisoner of war for perhaps thirty minutes," he took advantage of his guards' temporary absence, crawled across the road, and disappeared in the marshy underbrush.[22]

More than an hour later, some Hill County Volunteers found Dave lying in some underbrush down by the river. They took him to a clearing where other wounded Confederates were under the care of local housewives. Covered with dried mud and gore and still bleeding, Dave must have been a gruesome sight, for he wrote that the "women wept and tried to comfort me."[23]

Dave and two other badly wounded soldiers were placed in a white-topped wagon. Dave overheard the driver tell rangers standing nearby that they were bound for the hospital in Des Arc. Several minutes passed. Then without warning the concerned face of Little Will burst through the end-flaps of the wagon's canvas covering. He had lived up to the terms of his and Dave's "life or death" mutual assistance pact. Dave wrote: "Stuart, true to his promise, had not yet given up the search for me; for no one up to that time . . . knew what had become of me. So still searching with hope almost gone, he found me in the ambulance, and soon almost the whole company came to greet me. No one saw me dismount, or heard me cry out, for I was silent, and when Stuart found me I was still bleeding, and the flow did not stop entirely until my arrival at the hospital [in Des Arc] that night."[24]

The fight at Cache River, which lasted less than three hours, was not much of a battle by most standards. There even has been considerable disagreement over who won the contest, since both sides evidently retreated and suffered about the same number of casualties. Rust described the encounter as "a great victory" for the Confederacy, while Hindman lamented that Rust's forces "retreated in great disorder across the White River." Several of Parsons' and Taylor's soldiers blamed Rust for snatching victory from their grasp, claiming that he "at a critical moment failed to support Parsons."[25]

Even if the Federals were the tactical winners, they became the strategic losers when the final results of the battle were tabulated. The fury of Parsons' three charges, along with the strength and tenacity displayed by Sweet's troops fighting near Batesville a few days later, persuaded Curtis to abandon his plans to rendezvous with Colonel G. N. Fitch at DeVall's Bluff. Thus the Federal occupation of Little Rock was delayed for more than a year.[26]

In fairness to Curtis, however, it should be stated that the most compelling reason for his withdrawal to Helena was the poor state of his supply and his inability to live off the country. The region between the White and L'Anguille rivers had been totally depleted of usable resources, and the Memphis and Little Rock Railroad, which Curtis had hoped to use to transport reinforcements and supplies from Memphis, lay in shambles. Also Hindman evidently had convinced Curtis that he had reserves not yet committed. Hindman, a master of tactical diversion and deceit, had scattered rather than consolidated his Arkansas forces, creating the illusion of strength and numbers. Deprived of logistical support in a destitute country, convinced that Confederate reinforcements were approaching, hampered in his movements by sick and wounded soldiers, and burdened by thousands of runaway slaves that followed his army, Curtis made the only decision possible. But most Confederates attributed Curtis' withdrawal to Hindman's deception and to their own fighting tenacity. "It thus appears," Dave wrote, "that the vigorous fight of our little army . . . must have convinced Curtis that we had reserves, for he did not pursue." Fitch held DeVall's Bluff for several weeks waiting for Curtis, but fearing that his fleet might become stranded by the receding waters of the White and learning that Curtis had made Helena his destination, he also withdrew.[27]

As Fitch retreated and Curtis "diverted his line of march to Helena," the makeshift ambulance taking Dave and the other two wounded soldiers to Des Arc rumbled along, threatening to tumble to pieces on the rough road. With inadequate space for its passengers and neither "bed nor springs," it delivered a painful ride.[28]

Dave was conscious all the way to Des Arc. More than once he tried to make the young soldier next to him (also with a head wound) more comfortable by rearranging the boy's blood-soaked blanket which served as a pillow. Although Dave never learned the young soldier's name, he knew he was a member of the Ellis County Blues because of a blue strip of cloth sewn on his shirt. And Dave had recognized the other passenger the moment he saw him. He was Captain William J. Neal, the commander of the Slashers. The boy from the Blues moaned and moved occasionally, but Captain Neal showed no signs of life during the entire trip. Dave learned several days later that the commander of the Slashers had died.[29]

Finally after almost two hours on the road, the old wagon ground to a stop in front of a three-story building that Dave recognized as the Des Arc hotel, now serving as a hospital. He described the unloading: "[The] other two men were taken out first and carried in, leaving me all the room I needed. I made several ineffectual attempts to rise but failed. I had to give up and lie there till help came. However when once on my feet I walked in and up a flight of stairs to my room."[30]

Again Dave's wounds were bathed and bandaged, and that night he slept in a bed for the first time since leaving Texas. His troubled sleep was constantly interrupted by the suffering of a mortally wounded roommate. Dave wrote:

> There were two beds in that room. On one was a wounded soldier
> shot through the bowels, and I don't think I ever passed a night more
> horrible than that. The man's brother was with him, as also a friend or
> two. His suffering was so great he died at daylight next morning. He
> suffered with burning thirst and no sooner would he take a drink of
> water than he would throw it up. Tubfull after tubfull of water was
> brought until his bed was as wet as water could make it, and the whole
> room was drenched from side to side. Of course no one slept any,
> much less myself.[31]

By morning Dave's face was purple and swollen, his throat choked with mucus and other drainage, and his jaws so sore that he could not open his mouth to eat. An examining physician assured him that no vital organs had been punctured and that he would fully recover. A Des Arc housewife named Stubblefield appeared about ten o'clock and took Dave's clothes, laundered them, and returned them later in the day. While waiting for his clothes, he donned a shirt borrowed from Lewis Hardiman, another member of the Twelfth wounded at Cache River. "My clothes were stiff with dried blood and I had no others," Dave explained, "having lost all in battle."[32]

On the morning of July 10, Dave and several other seriously wounded soldiers were placed in "an ordinary two-mule wagon" and moved sixty miles to Little Rock. The journey required four "excessively warm" days, and the soldiers' discomfort was intensified by fogging dust and swarms of flies. "All this time the blow flies tried to get at our wounds," Dave wrote, "and once they deposited a lot of little worms right on the edge of the bullet hole in my shoulder."[33]

Shortly after noon on July 14, the creaking old wagon pulled up at St. John's College, which had been converted into a hospital. "The hospital at Little Rock was a five-story brick house," Nance explained, "[that stood] on top of a hill about one mile south of the ferry and about one-fourth mile east of the armory—state armory." Dave estimated that it contained about "500 patients sick and wounded—so many that large wooden additions had to [be] made to the building."[34]

Dave walked to his ward, a large room "about forty feet square" on the east end of the first floor. The room was hot and "literally full of sick and wounded men," and Dave was assigned a cot in "the northeast corner of the great east room, perhaps the coolest place in the house."[35]

"[Here] I spent the next two months, the most horrid in my whole life," Dave wrote, "in the St. John's College hospital where men died at the rate of eight every day for the whole time beginning with July 14th." Soldiers constituting so-called undertaking details made regular visits to the wards twice a day collecting bodies for burial. "[Not] far away is a forty-acre field of graves of young men like myself," Dave explained, "and for a long time I did not know what day they would come for me." [36]

During these terrible weeks in "the great hospital" Dave spent much of his time thinking, rejoicing that his life had been spared, and searching for an explanation for what had happened. He remembered his father's admonition not to join the army and his repeated warning that "God will punish those who kill." Dave knew that he had not killed. In fact he had not fired a shot at Cache River, having been knocked from the saddle before he could do so. Dave concluded that his recent suffering was God's way of repudiating war and his part in it. He also began to suspect that God must have a special reason for sparing his life, perhaps to accomplish some sacred mission which only he could perform. Therefore, Dave determined to give his life to God and strive to do His will. He wrote: "I was beginning to see that war is murder—cold-blooded murder. Then I promised myself that I would never shoot at another man. . . . I promised my God earnestly that if He would give me back perfect soundness, again in my father's home, that I would do my best to learn His will and do it." [37]

Seemingly in response to Dave's vow, a strange and wonderful thing took place at Heath Branch. Dave wrote in his theological treatise that apparently at the same moment he made his vow, God appeared to Quill in a dream "almost four hundred miles away" and assured him that his son would return safely from the war. "And although my father never relied on any other dream before," Dave explained, "he did rely on this [one], and Mother said [he] was never uneasy about me afterward but always insisted that I would return." [38]

For the rest of his days Dave believed that God heard his vow, provided divine intervention for his protection, and preserved his life during the war. In fact, Dave believed that God already had orchestrated his survival and prevented him from becoming a murderer. How else could one explain the events of the last several months? Sitting there in the Little Rock hospital, Dave recalled how his new Whitney pistol the year before had failed to fire when it otherwise would have blown off his foot, how the first shot at Cache River had incapacitated him to prevent him from killing a fellow human being, how he was captured but managed to escape after only thirty minutes, and how he now lived when so many of his comrades were in their graves. "[God's] constant preference for me was so conspicuous that I have never been able to persuade myself that it was only an accident," Dave confided in his theological treatise, "although I have never written this before and seldom mentioned [it] in my talk because it seems . . . like boastful egotism."[39]

As Dave's health improved, he borrowed a needle and thread from another patient, secured the strip of homespun he used to bind his neck at Cache River, and patched his only shirt. There was nothing he could do about the bullet hole in the right shoulder, but he carefully stitched a patch on the sleeve which had supplied the makeshift bandage that probably had kept him from bleeding to death.[40]

During these days of rapid recuperation, Dave established a close friendship with an "exceedingly kind" old surgeon who presided over his ward. Dave wrote:

> His name was Jones, and . . . [our] meeting seemed to be a case of love at [first] sight. When he came in, morning and evening, he would invariably come to me first, although I was at the very back side so that he passed many before reaching me. There were two regimental commanders in the room, one of whom had lost a leg, yet he always came to me first, and it was by the special care of this man that I survived at all. Once General Hindman, the commander of the Trans-Mississippi Department, came to the door; and as at all other times, Doctor Jones brought him first to me, at the same time saying, "Here General is one I want you to see." Those were his very words.[41]

At first restricted to liquids, Dave quickly returned to solid foods, and Doctor Jones would bring him "a biscuit in his pocket from his own table" and other "extras to eat." Many years later Dave recalled with pleasure the old surgeon's visits at least twice a day and sometimes more often. With the doctor sitting on the foot of Dave's cot and Dave nibbling on one of the old physician's biscuits, the two friends discussed the war, the suffering it had caused, the pointless questions it was supposed to answer, and—since the doctor also was a Texan—home![42]

One evening during one of these sessions, Doctor Jones shared some wonderful news. "[A] general order was issued to the army," the old surgeon reported, "allowing all men wounded at Cache River a sixty-day furlough." In other words Dave could go home as soon as he was able.[43]

But Dave's suffering in "the great hospital" had not run its course. Just as Dave seemed on the brink of complete recovery, he was smitten with a new affliction—erysipelas. What began as a small patch on his ear quickly spread to the rest of his body. "Erysipelas covered my head, neck, back of my waist, and right arm to my hand," Dave reported. "My eyes were so nearly closed by swelling I could scarcely see, and partial delirium set in and continued for several days." [44]

The moment Dave's malady was diagnosed, Doctor Jones transferred him to the erysipelas ward where a bad-tempered surgeon named Tolbert was in charge. This ward was in "an adjoining room but still on the north side of the building on the first floor . . . and contained about twenty patients." [45] Accustomed to the kind and considerate Doctor Jones, Dave detested his new ward boss, whom he described as "one of the most unsympathetic doctors" he had ever seen. "He would curse me when he should have sympathized," Nance complained. "I almost hated him; and once later after I had returned to camp, I met him on the street, but I thought so little of him that I did not make myself known." [46]

Finally after about two weeks in the erysipelas ward, Dave was returned to Doctor Jones' ward only to find that the kindly old physician had fallen deathly ill himself. The next day Dave was dismissed from the hospital but refused to leave the building without visiting with Doctor Jones. He wrote: "And the last act I did on leaving that horrid place was to go and find Doctor Jones and tell him goodby. He was sick in another part of the hospital and a few days later he died. May God remember his kindness to me and give him a double reward." [47]

After visiting the dying doctor, Dave wandered through the streets of Little Rock, having no weapons, money, or means of transportation. "I started back to rejoin my regiment . . . afoot," Dave wrote, having learned that the Twelfth was bivouacked somewhere east of Des Arc. [48]

Hitching a ride on a baggage wagon, Dave reached the Lonoke camp near Austin, where "a much larger army was being organized." He spent half a day visiting with members of a large infantry unit recently arrived from Texas. Then he caught another ride, this time on an ordinance wagon, which delivered him to his regiment's encampment. The camp was easy to find, since it rested on "the identical spot we occupied the night previous to the battle [of Cache River]." [49]

Upon his arrival Dave discovered that most of the men of the Twelfth were on furlough. Lonesome John and Bingham were the only members of the Long Branch present, and except for "a more emaciated appearance" they seemed in good condition. Many of the other rangers in camp were sick, suffering from a wide range of ailments including "Arkansas chills, diarrhea, and yellow jaundice." [50]

Dave, happy to rejoin his unit, found the atmosphere of the camp anything but pleasant. His comrades' reports on the course of the war and chances for the Trans-Mississippi's survival were not good. Another enemy offensive against Little Rock was expected; shortages were becoming critical; and the Twelfth seemed certain to be dismounted because of the loss of hundreds of irreplaceable horses in the battle of Cache River. The shortage of horses and forage already had resulted in orders specifying the future dismounting of Darnell's, Taylor's, and Fitzhugh's regiments. "Among those to be dismounted, there is great dissatisfaction," one of Parsons' rangers wrote, "and some of them have started home."[51]

But Parsons' regiment was brigaded rather than dismounted. The new brigade included George W. Carter's Twenty-first, Nat Burford's Nineteenth, F. M. Chrisman's Arkansas Cavalry, and J. A. Pratt's artillery battery. The Twelfth, still referred to as Parsons' regiment although now commanded by Bell Burleson, formed the "basis . . . [for] the brigade" and served as its core unit throughout the war. Although redesignated the Fourth Brigade after General T. H. ("Old Granny") Holmes became commander of the department, it initially was organized as the First Brigade, First Division, Second Corps, Army of the Trans-Mississippi. Parsons was appointed as the brigade's commander and held that position during most of the war, but as there was considerable turnover in the membership of the brigade, there were times when other officers held the top command. Other units later claiming membership in the brigade were C. L. Morgan's diminutive battalion, Sam J. Richardson's W. P. Lane Rangers, and finally R. Edward Gurley's Thirtieth Cavalry.[52]

But the brigading of his regiment was not among Dave's primary concerns after his return from the Little Rock hospital. After claiming his sixty-day furlough, he made arrangements to go home. He desperately needed the money he had hidden under the fallen tree during the Cache River fight, but he was not sure where the battlefield was located. He therefore enlisted the aid of Columbus Starkey, one of "that fated twenty" who had constituted the Twelfth's skirmish squad on the day of the fight. "[He] told me," Dave wrote, "he could point out the exact place I stood in the battle."[53]

Dave borrowed a horse, and he and Starkey rode out two or three miles east of camp. Dave soon found the fallen tree, its upper trunk resting on its branches so that it was about two feet off the ground. "I pointed out the log under which I lay and where my money was hidden in July before," Dave explained. "It required but a minute to find it—one hundred and five dollars, mostly in Confederate bills."[54]

Having recouped a measure of his former affluence, Dave collaborated with Lonesome John in the purchase of a mule for which forty dollars was his half. Then Dave bought a bridle and saddle for fifteen dollars and arranged with John to ride their mule to Texas. The next day he headed for home on his saucy little steed.

More than two weeks later, Dave dismounted in the dark shadows of his hilltop home, standing stark and silent in the Texas moonlight. A yellow glow from a single lamp was the only sign of life. "Mother," Dave wrote, "was preparing to retire for the night." Although everyone else already had retired, all but the youngest were told of his arrival and rushed to welcome him. "Well," Dave wrote, "of course they were all glad to see me."[55]

CHAPTER 6

Inferno in a Confederate Powdermill

*T*he Nance farmhouse sat majestically on its gentle hilltop silhouetted against the illumination of a predawn sky. In the shadows of the barn Dave Nance loaded the pack mule he jointly owned with Lonesome John. He was dressed in the ordinary costume of a Trans-Mississippi soldier of the day—an old felt hat, boots, and jeans and a jacket made from undyed cotton which had turned brown. A knapsack containing buckshot hung from one shoulder and a powder flask hung from the other. Having borrowed a young, spirited saddle mare from Quill and an old double-barreled shotgun from Uncle Otwa, Dave prepared to return to war.

It was less than an hour before sunrise, November 20, 1862. Dave's sixty-day furlough would expire in a few days, and he wanted to be punctual in reporting to his captain.[1]

As he pulled the last restraining ropes into place, Dave must have pondered the recent course of events. Federal troops had seized Galveston, and their presence in the state made his leaving more difficult. He knew that if South Texas railroads fell into enemy hands, a Federal invasion of the interior was likely. If Heath Branch and the upper Trinity had to be defended, he wanted to be here to defend them.[2]

Dave had said nothing of his fears to his family. And as was his custom, he had avoided mentioning his plans to leave until the time was near. Then, less than ten hours before his departure, he had said his good-byes and begun final preparations. Now, while the family slept, he climbed aboard his mare and, leading the old pack mule, hit the trail for Arkansas.

Dave crossed the Trinity at Miller Crossing and the Red at Laynesport to arrive in Little Rock on December 5. Parsons' rangers, he learned, were bivouacked near Des Arc, and two days later he rode into their encampment which was scattered along the west bank of the White. Dave estimated the distance between Heath Branch and Des

Arc at about four hundred miles, but somehow it seemed much farther.[3]

After locating Company E, Dave reported to Captain Brown in his headquarters tent. Dave delivered a snappy salute which the captain did not return. Instead he stared several moments at Dave as if he did not recognize him. Then after several moments, the perplexed commander asked Dave what he was doing there. Captain Brown explained that he thought the young soldier was in Texas making gunpowder.[4]

Noting Dave's bewilderment, the captain stated that he had received special orders that Dave was to be placed on assignment to manufacture gunpowder in Waxahachie, Texas. Brown in turn had mailed orders to that effect to Dave in care of the post office in Waxahachie. Dave knew nothing of this, since Quill had arranged for the assignment through the military committee of the Texas legislature without Dave's knowledge, and Dave had failed to receive Brown's orders, since Dave's post office was in Lancaster and not Waxahachie. This unfortunate mixup left Dave with no other choice but to retrace his steps to Texas.[5]

Dave was angry with Captain Brown for sending his orders to the wrong post office. "That little piece of carelessness on the part of my captain," he noted, "had caused me an unnecessary ride of eight hundred miles."[6]

After his return to Heath Branch, Dave learned more of the circumstances surrounding his new assignment. He wrote: "Old Mr. [William] Rowen, a neighbor of ours, had moved to Waxahachie and put up a powdermill for the manufacture of gunpowder for the Confederate army; and he had made application to the Texas legislature to have me detailed to assist him. . . . The State of Texas was furnishing Mr. Rowen all the sulphur and saltpeter necessary to be made into gunpowder on the halves."[7]

Although Dave knew nothing about making the explosive, he was eager to learn. So two days after Christmas, he entered a special phase of his military career—making gunpowder in Waxahachie.

Waxahachie, the seat of Ellis County, was situated in a lush region of natural beauty. Nestled among gentle hills, broken forests, and spacious meadows which abounded with wild game, it was a perfect site for the booming, rapidly-growing frontier community.[8]

Although Waxahachie was not the only town in the county, it was the major one. Having survived prairie fires, locust plagues, and at least one mild depression, Ellis County now boasted a population of 4,142 whites and 1,104 Negro slaves. There were twenty-two semi-

public "subscription" schools, two Masonic lodges, and the "most lux-
urious hotel (the Rogers' House) west of Jefferson." There was only
one saloon in the entire county, the remainder having been closed by
a temperance campaign conducted by local churches.[9]

A measure of wealth also was in evidence. The 1860 county census
listed 23,636 acres of "inhabited and improved" farmland valued in
excess of a million dollars. Although agriculture was predominant,
Waxahachie had three flour mills, two gins, a lumber plant, and the
new Rowen and Patterson powderworks where Dave became an ap-
prentice powdermaker.[10]

Dave made arrangements with Rowen and his wife to room with
them in their home on Red Oak Road while he worked in the powder
factory. He found this especially agreeable because of Rowen's vast,
private collection of books and periodicals. This library, unique for its
time and place, contained a wide assortment of titles on history, philosophy, religion, and the manufacture of gunpowder. During the
following weeks Nance spent many hours immersed in these works.

Rowen was a red-hot secessionist in his early fifties who worked
hard despite an emaciated body and an erratic heart. His bearing suggested aristocratic origins, and his speech reflected a sharp mind, a
good education, and the soft accents of the Deep South. Mrs. Rowen,
a wisp of a woman, worried about her husband's health and tried
without success to prevent his working endless hours in the powderworks. The good-natured Rowen always laughed at his wife's concern
and assured her that he would never allow a heart attack to deprive
her of a good husband.[11]

Like all Confederate powdermaking, Rowen's operation was fraught
with inherent dangers, filthy working conditions, long hours, and a
paralyzing shortage of workers. The importance of the powderworks
was never questioned, but few workers were available, since "most of
them were in the army." Those who might have been available became
expert in finding ways to avoid employment in the hot, grimy plant.[12]

In an effort to secure laborers Rowen had bargained with the Texas
government to allow army inductees to substitute powdermaking for
military service. This plan received the blessings of Austin and the
tacit support of Richmond, but the program had provided Rowen
with only one worker—Dave. And Dave might not have consented to
the substitution if he had been consulted. All the arrangements were
made by Quill and Rowen, and Dave evidently felt that he had no
choice but to accept the assignment.[13]

But Dave found that living in Waxahachie had its fringe benefits.
He learned to love the people of the community, who welcomed him
in a warm, friendly way, and he accepted dinner invitations from

prominent families, some with sons riding under Parsons' banner. He also visited Billy Parsons' grave in Shiloh cemetery on at least one occasion and spent almost every weekend and holiday with his family at Heath Branch.

Unlike earlier occasions when separated from his comrades in the Twelfth, this time he had no difficulty keeping up with their operations. In addition to receiving letters from Little Will and other members of his mess, he visited with Ellis County boys from his regiment when they came home on various types of furloughs. Also, since men from the county constituted the bulk of three companies in the Twelfth, Dave frequently found items about them and his regiment in the local newspaper, and of course relatives of men in his unit always were happy to share news obtained through correspondence with their boys in service.[14]

One incident involving the Twelfth that was widely discussed in Waxahachie during the spring of 1863 was the accidental shelling of Parsons' bivouac on the Arkansas River near Little Rock by a Confederate gunboat. Although described by other members of the unit in their letters and journals, it is not surprising that a description of the event found its way into Dave's recollections. In 1912 he wrote:

> Here at Argentia [present-day North Little Rock], . . . a Confederate gunboat . . . was bringing up one and one half million dollars in Confederate money to pay off the army. They fired a large shell which exploded in our camp. The shell was fired as a salute to the city, the men on the gunboat not knowing we were camped there. However it was a very reckless sort of salute. Though no one was hurt much, it exploded when it struck the ground under a horse, knocking the horse down by the concussion, I suppose, and bruising his rider slightly.[15]

For Dave the days in the powderworks passed quickly, and soon he considered himself an expert powdermaker. His joining Rowen's crew was applauded by the other powdermen, but the addition of only one worker did little to improve the plant's sagging production. The powderworks needed at least eight full-time workers to meet the quotas set by the military committee, but its crew never exceeded five workers at any one time, counting both Dave and Rowen. Other members of Rowen's crew during Dave's stint as a powdermaker were Tillman Patterson, Rowen's junior partner who did the glazing and pressing; Joshua Phillips, Rowen's first assistant (and only experienced powderman) who supervised the milling and drying; and Stephen Mulkey, an aged but capable chemist who processed the saltpeter and prepared the charcoal.[16]

State and independent contractors provided Rowen with supplies and raw materials. Local woodcutters delivered firewood for the charcoal burners and furnaces, and craftsmen in a nearby carpenter's shop provided cedar powder kegs. Saltpeter, shipped from South Texas by the army, always was in short supply, and Rowen occasionally had to suspend operations while awaiting the next shipment.

The powderworks, located north of the Waco (Little Rock–to–San Antonio) stage depot, was situated in the northeastern part of town on a major avenue (present-day North Rogers and McMillan streets). This normally busy thoroughfare, known as Mill Street during the war, curled among the buildings of the plant complex, linking downtown Waxahachie with Red Oak Road.[17]

The powderworks consisted of three clusters of dirty, barnlike structures interlaced with loading platforms, wooden tramways, service shelters, and storage sheds. The major buildings were the furnace shed, roller mill, and powderhouse. Each contained crude and sometimes makeshift machinery.

The furnace shed was isolated from the other buildings because of its open-hearth furnaces and ember-spewing chimneys used to produce charcoal and to heat an iron cauldron in which potassium nitrate (saltpeter) was purified and processed. Mulkey, who spent most of his time in this building, complained bitterly about the excessive heat. The charcoal, made largely from willow and maple, was produced in brick, ovenlike chambers built into the rear wall. After being crushed into coarse particles, the charcoal then was mixed with sulfur to form a gray compound called mash. While this was going on, the nitrate was cooked in the cauldron and thoroughly washed in drainage troughs to eliminate impurities. After the nitrate cooled into iciclelike crystals, it was crushed into a sparkling powder, and both nitrate and mash were transported by tramcart to the mill across the road.[18]

The roller mill and powderhouse, situated in a sharp, right-angled turn in the road, were the sites of greatest danger. The mill, with its dark, grimy interiors and cluttered piers, was by far the filthiest building in the complex, while the rambling powderhouse was the largest. These two buildings were linked by a tramway and a boardwalk. A large mule barn formed one of the rear walls of the mill, and a separate, barrackslike bathhouse stood nearby. The mill yard was divided into two sections by a large, reinforced barricade or firewall to shield the powderhouse from sparks or flying debris in the event there was an explosion in the mill. Towering above the mill yard on a ten-foot tower, a giant cistern provided water for drinking, bathing, and milling. A huge H-frame on an elevated platform served as a rack for dozens of cedar buckets, pulleys, and ropes suspended above the plant's only well.[19]

In his recollections Dave called the mill "my place in the powderworks" and described the machinery with which he worked: "The mill was operated by a treadwheel with ten little mules on it. It had ten mortars, each large enough to work twenty-five pounds. It also had an iron press capable of a pressure of about twelve hundred pounds to one charge. There was also a crushing machine, a shaving machine for graining the powder from the hard cake, and also a glazing cylinder."[20]

The foundation of the mill was as solid as iron and stone could make it, but the walls and roof were flimsy, designed merely to provide a measure of protection from the weather. If the building exploded, the force of the blast would be upward, destroying the superstructure. All the workers might be killed, but the floor and expensive machinery should remain essentially undamaged. If workers could be found to replace those killed by the blast, the mill could resume operation within a few days.[21]

Dave, working in the suffocating dust around the mortars, took on the appearance of a "shadowy creature from the recesses of hell" as the choking black dust darkened his clothing, face, and hands. But he and his co-workers, Joshua Phillips and Tillman Patterson, became good friends and worked well together. The crushing, blending, and pressing of the mash and nitrate were monotonous and grueling, but through dedication and tireless persistence Dave helped produce thousands of pounds of the explosive.[22]

As described in Dave's recollections, the crushing and blending were accomplished by rotating cylinders, powered by the treadwheel revolving inside the mortars. Water piped from the cistern was added at intervals to produce a gray paste, which was pulverized and allowed to dry into mill cake. After several hours of grinding, the cake was removed, shaved into uniform grains, glazed, and then transported by mule wagons to the powderhouse.[23]

The work in the powderhouse, by Rowen and other members of his crew not at the moment engaged in other operations, also was tedious and backbreaking. The powder was "blistered" in the sun or by some form of artificial heat, returned to the mill for pressing, and finally hauled back to the powderhouse for more drying before being placed in kegs for shipment. Large, dangerous stockpiles of kegged powder awaiting shipment usually occupied a large part of the powderhouse.[24]

Although most residents of Waxahachie were unfamiliar with the details of powdermaking, many recognized the "threatening presence" of the powderworks. Few doubted that the entire town would be demolished if the powderhouse exploded. And according to local prophets of doom, it was only a matter of time.

As fate would have it, on April 29, 1863, there was a small explosion in the mill followed by fire, more explosions, and finally a tremendous earthshaking blast that left the mill in ruins. Even part of the stone floor with its iron fixtures was blown away, and although the furnace shed burned to the ground, the powderhouse—shielded from the fire and explosions by the firewall—miraculously survived.

Most residents of North Texas learned of the tragedy by reading the *Dallas Herald* and other newspapers. The only survivor, the *Herald* announced, a resident powderman "who was employed in the mill," was a "young man named Nance, son of Allen Nance, Esquire, of . . . Dallas County," who was "considerably but not fatally burned." [25]

The initial explosion was a small one, taking place at 4:15 P.M., "about two hours before sundown." It was followed by rapid-fire blasts that seemed to grow in intensity until the final explosion blew the "mill . . . to atoms" less than three minutes later. [26]

Fortunately only three of the plant's five crewmen were in the mill. Shortly before four o'clock, Mulkey, who was working in the furnace shed, inadvertently let his charcoal burners go out and decided not to fire them again. Since he wanted to spend some time working in his garden before dark, he decided to leave the plant a few minutes early. As he left the furnace shed and started for the bathhouse, he was joined by Patterson, who also decided to quit work for the day. The two men went to the bathhouse, scrubbed themselves and their work clothes, dressed in their street attire, and left the plant.

Meanwhile, Dave was grinding 250 pounds of mill cake when Rowen arrived from the powderhouse. Since they and Phillips were tired and the hour was late, the three also decided to go home.

Suddenly after a blinding flash, a small blast occurred in one of the mortars, and the mill quickly filled with acrid smoke. Other explosions followed, violently rocking the floor and hampering efforts to escape. Phillips, who was fatally burned, lived long enough to attribute his delay in leaving the mill to being "knocked down several times . . . by explosions." [27]

The first explosion, though little more than a dull thud, set in motion larger blasts that blew out the rear of the building, demolished the mule barn, and killed most of the mules. This staccato of explosions also blew Dave, who had run toward the front door, closer to the main entrance, flattening him against the stone floor and igniting his powder-saturated clothing. A multitude of strange sounds, like thousands of whispering voices, reverberated through the smoke-filled mill, but Dave had no time to try to locate their source (probably smoldering mash in the mortars). With fire searing his entire body, he scrambled to his feet and ran through the front door clawing at his clothing. "My clothes were literally burned off of me," he wrote, "[and] . . . I was badly burned."[28]

At least another twenty seconds passed, punctuated by other explosions, before Rowen and Phillips emerged from the mill. The initial blasts had thrown them into the rear of the building among flaming wreckage that had been one wall of the mule barn, and they were fifteen or twenty feet from the front exit.

Scorched and blinded by smoke, Rowen and Phillips realized that they had little time to escape the inferno. Eternity, indeed, was only a heartbeat away. At this point they probably were burned less severely than Dave. At least their clothing had not yet ignited. Only seconds later, however, as subsequent detonations again knocked them off their feet, Phillips' clothing caught fire. The situation had worsened, but escape still was possible. Rowen probably suffered more at this point from cuts and bruises than from burns, and the front door was well within the reach of both men.[29]

But time ran out. Rowen and Phillips were about "ten steps from the door" when in his agony Phillips tripped over an open "barrel of powder which had been sent from San Antonio for reconditioning." The powder ignited, and both men were engulfed in flame. Transformed into human firebrands, Rowen and Phillips ran through the front door and leaped into the well. Seconds later the final explosion, which "shook the town like an earthquake," occurred. Flaming debris amid a huge, churning cloud of smoke shot skyward and created a rainstorm of embers.[30]

Waxahachie's brief history contained no other tragedy of this magnitude. More than "800 pounds of powder in the process of manufacture" had gone up, creating momentary panic among the town's residents. The mill, mule barn, and bathhouse were demolished, and the firewall, furnace shed, tramway, and several service buildings were aflame. Small fires also appeared on the roof of the powderhouse, containing "eight or ten thousand pounds of powder ready for market," but they quickly were extinguished by volunteer firemen who mounted exterior ladders and swarmed over the structure. If the powderhouse had exploded, damage to the town would have been greater, and more people probably would have been injured or killed. As it was, the flaming holocaust claimed only three victims. Dave was seriously, though not fatally, burned, but Phillips was burned so badly that he was distinguishable only by identifying Rowen and determining that Mulkey and Patterson were not in the plant. Phillips died about five hours after being pulled from the well, and Rowen expired "at daylight the next morning."[31]

The dawn of the following day revealed the extent of the horror. Small knots of tight-faced and silent spectators formed along Mill Street to view the charred wreckage. Except for the powderhouse, the plant in which Dave had worked was gone. Debris littered the northeastern section of town, streets two blocks away were strewn with smoking rubble, and several dwellings on Mill Street were blackened by fire or otherwise damaged.

Early that afternoon the mayor issued a proclamation declaring May 1 a day of mourning and joined several members of the town council for another visit to the disaster site. By this time scores of rural residents and inhabitants of outlying hamlets were on hand surveying the damage and discussing the miracle of Dave's survival.[32]

Dave's parents, Quill and Elizabeth, were among the out-of-town visitors, but they did not stop to view the wreckage along Mill Street. Instead they drove their carriage directly to the Rowen residence on Red Oak Road, where Dave was under the care of a local physician. "Well I was badly burned, of course," Dave wrote, "and my father and mother came and hauled me home this time on a feather bed."[33]

The cause of the April 29 disaster was never determined. Most Waxahachians suspected foul play, concluding that the fire was set by a "Yankee Abolitionist" or a "Northern spy." Newspapers emphasized the presence of an unknown "stranger . . . seen at the mill site immediately after the explosion." According to the most popular version, the stranger "had visited . . . [the plant] for several days" prior to the disaster and must have "dropped a match, which later became ignited, in the mill." The mysterious stranger, however, was never found, disappearing "before any action could be taken."[34]

But there is another more likely explanation. Dave, who was running the mortars, really was not a seasoned powdermaker. Tired and perhaps eager to go home, he could easily have overlooked danger signs that a more experienced eye might have caught. Extreme care had to be taken as the mortars crushed and mixed the sulfur, saltpeter, and charcoal. If the powder became too dry or remained in the mortars too long, the rotating cylinders tended to push the mixture rather than roll over it. If a metal roller scraped on a mortar bed and created a spark, the mixture in the mortar could ignite. Although Dave apparently was unaware of it, this probably is what happened, leading to the first explosion. Subsequent explosions, set off by flying sparks from the first, then ignited the dust generated by the rollers, the mixture in the other mortars, and finally the accumulated mill cake ready for the next stage of manufacture.

If this is what happened, Dave never knew it. There is nothing in his papers to suggest that he ever looked beyond the mysterious stranger theory. "The destruction of the powderworks," Dave concluded, "was accomplished by a traveler . . . who with his wife was then stopping at the . . . Rogers Hotel." [35]

For young Dave the first weeks recuperating at Heath Branch were filled with pain and discomfort. He remained helpless in bed for almost two months because of his burns, and during this time his mother had to feed him "with a spoon as one feeds an infant." [36]

Once again Dave marveled at his survival. He alone remained alive while everyone else in the mill had died a horrible death. He wrote:

> In the battle [of Cache River], the first ball fired from the enemy's guns hit me; and when I tried a second time to shoot at a man a stray ball from a gun right at me prevented me again. Then . . . [the enemy] captured me and I got away a half hour later. Then all who had erysipelas in my ward in St. John's hospital died but me, and now in this awful explosion I alone was left again. These facts impressed me in a way I cannot describe. [37]

Dave pondered the meaning of these seemingly miraculous events, concluding that God's guiding hand was the only explanation. The strange sounds resembling loud whispers he had heard in the burning powdermill puzzled him at first, but he soon become convinced that he had heard the voices of angels delivering a sacred message. "Of course no one could know but me," he wrote, "and to me they . . . [were] Heaven's words—rough, but they made me hear. They said to me, 'You must show mercy to men.'" Dave did not know how he was going to fulfill his duties as a soldier and show mercy at the same time. "Still I meant to keep my resolve [not to kill]," he later wrote in his reminiscences, "come what would." [38]

Once Dave's recovery was certain, every day brought improvement. By the middle of June he was able to spend several hours each day sitting on the gallery enjoying the view of the garden, and though his horribly burned hands healed slowly, he soon began doing small chores around the farm. During the first week in July, while Confederate forces were being defeated at Gettysburg and Vicksburg, Dave spent the summer days on the farm with his younger brothers and sisters, roaming the banks of Pleasant River, picking blackberries in the lowlands, and wading the sparkling streams.

This interlude of happiness abruptly ended, however, with the ar-

rival of news of the Confederate disasters at Gettysburg and Vicksburg. Dave knew that his brigade was somewhere near Vicksburg, but
it was only later that he learned that Parsons' role in the campaign had
been minimal.

Relieved that his brigade had not suffered heavy casualties, Dave
nevertheless became deeply troubled by the fall of Vicksburg. In one
bold stroke, the North had gained control of the entire length of the
Mississippi, isolated the Trans-Mississippi Department, and secured
naval access to the Red River from two directions. The Red, of course,
led directly into Northeast Texas, only a stone's throw from Heath
Branch. General E. Kirby Smith, the new commander of the western
Confederacy, would need all the fighting men he could muster to defend his department, and despite his vow, Dave realized that he had
no choice but to be one of them.[39]

Toward the middle of July, Dave went to work in his Uncle Otwa's
wool-processing plant. "So I went then to the great carding mill
at Lancaster and got a job," Dave explained, "where material was being prepared every day and every night except Sunday to clothe
the people."[40]

Dave worked in the mill about two weeks, quietly making plans to
join his unit while allowing his badly burned hands to regain their resilience. "I labored six hours on and six hours off," he wrote, "while
the oily wool was helping harden my hands."[41]

Again refusing to confide in his family concerning his plans to return to his unit, Dave learned from some of Parsons' boys home on
leave where the brigade currently was located. Since Parsons had in-
stigated a new furlough system that allowed four men from each company to go home on a rotating basis, several rangers from Ellis and
Dallas counties were on hand to advise him.[42]

Soon thereafter, as splashes of color appeared in the hollows and
ravines around Heath Branch, Dave again left "the beautiful old home
place" behind. Marked by multiple bullet wounds, scarred from acute
erysipelas, and wearing the discolorations of freshly healed powder-
burns, Dave refused to contemplate the horrors that lay ahead. Instead he preferred to think of the omnipotence of an omnipresent
God, his source of strength and hope.

CHAPTER 7

Shadows of Impending Defeat

*D*ave's ride across North Texas in the fall of 1863 to join his unit in Louisiana was depressing. Everywhere he looked, he saw more evidence that the western Confederacy was failing—in manpower, in rations, in equipment. The region's defenders, encountered along the road, were stooped, spindle-shanked, sickly, and shabbily dressed. Some had no weapons. Others carried only pikes, knives, axes, antiquated shotguns, or muskets of Mexican War vintage. Many were crippled or weak from hunger or disease, and several hobbled along with makeshift walking sticks. With dirty, threadbare blankets, tents, or bundles of clothing tied on their shoulders, they were anything but an imposing array of armed might. These men, Dave must have marveled, were supposed to defend the department.[1]

When Dave reached Shreveport, the headquarters of the Trans-Mississippi Department, he saw more of the same: more ragged and poorly armed soldiers, more dilapidated wagons, and more pitifully thin horses and oxen, their ribs painfully visible, moving with great difficulty through the cluttered streets. Dave knew that this city must be the best fortified in the department, but somehow he felt unsafe, that the western Confederacy was falling apart, and that the end was not far away.[2]

In a very real sense he was right. Enemy forces, after overcoming stiff resistance at Cane Hill and Prairie Grove, had tightened their stranglehold on Arkansas by occupying Little Rock. Union troops in Southwest Louisiana, after holding Alexandria for two weeks, had withdrawn to New Iberia and Berwick Bay, where they enjoyed a three-to-one advantage over Dick Taylor's less than ten thousand ragamuffins, who were poorly armed, sick, and beset by desertion.[3]

Nor was the war going well in other parts of the West. Confederate authority in Indian Territory was minimal. Rebel raids into Union-occupied portions of Missouri had accomplished nothing. Strikes against the Texas coast by the United States Navy were commonplace, and Federal beachheads on Matagorda Bay and the lower Rio Grande posed a continuing threat to that state's poorly defended interior.[4]

Dave spent part of a day and a night in Shreveport, sleeping in a livery stable filled with other transients. The stable was only a few blocks from the Brice Building, where E. Kirby Smith maintained his departmental headquarters. If Dave could have seen through the walls of the building, he might have found additional reasons for worry and despair.

At times near panic reigned in Smith's headquarters. He and his staff believed that as many as eighty thousand Federal troops were preparing to descend upon the Trans-Mississippi from several directions. After informing Jeff Davis in Richmond that he could muster only about fifteen thousand effectives to defend his department, he pled in vain for reinforcements, food, and firearms. On September 21 he made the startling proposal that new troops be created by building "a military force from amongst the slave population," although he doubted that he could supply them with the necessary arms. "With the exception of a few hundred unserviceable . . . flintlock muskets," Smith informed Richmond, "nothing has been received by this department."[5]

During these weeks Smith resorted to every means at his disposal to prepare the department for the forthcoming onslaught. Revoking the noncombatant status of hundreds of soldiers, he assigned them to fighting units and ordered the formation of civilian vigilance committees for local defense. He stepped up his war on slackers and assigned several cavalry units, including seven companies from Parsons' Brigade, to work for the Conscription Bureau as so-called Jayhawking squadrons rounding up the draftdodgers, deserters, and other itinerant troublemakers. Late in September, Smith assessed his chances of defending his department and again prevailed on Richmond to send supplies. He wrote: "A decisive blow struck by us may turn the tide of events; but assistance from without or success within the department can alone prevent the occupation of Arkansas, Louisiana, and the Texas coast this winter. Cut off as we are, I know not what aid you can give us. Arms and money are our most pressing wants, to pay the troops and meet current expenses."[6]

In the meantime Dave stumbled upon a large cavalry and infantry camp thirty-five miles northwest of Monroe near the little town of Vienna. The bivouac consisted of several hundred ragtag tents and shanties scattered along a small tributary of the Ouachita, occupying the gentle slopes of several small hills that converged on the stream.[7]

Dave was surprised to find the headquarters of Paul Hébert, the commander of the Subdistrict of Northwest Louisiana, at the foot of one of the hills, situated near an old, abandoned well. Dave later learned that the well was supposed to provide Hébert and his staff with a convenient water supply, but the discovery of decaying human hair in the well had forced them to seek another source. Speculation had it that the hair belonged to long-deceased residents of a hilltop cemetery that somehow had found its way into the underground water supply.[8]

Dave also found Parsons' headquarters nearby with sizable contingents of the Twelfth and Nineteenth clustered around the colonel's tent along the creek. Dave's company's baggage wagon was nearby, but most of the men of his company were not, having ridden out of camp several days earlier as part of a Jayhawking squadron. Since the current location of the squadron was unknown, Dave had no choice but to wait in the Vienna encampment for its return.[9]

During the days that followed, Dave must have learned a great deal about the brigade's recent history. He was surprised that Parsons' command at this point consisted of only two regiments, the Twelfth and Nineteenth. Carter's and Pratt's boys were in Arkansas in the vicinity of Union-occupied Little Rock, and Morgan's Battalion, for the moment operating as an independent unit, was in Shreveport.[10]

Elections, casualties, transfers, and special assignments had altered the two regiments, and a recent feud over command had divided the loyalty of the men, created considerable hard feelings, and contributed to an unofficial split in the brigade. George W. Carter, the commander of the Twenty-first, who led a large expedition into Missouri during the summer, had returned claiming that his appointment to colonel predated Parsons' and that therefore he should be commander of the brigade. Carter received the support of the men of the Twenty-first, but the men of the Twelfth and Nineteenth disputed Carter's claim and declared that they would not serve under anyone except Parsons. As Carter and his boys departed for Arkansas the next month, he requested a ruling from the war office in Richmond to determine the senior colonel. The war office's reply finally established Carter as the ranking officer. But by the time this question was decided, Carter's command was in a different theater, and it was too late in the war to make any difference. Nevertheless, for the rest of the war both Carter and Parsons claimed the status of brigade commander and unsuccessfully sought promotions to the rank of brigadier general. Although E. Kirby Smith's final organization chart in the *Official Records* lists Parsons merely as a regimental commander (commanding the Twelfth) in William Steele's brigade, Parsons nevertheless claimed the rank of brigadier after the war and liked to be addressed as "General."[11]

As Dave waited in the Vienna encampment for news of his company, he must have marveled at the battle scars of the men of the Twelfth and Nineteenth. They had spent the last several months occupying observation posts along the Mississippi, breaking up Union-operated plantations in Arkansas and Louisiana, and destroying everything that might "give the enemy facilities for invasion." Running clashes with the enemy had been frequent, and contrabands (slaves in the service of the Union) were rounded up by the hundreds. "Our command [has] . . . taken upwards of 1,300 Negroes in the employment of the Feds on plantations around Lake Providence," one of Parsons' boys wrote, "and burnt every dwelling, gin, crib, etc., in that country."[12]

Parsons' most recent clash with the enemy had been near Monroe, and it also had involved him in another internal dispute, this time with Hébert. Hébert, with the consent of the Monroe city council, had ordered the surrender of the town to prevent its destruction, but Parsons repudiated the order and announced his intention to stay and fight. Hébert, angered by Parsons' insubordination, gave Parsons a direct, hand-delivered order to withdraw. "Colonel Parsons, I have heard, was much displeased with this," a soldier in the Twelfth wrote, "but we fell back across the [Ouachita] River."[13]

Although the Federals had marched into Monroe unopposed, they held the city for only about forty-eight hours. After torching a textile mill, a tannery, and several freight warehouses, they withdrew to Vicksburg.[14]

Dave could see that Parsons' rangers had become a hard, angry, pitiful-looking lot. They were dejected, impoverished, and filthy. Their headgear consisted of everything from battered felts to strips of homespun wrapped around their heads like turbans. Their undyed brown coats and jeans reflected their continuous abuse and contained innumerable rips, makeshift patches, and colonies of grayback lice. These little wingless insects lined the seams of their clothing, lived in colonies in their beards and hair, and infested their underwear.[15]

Oddly enough, the larger, more aggressive graybacks provided Parsons' boys with a spectator sport which became very popular. A member of the brigade who spent most of the war under Carter's banner described one of the grayback contests:

> It is true that the grown bugs, when taken from the bodies of different
> men and placed close together, will rush at one another like bull dogs
> and fight to the death—or until one, being whipped and wounded,
> will scramble out of reach of his adversary. This I saw tested one day
> when a number of our men was gathered together watching very

intently such a fight. They had two "big fellows" on top of a hat, smoothed out. There was considerable excitement, and the men had their Confederate money and were flourishing it as I have seen men do at a horserace. I walked up to see what was going on and saw the whole fight. The bugs were just coming together, and they certainly were mad. The gladiators, unarmed save for their natural weapons, joined in conflict. It was a battle royal. They stood up on their hind feet. They closed in, grappled, and would roll over and over. They seemed never to weary. The battle lasted five or six minutes. The blood was very perceptive on each side. Their legs were broken and wounds [appeared] on their bodies to such an extent that they were maimed, but neither could run from the other. The two warriors could do nothing but lay on the field of battle and . . . die.[16]

After waiting several days in the Vienna camp for news of his company, Dave was rewarded one morning when four men from the squadron he sought rode into camp. Having delivered prisoners to the provost in Shreveport, they were on their way to rejoin their squadron. The squadron, Dave learned, was commanded by Bell Burleson and contained most of Company E, including the men of the Long Branch. The rest of the squadron consisted of parts of other companies from the Twelfth and Nineteenth and currently was southwest of Monroe combing the forests of Winn and Jackson parishes looking for deserters.[17]

The next day Dave accompanied the four rangers as they returned to their squadron, and once again he was united with his messmates. He found that they also had changed in appearance and disposition. Like their comrades in the Vienna camp, they were emaciated, dirty, and dressed in rags. And they somehow seemed more cruel, vicious, and belligerent. They were reflective, preoccupied, troubled, and silent. Even Little Will and Lonesome John were distant, untalkative, and strangely reserved. Dave noted that his messmates and the rest of the squadron stalked deserters and draftdodgers totally without compassion, and once their quarry was cornered, they seemed to prefer killing to capture.[18]

Since Burleson's rangers, like all Confederate troops, had to live largely off the country, their quest for food for themselves and their horses had turned decent, considerate, law-abiding farm boys into shameless, unabashed thieves. The pilfering Dave had witnessed earlier had been furtive, a matter of a few rangers sneaking away from their company, raiding a hen house or clothesline, and running for cover. Now they operated in the open, using force rather than stealth to accomplish their ends. They emptied smokehouses, corncribs, and root cellars. They swept up chickens, hogs, cattle, sheep, and anything else that might prove useful. If their victims protested, they either were threatened with violence or forced to accept worthless script as payment.[19]

But the men of Burleson's squadron and Parsons' Brigade were not the only Southern troops guilty of "wholesale and indiscriminate . . . plunder" of civilians. Complaints from residents all over the department poured into Shreveport concerning "our soldiers' . . . extraordinary depredations on private property." In a few instances overzealous foragers bludgeoned old men, assaulted young women, and carried off priceless heirlooms and keepsakes.[20]

Smith responded from his Shreveport headquarters with stern warnings. He notified Hébert, Taylor, and other commanders that he would hold them personally responsible for the conduct of their troops. Unscrupulous looters were to be "put in irons and sent to departmental headquarters with proper evidence of guilt . . . [or be] shot down." Even so there was little that could be done to stop desperate, hungry men—especially in independent units "acting under superior orders" from Richmond—from committing unreasonable acts of violence against civilians. Field commanders realized this and evidently made little serious effort to stop it. As a result "outrages upon private property" and mistreatment of civilians by foraging parties went largely unpunished.[21]

Burleson's squadron finally returned to the Vienna encampment late in September. During the weeks that followed, Dave joined the other men of the Twelfth in convoying freight, scouting the banks of the Ouachita, and foraging for the Central Commissary and Rations depot in Shreveport.

In the latter capacity Dave and his messmates served on a "bacon-impressing" detail that hunted wild hogs in the Louisiana and Arkansas backwoods. They delighted in this assignment which required the delivery of fresh pork to a meat-packing plant in Jefferson, Texas. Taylor, who was desperately in need of mounted troops for scouting in Southwestern Louisiana, repeatedly harangued Smith about his use of valuable cavalry for hog hunting, but Smith insisted that the wild hogs were "elusive and fleet of foot" and that "securing of stock . . . was of great importance" to the department.[22]

But during the first week in November, orders from Shreveport shifted Parsons' scouting and bacon-impressing base of operations from Louisiana to Arkansas. Smith, distressed by Federal naval activity around Helena, instructed Parsons to take "that part of . . . [his] brigade immediately available," proceed to Camden, and report to General Theophilus ("Old Granny") Holmes, the Confederate commander of the state. There he was to unite with Carter's forces and attempt to disrupt enemy supply in the L'Anguille Valley. "[As] soon as . . . Parsons' Brigade is reunited," Smith explained to Taylor, "Lieutenant General Holmes has been directed . . . to order it in the direction of the Mississippi to operate above on that stream." [23]

Several days later, however, Smith changed his mind and directed Holmes to retain Parsons near Camden, where Parsons could continue his bacon-impressing operations and at the same time help Sterling Price keep U.S. General Frederick Steele bottled up in Little Rock. As a result Parsons' Brigade, now including the Twelfth, Nineteenth, Twenty-first, and Morgan's Battalion, spent the next ten weeks in central Arkansas. [24]

Dave and his comrades were disappointed that they had not been ordered to return to Texas; nevertheless, they knew that they now occupied a central position in the future military operations of the department. Everyone agreed that there were only three feasible routes the enemy could take to seize Shreveport and occupy the heartland of the western Confederacy. These were up the Ouachita and Red rivers from Bayou des Glaize, south and west from Little Rock using the Arkansas River as a partial line of supply, or through Galveston or Velasco, where railroads might facilitate drives into the Texas interior. [25]

With an eye on all three routes, Smith prepared to shift his troops as needed; therefore, he established a series of forage depots along "the shortest line . . . between the Red River and the troops serving in Arkansas and Texas." [26]

But Smith understandably was worried, for he believed that the Federals enjoyed all of the advantages. In a message to Jeff Davis dated January 20, he wrote: "The facilities which the enemy possess in transportation and operating on interior lines give him advantages which, with his superior numbers, will tell in the early operation of a campaign. In five or ten days he can shift his whole force from Louisiana to the Texas coast, requiring us to march a distance of 300 miles or more through a country destitute of supplies and at this season offering almost insurmountable physical obstacles to the march of armies." [27]

There were wide differences of opinion among Confederate commanders over which invasion route the Federals would take. "Prince John" Magruder, the commander of Texas, was convinced that the Federal invasion would originate on the Texas coast. "Old Granny" Holmes was inclined to believe that Frederick Steele, reinforced by troops from Helena, Memphis, and Fort Smith, would march on Shreveport from Little Rock. Although Smith seems to have vacillated slightly at the time, he later claimed that from the beginning he believed the Federal invasion would be up the Red River in Louisiana, using Vicksburg and New Orleans as staging areas and bases of supply. "Though twenty-five thousand . . . [Federal troops] were reported on the Texas coast," Smith wrote after the war, "my information convinced me that the valley of the Red River would be the principal theatre of [enemy] operations and . . . I continued steadily preparing for that event." [28]

Smith's preparations included putting pile-driver crews to work along the lower Red pounding great beams into the bed of the river to form "permanent obstructions," reinforcing and strengthening Fort DeRussy near Marksville, and beginning construction of a new fort near Simmesport called Fort Yellow Bayou. Believing that such fixed fortifications required fewer defenders, he moved Tom Green's Texas cavalry division from Louisiana to Texas, thereby stripping Dick Taylor of most of his mounted troops. Already short on cavalry, Taylor's response was a flurry of charges aimed at Smith which bordered upon insubordination. Attempting to explain his actions, Smith sent Taylor a lengthy reply:

> General Green's division is the only reinforcement sent to Texas. I still think the Red and Washita [Ouachita] rivers, especially the former, are the true lines of operation for the invading column, and that we may expect an attempt to be made by the enemy in force before the rivers fall.
>
> . . . .
>
> Had [Alfred] Mouton's division gone to Arkansas, Parsons' Brigade would have gone to you. It is now engaged in driving out hogs from the lower Arkansas and Bartholomew for the packing establishment at Jefferson. Having accomplished this duty, it goes to either Louisiana or Texas as the development of the enemy's plans may require.[29]

Meanwhile, Dave and the other members of Parsons' Brigade spent the coldest winter of the war on the Ouachita River not far from Camden. "Parsons' and Burford's regiments and Morgan's Battalion were camped on the south side of the river near town," a ranger in the Twenty-first wrote, "and Carter's regiment, Lieutenant Colonel Giddings commanding, was camped on the north side in a bottom that was subject to overflow." [30]

Segments of John Marmaduke's and J. F. Fagan's divisions were nearby, camped several miles upstream, and other troops under Price's command were bivouacked near Woodlawn, a little town about eighteen miles to the southwest. Among the units spending the winter of 1863–64 in Arkansas were C. D. McRay's Eighth Texas Cavalry,

D. M. Frost's dismounted brigade, J. C. Tappan's Arkansas cavalry, and several brigades from M. M. Parsons' Missouri infantry division.[31]

The severity of the winter and the shortage of cold weather equipment caused untold hardship among Confederate troops along the Ouachita, Dave and his comrades among them. For Parsons' boys, tents merely were memories of better times, and they devised whatever shelters they could and ate whatever they could find. In the tradition of George Washington's ragamuffins at Valley Forge, they battled sickness, privation, and the murderous cold. Their letters contain references to having "nothing to eat," being "poorly clad," and suffering from the awful "malaria found in the terrible Arkansas swamps." A ranger in Maddox's company wrote that sometimes the cold became "almost unbearable" and lamented that they "had only one blanket to a man and had . . . [to take] the rain, sleet, and snow as it came." A member of one of Parsons' hog-hunting details, returning to camp on New Year's Day 1864, described the suffering produced by the frigid setting: "It was bitter cold, everything is frozen stiff and hard, but the sky is clear. . . . A cold and dreadful march we have had, men and horses have suffered exceedingly. The cold was so intense that we walked more than half the distance marched. Frozen, almost, we arrived at camps."[32]

Dave and the residents of the Ouachita camp devised several survival techniques for the long winter nights. "[When] it was very cold, we would pile up logs and burn them for awhile till the ground was warm," one of Veal's rangers wrote, "and then we would move them to another place and make our beds on the warm ground." They also slept in shifts, always making certain that someone was awake to feed the fires and awaken the next shift.[33]

Fortunately the weather moderated somewhat during the middle of January, and Smith seized the opportunity to make some adjustments in his defenses. On January 14 he instructed Holmes to order Parsons to report to General Tom Green near Hempstead, Texas, where Parsons was to stand ready to challenge any threatening moves made by the Federals on Matagorda Bay. Again Parsons promised each of his companies twenty days of free time "to go . . . [by] its own county" after the brigade had crossed the Sabine. Dave and his comrades were overjoyed at prospects of going home, being stationed indefinitely in their home state, and serving under Green, perhaps the most colorful cavalry commander in the department.[34]

But their rejoicing was premature. The brigade's destination was changed repeatedly during the next several weeks, and Dave and his companions finally were ordered to Shreveport, where they were at-

tached to the Confederate Conscription Bureau. Although their primary duty was to deliver deserters and draftdodgers to the provost in
Shreveport, Parsons set up his bivouac in Texas at a military campground (Camp Davis) on the Shreveport road about seven miles east
of Marshall. Carter, again commanding his regiment, expressed the
sentiment of most of Parsons' boys when he said that he "didn't think
our brigade would see Hempstead." [35]

Smith, however, having changed his mind repeatedly during the
last several weeks, seemed satisfied with his decision to keep Parsons
in the vicinity of Shreveport. He explained in a dispatch a few days
later that Parsons' Brigade could be dispatched "to either Louisiana or
Texas as the development of the enemy's plans may require." Smith
also informed General Samuel Maxey in the Indian Territory that
Parsons' Brigade of fifteen hundred men, although "on duty under
the direction of the Bureau of Conscription," would be "within sup-
porting distance . . . in case of emergency." [36]

During the weeks that followed, Dave and his comrades combed the
backwoods of three states and Indian Territory rounding up deserters and draftdodgers for the Conscription Bureau. "Our orders were
to explore the section that was allotted to us," one of Dave's companions wrote, "and to arrest every man who was subject to conscription
but had not yet joined the army." Although intervals of bad weather
sometimes complicated their work, Parsons' boys kept a steady stream
of draftdodgers and deserters pouring into Shreveport. "[We] were
in the saddle almost everyday," Dave wrote in his reminiscences, "no
matter what the weather was." And one of Dave's companions in the
Twelfth wrote that "the command has been doing a good business" in
its special line of endeavor, having recently "sent up over two hundred [prisoners] to Shreveport." [37]

Dave, however, was convinced that apprehending deserters and
draftdodgers would never solve Smith's critical manpower shortage.
The size and morale of Confederate armies in the Trans-Mississippi
continued to decline, and Dave concluded that Smith's only hope
rested on his signing some sort of alliance with one of the political fac-
tions in Mexico. Otherwise, Dave was convinced that the end was
near. Spring certainly would bring the anticipated Federal offensive.
He believed its outcome would tell the tale. [38]

CHAPTER 8

Red River Battleground

The spring of 1864 found Dave at Heath Branch. Serving as an escort rider for an ammunition train bound for Shreveport, he had seized an opportunity to go by his parents' farm for a brief visit, and it was here that the first rumblings of the Red River campaign reached him. Early reports were spotty and often contradictory, and for the time being, at least, he chose to ignore them.

But it soon became apparent that the Federal thrust up Red River was the enemy's long-anticipated offensive to occupy Shreveport and conquer Texas. Dave described the situation in his reminiscences written after the war: "U.S. General [Nathaniel P.] Banks came up Red River with a strong fleet of ironclads and an army of 51,000 men. The Confederate forces had perhaps 15,000 to meet them. At the same time U.S. General [Frederick] Steele started south from Little Rock with a similar army, the ultimate intention being to form a junction of these two armies at Shreveport, Louisiana, and then move west to Dallas, and south to Galveston, and so overrun the State of Texas."[1]

Although Dave's description of the enemy troops' strength and disposition were slightly in error, his grasp of Banks' intentions was correct. The main invasion force, in the company of a fleet of Admiral David Porter's gunboats and commanded by Banks, moved up the Red to Alexandria, where it rendezvoused on March 21 with General William Franklin's army from Opelousas. In the meantime, General J. M. Thayer set out from Fort Smith to merge his forces with those of Frederick Steele, who was moving southwest out of Little Rock. If these troops, along with other Federal troops in the region, were able to combine and converge on Shreveport as planned, Banks would have an army of perhaps forty-five thousand men supported by gunboats with which to seize the city, his springboard into Texas.[2]

This campaign, if successful, promised great rewards. Not only could Banks occupy the headquarters of the Confederate Trans-Mississippi Department, but he would be in a position to seize up to 100,000 bales of cotton awaiting shipment along the Red; destroy vital industries and storehouses around Alexandria, Shreveport, Marshall, and Jefferson; take possession of the rich grain and cotton fields of East Texas; and merge his forces with Federal troops along Matagorda Bay and the lower Rio Grande. Except for the unsettled and insignificant Texas Panhandle, all of the Lone Star State would fall under his control.[3]

A Federal officer, assessing the value of the potential conquest of this part of the Confederate Trans-Mississippi Department, wrote: "The department depot for provisions is at Jefferson. . . . At Marshall there is a government tannery; a shoe factory; a foundry for cannon, shot, and shell; a factory for percussion caps; a powder factory; and the headquarters of the Treasury Department for the Trans-Mississippi Department. Lead is brought to Marshall from Mexico. At Shreveport is a foundry for casting cannon shot and shell; also the depot of clothing which is full of blankets [and] shoes. . . . All shoemakers and tailors are obliged to work there."[4]

Dave's unexpected visit to Heath Branch in the spring of 1864 was made possible by a combination of unique circumstances. He, Little Will, and a handful of Parsons' boys were escorting an ammunition train from Austin to Shreveport when several wagons in the train broke down near Eutaw, a small town twenty miles south of present-day Groesbeck. Leaving the wagons to be repaired by local smiths, Dave and the escort riders scattered to visit their homes after agreeing to return to Eutaw on March 22 to continue their journey.

As the day of the Eutaw rendezvous approached, news from the front in Louisiana worsened. Alexandria and Pineville were reported in enemy hands, and Dick Taylor and his ragamuffins were said to be retreating from Natchitoches.[5]

Dave knew that he had no choice but to keep the Eutaw rendezvous, but the temptation to remain at Heath Branch was overwhelming. An influenza epidemic had swept North Texas, and several members of his family, including Quill, were ill. Aside from this current health problem, Quill's general physical condition in recent months had not been good, and with the shearing season approaching and Elizabeth expecting her ninth child (two had died in infancy), Dave knew that he desperately was needed at home.[6]

Perhaps desertion was the answer. It certainly was a common practice among the troops of the Trans-Mississippi; but with enemy soldiers headed toward Heath Branch, Dave chose to ignore his vow not to kill and determined to do everything necessary to stop the Red River invaders.[7]

On March 22 Dave found Little Will waiting for him at a predesignated spot, and late that afternoon the two friends jingled into Eutaw. They found their wagons repaired, loaded, and under the watchful eyes of some aged but fiercely patriotic militiamen. Since two members of the escort had not returned, the lieutenant in charge delayed departure until daybreak the next morning. But the coming of daylight did not produce the missing men, and the train was obliged to leave without them.

Settling down to a steady, ground-eating pace, the old wagons creaked and groaned but moved with a refreshing, well-greased smoothness. Since the weather was clear and the roads good, the train and its escort made good progress during the next two days. But on the evening of March 26, rain fell and travel was impeded as low-lying areas became lakes and sections of the highway became bottomless quagmires. Two days were lost at the Sabine because of high water, but on March 30 the river was negotiated and the journey resumed.

The last miles into Shreveport also were difficult. Refugees, seeking to escape a city earmarked for destruction and enemy occupation, clogged the road and reduced the flow of traffic to a snail's pace. Their collision with Confederate columns en route to sundry destinations added to the confusion, but this scene of humanity on the move was commonplace throughout northeastern Texas. Since the Federals were said to be in Logansport, reinforcements rushing to join Taylor were routed through Keatchie and Shreveport jamming these roads to overflowing. Some Southern reinforcements were infantry and artillery, but Taylor's cry for mounted troops at last was being answered and most were cavalry. "All the cavalry forces in this region of the country . . . are now in full march toward Louisiana," a soldier in Northeast Texas wrote, adding that "there soon will be heavy fighting."[8]

Somehow Dave and his comrades made their way through the tangled humanity west of Shreveport and entered the city, and about noon on April 3 their train rumbled through the gates of the Shreveport Arsenal and Ordnance depot. Both soldiers and slaves swarmed the wharves and loading piers stacking supplies and preparing guns, powder, and shot for movement to the front.

The delivery of the ammunition from Austin was a most welcome event. Only hours after its arrival Kirby Smith notified Taylor at Pleasant Hill that a shipment of ammunition had arrived and was being "organized and prepared" for distribution. There is no way to determine whether this was the ammunition that Dave helped deliver,

but it seems likely that it was. At least part of the shipment was scheduled for Sterling Price in Arkansas, but Smith informed Taylor that
he would send the ammunition "in any direction that circumstances
. . . [might] demand."[9]

Their mission accomplished, Dave and Little Will rode together to
Parsons' main camp east of Marshall. There they learned that Parsons
was under orders to consolidate his brigade "at the earliest moment
. . . to be in readiness for prompt and active service."[10]

This standing alert, when coupled with news of continued Confederate reverses in the Valley of the Red, underscored the anxiety and
desperation that characterized the camp. U.S. Admiral David Porter,
temporarily stalled by shallows in the Red at Alexandria, now had
thirteen gunboats and thirty transports in the upper channel ready to
sail for Shreveport. Also Banks' army in Natchitoches, about thirty-
seven thousand strong after the arrival of Franklin, was said to be
pushing Taylor back with relative ease. In addition U.S. General J. M.
Thayer was expected within the week to link up with Frederick Steele
southwest of Little Rock for a combined thrust on Shreveport from
the northeast. Indeed the future of the western Confederacy looked
bleak.[11]

Parsons' main camp, designated Parsons' Number One by the boys
of the brigade, occupied both sides of the Shreveport road and filled
several dozen acres between the highway and the Memphis and El
Paso Railroad. Convenient to both Marshall and Shreveport, the site
was well watered, adequately timbered, generously carpeted by grass,
and, except for unsightly sandhills, richly adorned by nature.

Four miles down the road toward Shreveport, Carter's Twenty-first
and several independent companies occupied a similar campsite—
Parsons' Number Two. Although presumably part of the brigade,
Carter still claimed independent brigade status and the separate campsite served as a reminder of that claim.[12]

The organization and overall strength of the brigade at this time
are difficult to determine. The *Official Records* indicate that Parsons
had fifteen hundred effectives in the spring of 1864, although many
of these men were away on scouting and Jayhawking patrols, ignorant
of orders to consolidate. Burleson's and Burford's regiments, along
with Morgan's Battalion, constituted the bulk of Parsons' Number One.
Although Morgan's command now included a new company known as
the W. P. Lane Rangers, most of its members either served as guards
at Camp Ford near Tyler, the largest Confederate POW camp west of
the Mississippi, or scouted the Logansport region for Taylor. Pratt's
Battery, which had been part of the brigade since 1862, was now in
Shreveport attached to another unit. Whether the fifteen hundred

figure included Carter's command, recently arrived from Arkansas and occupying Camp Number Two, is not clear.[13]

Each day that passed, the boys in Camp Number One became more angry, frustrated, and unruly. Tired of waiting for marching orders, they could not understand why they were inactive while Taylor was being mauled in Louisiana only a couple hundred miles away. Much preferring "active service in the field" to the dull routines of camp duty, Dave and his comrades agreed that this was not "the kind of soldiering that the Rangers [had] bargained for."[14]

And Dave soon learned other reasons for widespread discontent. Parsons' boys despised Marshall, a rich man's community either unable or unwilling to extend courtesies to common soldiers with little or no money. Denied visits to Shreveport because of the greater distance and the standing alert, they found Marshall overrun by black market scalpers, shifty-eyed civilians, and fancy-dressed officers. A resident of Camp Number One complained that the town always was "filled with strangers" and that the streets were jammed to overflowing with "brass buttons and gold lace."[15]

Still another chronic cause of unhappiness was debilitating illness. Because of their foraging, escorting, scouting, and Jayhawking over a wide area, sick and disabled men of the brigade were scattered all over the department, situated in private homes, field infirmaries, and public hospitals as far away as Houston. They suffered from a variety of illnesses, including "dearrangement of the bowels," recurring Arkansas fever, measles, mumps, and smallpox.[16]

Smallpox, the most dreaded and feared disease of all, struck quickly, spread rapidly, and frequently was fatal. The army's immunization program, based upon little but hope in the beginning, had degenerated into disaster because of the inadequacy of the vaccine, shortages of skilled personnel to administer it, and the scourge of infection that usually accompanied the injections. One supposedly immunized soldier wrote that his vaccination almost ate his arm off and caused a large hole to putrefy in his shoulder and breast.[17]

Just as the men of Number One seemed ready to desert, another alert from Shreveport arrived by wire. At midmorning on April 9 the clattering field telegraph directed all mounted units in Northeast Texas and around Shreveport to "stand ready to march" for Mansfield, Louisiana, where "a battle of tremendous proportions" was raging.[18]

The Confederate government had suspended military exercises and set aside April 8 "as a day of fasting, humiliation, and prayer," and many of Parsons' boys were enjoying the holiday and playing town ball or pitching horseshoes when the second alert arrived. Although many men in camp had not had breakfast, preparations for departure began immediately. Evidently some of Carter's boys in Number Two ignored the "stand by" order and started at once for Louisiana. "Some of us rode hard toward Mansfield, hoping to get there in time to participate in the battle," a member of the Twenty-first wrote, "but we were too late." [19]

Dave and the men of Number One, however, waited for orders to move out. Less than an hour later they came. In a flurry of activity Parsons held a brief conference with his officers, assembled his troops, and announced the brigade's destination. "We have been ordered," he explained, "to proceed as rapidly as possible to report to Major General Taylor at or near Mansfield." The baggage train was to stay on the road and travel at a more leisurely pace, but the rest of the brigade was to concentrate on speed and cut "cross country" to save time. The general line of march, as outlined by Parsons, was to extend south to Logansport and then east to Mansfield. If enemy troops were encountered, Dave and his comrades were to defend themselves but to avoid pitched battles where possible. Part of the route sliced through dense woodland and promised additional woes to cross-country horsemen, especially at night. Care for their mounts was essential, since lame horses could not be replaced. Without question this headlong race against time promised to be a most hazardous affair for both man and beast. [20]

Shortly before noon Parsons' bugler sounded "to horse." Resentful because most of Carter's troops already had gone, Dave and his comrades mounted their horses. Minutes later the brigade, composed of scaled-down versions of three regiments (the Twelfth, Nineteenth, and Morgan's Battalion), "took up the line of march" for Louisiana.

Parsons' regimental columns-of-two quickly dissolved into competing, leaderless bands, the composition of each determined by the riding skills of the rangers and the speed and strength of their mounts. Since most soldiers rode old or broken-down horses, they quickly were outdistanced by their better-mounted comrades. Others, whose mounts broke down completely, were obliged to hitch rides on the baggage wagons which brought up the rear.

A full moon was rising when Dave, Little Will, and a small band of companions rode into Mansfield. They were not prepared for what they saw. Dead and wounded soldiers were everywhere. One recent arrival described the town, streets, and surrounding countryside as "a huge hospital full of wounded soldiers." The local female college served as an all-purpose operating room, where local housewives and college students with little or no medical training assisted country doctors and army surgeons in removing shattered arms and legs without anesthetic.[21]

As Dave and his companions guided their exhausted horses among the human wreckage, they sickened at the stench of seared flesh, clotted blood, splintered limbs, and dismembered corpses. Dozens of wounded, disoriented by pain, blindness, or shock, wandered aimlessly around the streets, some treading on dead or wounded comrades. Most of the soldiers in the streets were Confederate, but some were prisoners wearing the telltale blue of the enemy. "Mansfield crowded, the streets full of prisoners," one Southerner reported, "some of whom are going at large without any guard."[22]

Three miles down Pleasant Hill Road, Dave and his companions came upon the main battlefield. The panoramic scene of death and destruction took on dark and eerie dimensions in the uncertain light of the full moon. Dead soldiers, burst open, mangled, and frightful, sprawled among splintered trees and wagons. Scavengers, mostly runaway slaves and stragglers, drifted among the human carnage in the semidarkness "plundering the battlefield—robbing the pockets of the dead and stripping them of their best clothing."[23]

Dave and Little Will camped that night near the battlefield. They learned from some rangers from Peter Woods' Thirty-sixth (also designated the Thirty-second) that a "general consolidation" of mounted troops was taking place near Pleasant Hill, where a battle of major proportions was raging. The flow of traffic on the road remained constant and continued well into the night, another indication that fighting still was in progress around Pleasant Hill. "I saw about a thousand prisoners brought into Mansfield by our troops on the 8th and 9th," one of Woods' boys reported, "besides a large number of wagons and army supplies."[24]

Some of the prisoners, later incarcerated at Camp Ford, were New York Zouaves, whose resplendent uniforms evoked considerable merriment among the Texans. A soldier in Horace Randal's Twenty-eighth wrote: "Then General Taylor . . . [captured] about 2,500 prisoners, amongst them was a regiment of New York Zouaves all dressed in red flannel trousers, looking somewhat like the ladies' bloomers of later times. They wore dainty red caps with tassels and made a sight for the Texans to look at, and when they were marching by and halted, the Texas troops pretended to get mad, swore because they had been compelled to fight women. Some of them threw down their guns and declared that if they were to fight any more women they would go home."[25]

Dave and Parsons' little band of rangers had little appetite for breakfast the next morning, but they went through the motions. Burial squads appeared shortly after dawn and began collecting the bodies of their fallen comrades and stacking them like cordwood in wagons blackened by dried blood. Bodies of Union soldiers for the time being were left where they lay. Since several days passed before they were collected, they became bloated, reeking fly-infested mounds of rotting flesh that turned the stomach and poisoned the air. Mutilation by dogs and wild animals added to the scene of horror, prompting passersby to complain. "All our dead are buried," a Confederate soldier wrote on April 11, "and the enemy's dead are now being buried the third day from the fight."[26]

About midmorning on April 10 Dave, Little Will, and a handful of rangers from other units took the road to Pleasant Hill. Evidences of bitter fighting were everywhere. Dead horses, wrecked wagons, and various items of clothing and equipment cluttered the forests and lined the tumbled-down rail fences that zigzagged across the landscape. The forests on both sides of the road were deathly silent. "Not even a bird was seen," one soldier observed, "nor any living thing that could get away."[27]

Occasionally more human corpses wearing Union blue were seen, stiff in death, mute evidence of the ferocity of the fighting which accompanied the Federal retreat into the forests south and east of the main battlefield. Most lay in clusters among bullet-splattered trees near the road, but some had fallen in the road and had been crushed by wagons and trampled underfoot by fleeing troops. One Union soldier, evidently a member of a black regiment, was so badly mauled that a traveler noted that he no longer bore "any resemblance to human shape."[28]

Learning the location of Tom Green's cavalry bivouac southwest of Pleasant Hill, Dave and Little Will made their way to it. The campsite, a place "where citizens . . . held their camp meetings" before the war, was strewn with bare-tongued wagons, knapsacks, cooking utensils, smashed weapons, hundreds of dead horses, and more dead soldiers. About five hundred Federal prisoners, dazed and dispirited, huddled together nearby under the watchful eye of Confederate sentries. In the distance the fire-blackened chimneys and burned-out buildings of the town were clearly visible, and everything halfway habitable within a radius of five miles was occupied by Confederate troops. "[Scores] of sheds have been erected here," one ranger wrote, "and . . . adapted to the camping of soldiers." The earlier fighting along the road east of town had chopped up the forest so badly that occasionally broken and bullet-splintered limbs crashed to earth. A member of Nicholas Gould's

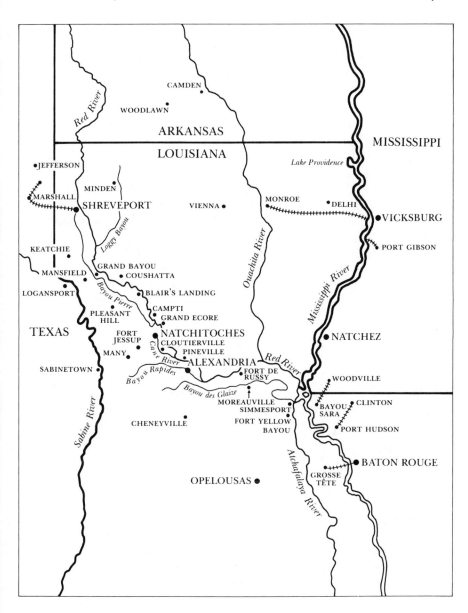

Map 4. The Red River Valley of Louisiana, 1864

Twenty-third wrote that he thought he was "more in danger from falling timber than from bullets or cannon balls."[29]

Although thousands of mounted troops maintained bivouacs southwest of Pleasant Hill, Dave and Little Will found that some of Parsons' boys had already arrived and were living with Woods' and Gould's troops. They found their comrades happily expectant at the prospects of pursuing a retreating enemy and greatly relieved that an invasion of their home state had been thwarted.

Dave shared their feelings. For the moment at least, Heath Branch was safe.

Banks had made his decision to withdraw the night before. The unexpected Confederate resistance, the uncertainty of supply, the unpredictability of the river, and his inability to follow his timetable had made his drive on Shreveport too precarious to continue. Another battle like the one at Mansfield could wipe him out. So about 10:00 P.M. on April 9 Banks had ordered a general withdrawal.[30]

The fighting on April 8 and 9 around Mansfield and Pleasant Hill was costly to both sides. Taylor's number of killed and wounded soared to more than two thousand, but Banks lost about three thousand killed and wounded with another three thousand including noncombatants captured. Also to the delight of Taylor and his men, the Southerners seized 250 wagons loaded with guns and supplies, twenty-one pieces of artillery, and thousands of draft animals.[31]

On April 10 some of the captured guns were delivered in Federal wagons to Green's Pleasant Hill camp for distribution among his troops. The wagons became a source of amazement and relief as Texas troops noted destinations painted on them. "Banks' wagons . . . were labeled 'Austin,' 'San Antonio,' 'Houston,' [and] 'Galveston,'" leaving no doubt that they were bound for the heart of the Lone Star State. Dave and his comrades were relieved that the bloody showdown with the invaders had not taken place on Texas soil.[32]

That afternoon Dave and Little Will witnessed the distribution of some of the captured weapons. Veal and Weir, who had arrived that morning, made certain that at least some of Parsons' boys received powerful Enfields, perhaps the most desirable of all cavalry pieces. "On the battlefield of Pleasant Hill nearly all of our company got Enfield rifles," one of Veal's boys wrote, "which will shoot half a mile." Although some soldiers in Dave's company received the shiny new weapons, he and Little Will, armed merely with shotguns, did not. There simply were not enough to supply all the rangers who needed them.[33]

About 5:30 P.M. a message from Taylor arrived, instructing Green to leave immediately to intercept Porter's retreating fleet bound for

Grand Ecore. Earlier in the day Arthur Bagby with two mounted regiments with artillery had attempted an interception at Grand Bayou, twenty miles north of Blair's Landing, but by the time he had reached the river, the Federal flotilla already had passed.[34]

Green realized that he must have artillery if he was to attack gunboats. He therefore issued an urgent call for a field battery but found none readily available. The battery with Bagby, now racing downriver in an attempt to overtake Porter, was not likely to be available when he needed it. Therefore, Green decided to gamble on a battery's being sent to him in time and began preparation immediately to depart. A special courier on a fast horse was dispatched to Colonel John A. A. West's camp, known to be somewhere on the Natchitoches Road. West, whose battery contained several 2.9-inch rifles and three 12-pound howitzers, was instructed to move rapidly to the Blair Plantation, where he was to report to Green.[35]

About 6:00 P.M. on April 10 Green and his commanders held a council of war. Since Parsons was not present, having been delayed in Shreveport, Burleson, Weir, and Burford represented Parsons' Brigade. Shortly thereafter Greens' bugler sounded "boots and saddles." Porter's progress downstream was reported slowed considerably by the hazards of low-water navigation, and the Federals appeared vulnerable to attack if Green could reach Blair's Landing in time.[36]

Although it was nearly dark, Green's huge cavalry force, almost twenty-five hundred strong, thundered out of Pleasant Hill to fight one of the most celebrated battles of the Western war. Green and his brother-in-law, Brigadier General James W. Major, rode at the head of the column that contained part of Major's division, Gould's Twenty-third, Woods' inexperienced Thirty-sixth, and, of course, Parsons' Brigade, including the Twenty-first.[37]

Parsons' boys, consisting of segments of about fifteen companies, composed about one-fifth of Green's total force, and most were destined to play major roles in the forthcoming battle. Rock-jawed and steely-eyed, they once again prepared to face hostile guns. Dave, armed with an antiquated shotgun and troubled by his belief that further action against the enemy was unnecessary, had no choice but to tag along.

CHAPTER 9

Ambush at Blair's Landing

*I*t was early in the afternoon, April 12, 1864, when Dave and Little Will, riding with the vanguard of Green's cavalry, reached Bayou Pierre. The river and woodland beyond shimmered in a blue, foglike haze. The Red River was five miles farther east, running parallel with the Pierre; and Porter's fleet was somewhere on the Red headed for Grand Ecore. Tired and bleary-eyed, the two boys dismounted with their comrades to rest their mounts, wait for the remainder of their unit, and give their commander a chance to ponder their next move.[1]

The Pierre posed a problem for Green. His horses were exhausted, many incapable of swimming the river; and since he had no pontoon train, he feared that the enemy fleet would escape. If he and his boys were going to ambush Porter's flotilla before it passed them, he must act quickly.

Although the Red was a considerable distance away, Green called for silence and listened for distant gunfire. But except for the sounds of birds frolicking in the forest, he heard nothing. This was not as he had hoped. The absence of gunfire meant that Bagby, pursuing Porter downriver toward Grand Ecore, evidently had not yet overtaken the enemy fleet. Since Green had no artillery, he had hoped to make use of the battery traveling with Bagby. Now if Porter was going to be stopped, Green realized that he and his boys would have to do it, using only Enfields, Mississippi rifles, shotguns, and pistols. Considering the inexperience of some of his troops and the destructive power of Porter's naval guns, this indeed was a tall order.[2]

But Green did not waste time in deploring the situation. Shouting orders that sent men scurrying in all directions, he transformed the west bank of the Pierre into a flurry of activity. Pickets were thrown out, housekeeping details organized, and a camp erected. Two scouting squadrons, composed of Dave, Little Will, and about four hundred members of Parsons' command (selected because of their sturdy mounts), splashed across the Pierre to reconnoiter the woodland between the rivers and search for Porter's fleet.

But Green decided to leave his baggage wagons and the rest of his horses in his camp on the west bank of the Pierre. This meant that the main body of his troops must proceed to the Red on foot. Therefore, he directed his captains to select every tenth man in each company to stay behind with the bulk of the horses, and he put construction crews to work building barges to transport his grumbling troops across the river.³

Green's boys knew that time was their enemy, so they moved quickly. When the barges were completed, they crowded aboard and ferrying operations got under way. Within two hours Green and his rangers stood on the east bank of the Pierre.

Meanwhile in the forest beyond, Dave and Little Will, riding with a scouting detachment, were among the first to sight Porter's fleet. The alarm went out, and other riders converged on the spot, lining the high banks of the Red to study the array of enemy vessels passing below.

Dave and his comrades counted nine gunboats and twenty-four transports in two columns about a mile apart. The vessels were crammed with soldiers, equipment, runaway slaves, and cavalry horses. They were strung out over several miles. Most of the riverboats had sacked grain and bales of hay piled high on their decks to provide protection against sniper fire.⁴

But up to this point it had been the river and not Confederate arms that had posed the biggest headache for Porter. The Red, scarcely navigable under normal conditions, was at its lowest level in a decade, and like a living thing, it had clawed the keels of the Federal vessels, challenging them with rockbound shallows, right-angled turns, treacherous currents, and submerged tree trunks. Seemingly with fiendish delight, the river had reaped its harvest of cracked hulls, broken rudders, detached wheels, and tight-bend collisions. Federal dispatches contained harrowing descriptions of the fleet's endless struggle to stay afloat, leading Banks to conclude on April 13 in a message to Grant that the river was "as treacherous as the enemy we fight."⁵

Realizing that the Confederates also would do all in their power to damage his fleet, Porter had divided his flotilla into the two columns, leaving each largely responsible for defending itself. The first column, commanded by Porter himself, consisted of the flagship, all but two of his gunboats, various troop and baggage transports, a large commissary vessel, and several service craft. The second column, smaller and therefore more vulnerable, was commanded by General T. Kilby Smith, an astute officer and one of Banks' most trusted lieutenants. It contained a wooden gunboat, a damaged ironclad, and five transports carrying twenty-five hundred soldiers from A. J. Smith's corps and several hundred horses. The *Gazelle,* a speedy dispatch vessel, scurried back and forth between the columns, keeping Porter and Smith in touch.[6]

From their vantage point along the river, Dave and his companions calculated that Smith's column should reach Blair Plantation in about two hours. If Green's boys could reach the plantation in time, they believed an ambush might be successful. So leaving a few fun-loving rangers sniping at the transports, Dave and his friends raced back to report to Green.

Upon reaching the ferrying site on the Pierre, the scouts found their comrades rejoicing over the arrival of J. A. A. West's artillery, consisting of three howitzers and two 2.9-inch rifles. Those in Green's command who had never engaged riverboats unfortunately concluded that their forthcoming ambush now would be a turkey shoot. Parsons' boys, who earlier had faced naval guns on the Arkansas and Mississippi, knew better.

Dave and his companions reported their sighting of the enemy vessels to Green, and plans for a surprise attack on Porter's second column (the one commanded by T. Kilby Smith) were laid. Green formed his dismounted troops into columns of brigades, placed Burleson in charge of scouting and prepared to move out on the double.

The dehorsed cavalrymen, griping at having to walk while Dave and the rest of the scouts rode, nevertheless seemed eager to vent their anger on somebody. Green galloped to the head of the column and took his place next to his brother-in-law. Turning in his saddle, he studied the formation a few seconds, rose high in his stirrups, and then brought his arm forward in a great sweeping arc. The column jerked into motion and started down the well-traveled road that connected the Sabine with Blair's Landing. Minutes later Green's boys were deep in the woods, moving with an air of urgency, each hoping to be the first to sight the Red.[7]

The ludicrous spectacle of Green's boys plodding down the road would not have intimidated potential adversaries. These sloppy, rout-stepping rangers, looking more like farmers on their way to market than soldiers, were accustomed to riding, and their disdain for walking manifested itself in their clumsiness. They frequently stumbled, fell to their knees, dropped their weapons, and cursed the occasional traffic jams which they themselves created.[8]

Dave and Little Will, riding rear guard, trailed their pedestrian comrades by about two hundred yards. The deeper they penetrated the swampy forest, the darker it became as the late afternoon sun disappeared behind overhanging branches. Except for the distant chatter of birds, there were few sounds, and the eerie woodland became a captivating world of silence, shade, and shadow. Occasionally Dave caught glimpses of other members of the Twelfth, roaming their flanks, vigilant and alert, combing the surrounding forest, and in general carrying out Green's charge to protect the column from surprise attack.

Riding stirrup to stirrup, Dave and Little Will hunkered in their saddles, slapped at swarming mosquitoes, occasionally ducked under low-hanging branches, and methodically guided their exhausted horses down the narrow trail. About ninety minutes dragged by. The woods seemed lighter now, since the trees along the road stood more in clumps than in mass. Then suddenly the column topped "a long line of hills" that skirted the Valley of the Red, and the forest fell away revealing the rooftops and fields of the Blair Plantation. Below, among the cottonwoods and limestone cliffs which marked the course of the Red, the smokestacks and masts of Porter's last column of riverboats bearing T. Kilby Smith's troops were plainly visible.[9]

At this point a rider with a white plume in his hat galloped past and drew rein at the head of the column to address Green. It was Parsons, who, having been in the saddle for almost twenty-four hours, finally had caught up with his brigade. He wrote:

> By forced marches on one of my fleetest horses, I overtook the command just as it was descending in a long line the hills that encompass the valley, denuded of timber for a width of three-fourths of a mile, which composed Blair's plantation, and the site of the ferry, which was a famous crossing from the west to the east bank of Red River from the Sabine.
>
> Never shall I forget the low murmur of greeting by my old veterans who had never gone into action without my leadership, as I swiftly passed and moved up to the head of the column, which at that very moment rested momentarily at the edge of the valley in full view of the smokestacks of the gunboats and transports, which were the objective of our proposed attack, and where, as I expected, I found General Green, surrounded by his staff, to whom I at once reported for service.[10]

After conversing with Parsons several moments, Green led the column down into the valley and halted in a shallow, sparsely timbered ravine that paralleled the river. After dispatching several reconnaissance teams to search the plantation houses, Green asked Parsons to serve as his field commander and placed James Major in charge of a reserve force of several hundred troops which included Dave, Little

Will, and about three dozen members of the Twelfth and Nineteenth. The primary objective of Major's contingent was to stand ready to swing into action if Kilby Smith's soldiers came ashore from the transports. Parsons, commanding the main assault force, immediately made use of the remainder of his mounted troops by ordering "Captain Veal and Lieutenant Colonel Burleson to cover and protect the flanks of . . . [his] line while in action with two squadrons of cavalry, each from the Twelfth Texas." [11]

Meanwhile, the reconnaissance teams scouting the plantation found the outlying slave quarters abandoned; but a search of the mansion turned up the proprietress, Mrs. John Blair, along with several Negro servants. "In this fight Mrs. Blair was in a house on our line and remained in the house," a member of the reconnaissance party reported, "because her husband told her to stay there until he came back—and he was a prisoner on a gunboat." She refused therefore to move to a place of greater safety until several "cannon balls passed through the house." When that happened, Green's scout reported, she and her retinue consented to move elsewhere. [12]

By this time Parsons' main assault troops, occupying the ravine, large sections of the open fields, and the denuded hills in the rear, prepared to move to the river to launch their attack. Concerned about the lateness of the hour, Green turned to Parsons and asked if he thought darkness would foil their ambush. "The moon is at its full," Parsons replied, "we are deficient in artillery and the approach on [the] ironclads may be made and we may retire if necessary without incurring serious loss in a night attack as the initiative is in our hands." [13]

So, as the main assault force waited for a hand signal from Parsons, Major's reserve force, composed of Dave, Little Will, and several hundred troops, retired to the rear to await further orders. Incredibly, these troops under Major's command remained uncommitted during the entire battle. Only when the struggle was in its last phase and the escape of the enemy vessels a certainty, too late to make any difference, did Major order them to rush to the aid of their badly mauled comrades along the river. [14]

Before the battle started, however, as Green and Parsons sat side by side on their horses, Green addressed the men of the main force, congratulating them on their courage and fortitude. They were, he predicted, about to "perform one of the most glorious feats of the war." After warning them to stay out of sight of the Federal vessels in the hope that they had not yet been seen, he raised his saber above his head and signaled the first wave to charge across the open fields and take positions along the river. [15]

So while Dave and the rest of Major's reserves watched, Parsons' main force poured from the ravine like ants from an anthill. The first wave swarmed across the fields, filtered through clumps of cotton-woods, and assumed positions among the "high and almost perpendicular banks" that formed a natural levee for several hundred yards on each side of the landing. Then the second wave raced across the fields, taking positions among the first, digging in for the onslaught to come.[16]

Meanwhile, six transports and two gunboats glided into the potential death trap. Unaware of the enemy presence, the transport *Hastings* tied up at the landing to repair a broken wheel. Fifty yards behind, the *Alice Vivian*, jammed with four hundred cavalry horses, suddenly veered from the main channel and smashed into shoals along the opposite bank. Two trailing transports, the *Clara Bell* and the *Emerald*, immediately sailed to the aid of the *Alice Vivian*. The *Lexington*, a wooden gunboat, and the *Rob Roy*, a transport, came next in line, jammed stem to stern in flagrant disregard of Kilby Smith's orders to maintain safe intervals between vessels. Because of the narrow confines of the channel, these two vessels had no choice but to drop anchor to wait until the *Alice Vivian* could be returned to deep water. A quarter mile farther upstream, the converted transport *Black Hawk* and the ironclad *Osage* brought up the rear.[17]

But the river had one more trick to play on Smith's errant column. As the *Osage* prepared to drop anchor, the huge ironclad was caught in the swirling currents near some shallows, slipped sideways, and slammed into some shoals which lined the west bank, squarely under the guns of Burleson's and Burford's sharpshooters, its "starboard broadside bearing on the right bank." The nearby *Black Hawk* immediately moved into position to assist the *Osage*.[18]

It was at this point, however, that the officers on board the *Osage* and the *Black Hawk* began to suspect the Confederate presence. As operations to float the *Alice Vivian* got under way, the pilot of the *Black Hawk* sighted some of Green's troops, some seemingly dressed in Federal uniforms, gathering in the woods almost three miles away. Because of the distance, he could not be sure that the figures he had seen were Southern soldiers, but he reported that possibility to Captain Thomas Selfridge of the *Osage*. While rescue workers labored furiously to free his vessel, Selfridge stationed himself in his pilothouse and scanned the countryside for several minutes looking for intruders.[19]

After a time workers swung the bow of the *Osage* around and again pointed the ponderous vessel downstream. But because of a smashed steerage, the *Black Hawk* was lashed to its starboard to try to keep it in midchannel. The *Osage* now was ready to get under way, but Selfridge discovered that the grounded *Alice Vivian* blocked his passage. Therefore, the *Osage* and the *Black Hawk,* lashed together like Siamese twins, again dropped anchor, still under the guns of Burleson's and Burford's sharpshooters lining the north end of the levee.

Meanwhile, Parsons, his troops as yet not identified as Confederate soldiers, positioned the rest of his men along the landing and riverbank as Green had directed. Green's plan was simple. If Confederate artillery and small arms could explode the boilers or magazines of one or more of the riverboats at the head of Smith's column, the wreckage could block the channel and prevent the escape of the remaining vessels. Then when Federal troops came ashore from the transports, which should be an undertaking costly in enemy lives, they would be set upon by Dave, Little Will, and the rest of James Major's reserves waiting in the fields beyond the ravine.[20]

The Confederate battle line extended almost two miles along the west bank of the Red. Gould's Indian fighters were below the landing on the right, with Burleson's and Burford's veterans more than a mile upstream on the left. Major's, Woods', and Carter's troops with two pieces of West's artillery occupied the center. Hoping to prevent vessels from downriver returning to aid those under attack, Green positioned one of West's howitzers near the bend; but at Parsons' insistence moved it to the landing to try to broadside the crippled *Hastings*.

But at this point Green's plan began to go awry. Once the Federals on Kilby Smith's vessels had been alerted to the presence of unidentified individuals on the west bank, reports of additional sightings became commonplace. "I ascended to the pilot-house, and scanning them carefully, made sure they were Confederates," Selfridge wrote, "and at the same time directed Lieutenant Bache of the *Lexington* to go below and open an enfilading fire upon them."[21]

So the first shot was fired by the proposed ambushee rather than the proposed ambusher. Sharpshooters on board the *Lexington* opened fire, delivering a fusillade that accomplished little except to sound the alarm. In response a flurry of activity erupted on the other vessels as blue-clad soldiers, Union sailors, and runaway slaves sought safety behind hay bales and sacks of grain. Some of the Confederate troops already were in position, but some were not and West's howitzer on the landing was not even pointed in the right direction. Nevertheless, Parsons had no choice but to signal his boys to open fire.

The *Hastings* immediately cast off to escape the pointblank range of the howitzer on the landing. But the Confederates finally got their howitzer into action only to miss their target—not once but several times! Their first rounds fell short, and the rest sailed over the *Hastings*, landing among canebrakes on the opposite bank. In his report Kilby Smith marveled at these miscues and poked fun at the Confederate gunners, suggesting that their "practice . . . [must have been] defective." [22]

Although Confederate small arms fire also was erratic in the beginning, it quickly swelled into a withering barrage of smoke and lead. Burleson's and Burford's sharpshooters unleashed a thunderous fusillade that sent a shudder through the *Black Hawk* and the *Osage*, engulfing both vessels in blinding smoke, singing miniés, and flying splinters. One of Burleson's rangers later gloated that he and his comrades "behind the levee" had filled the portholes of the "several boats in the river" so full of minié balls that the Federals had trouble manning their guns. Selfridge described the musket fire as "the heaviest and most concentrated" that he had ever seen. Troops on the wooden *Black Hawk* eventually were forced to abandon their vessel in favor of the ironclad *Osage*, but Selfridge wrote that "everything that was made of wood on the *Osage* and *Black Hawk* was pierced with bullets." [23]

Carter's and Gould's boys, although armed largely with Mississippi rifles and shotguns, also poured a devastating fire into the *Emerald*, the *Clara Bell*, and the *Alice Vivian*. Federal soldiers and sailors struggling to dislodge the *Alice Vivian* had to work in the open, and a few paid with their lives. Others tumbled to the deck clutching an arm or leg or clawing at sightless eyes seared by acrid smoke or pierced by flying splinters. Gunners on the *Alice Vivian*, in danger of being trampled by the terrified horses jamming its decks, despaired of ever getting their guns into action. With wounded horses piling up around them and plunging over the side, they suffered significant losses and twice had to retreat below decks before finally reaching their deck guns. Intense Confederate small arms fire also delayed gunners on the *Emerald* and the *Clara Bell*.

But when the tide changed to favor the Federals, it did so permanently. The *Lexington,* spared the full weight of Green's initial onslaught because of its position, was the first vessel to open fire with its big guns, and it concentrated largely upon Confederate artillery. Displaying astonishing maneuverability, the gunboat braved sharpshooter fire and defied shallows and shoals to spray "the west bank . . . with grape and cannister . . . for two miles . . . up and down the river." During the first thirty minutes of the battle, the *Lexington* damaged West's howitzer on the landing, killed or disabled more than half of his artillery horses, and wounded two of his cannoneers, one critically. Then, supported by the Parrotts of the *Rob Roy,* the gunboat pulled astern of the *Alice Vivian* and laid down a barrage that enabled the *Osage* to get its guns into action and the troops on the *Black Hawk* to complete their transfer to the *Osage*.[24]

The proximity of Parsons' sharpshooters, however, posed a serious problem for Kilby Smith's gun crews. The big weapons were intended for long-range bombardment, and since Green's boys were under their muzzles, it was like trying to swat flies with a sledge hammer. "Shelling under the circumstances was almost useless," Selfridge wrote. "The great guns of the *Osage* were loaded with grape and canister, and, when these were exhausted, with shrapnel having fuses cut to one second."[25]

But the *Osage* and the *Lexington*, supported first by the *Rob Roy* and then by the *Emerald* and the *Clara Bell*, rained death and destruction upon Green's hapless rangers. West's gunners, broken and bleeding, watched in dismay as their last caisson was wrecked, most of their remaining horses disabled, and two more cannoneers wounded. Forced to wheel their remaining howitzer to each new location by hand, they struggled to continue the fight. But suddenly the big fieldpiece was completely destroyed by a direct hit by one of the *Lexington*'s 8-inch guns. This left West's boys with only one 2.9-inch rifle, now fired sparingly because of critical shortages of ammunition.[26]

Some of Woods' boys, pounded relentlessly by the fleet's big guns and facing increasing small arms fire, abandoned their positions and fell back a hundred yards. Federal sharpshooters on the *Osage*, under the cover of the vessel's big guns, now began to take careful aim and pick off anything on shore that moved. "My soldiers were all upon the hurricane decks protected by cotton bales, bales of hay, and sacks of oats," Kilby Smith wrote, "enabling them to mark the enemy with deadly aim."[27]

Meanwhile, the *Emerald* and the *Clara Bell*, their decks shrouded in smoke from their bow guns, hauled the *Alice Vivian* into deeper water. But this was not accomplished without another near disaster. As the *Alice Vivian* broke free, she collided with the *Emerald*. Both vessels were swept into the current and almost capsized, dumping both men and horses into the debris-infested river. Most of the soldiers were picked up later downstream, but a few drowned or were picked off by Confederate sharpshooters. "The men tried to swim out on the opposite side," a member of the Twelfth wrote, "but there was such a hail from the small arms that many a poor fellow could not get over the shoals."[28]

Moments later Smith's riverboat procession again got under way, still pouring a devastating fire into Confederate positions. Some of Woods' troops, having already fallen back about a hundred yards from the river, now broke for the open fields, some losing their weapons in their mad rush for safety. Many of Gould's boys followed, leaving only about twelve hundred Confederate sharpshooters in riverside positions. "Before sundown we had silenced the enemy's batteries," Kilby Smith wrote in his report, "and shortly after . . . [the Confederates] fled the field, leaving many dead."[29]

The men of the Twelfth, Nineteenth, and Twenty-first, reluctant to admit defeat, were the last to leave the levee. Low on powder and shot, dazed, exhausted, and streaked with smoke, blood, and grime, they responded gallantly to Parsons' plea to stick to their positions. Having learned from experience to lie down while reloading to avoid the full force of naval bombardments, they fired less frequently but with the pinpoint accuracy that bespoke their frontier origin.[30]

Leaving a haze of blue smoke in their wake, the last vessels of Smith's column rounded the bend below the landing. Once they were screened from Confederate small arms fire, Federal gunners unleashed a blistering bombardment that blew the landing apart, forcing the men along the levee to scatter. When the smoke cleared, the landing was gone and so was the Confederate will to fight.

This final Union salvo, however, cost the Confederates more than just their pride. It altered forever the course of the Western war by removing one of the Trans-Mississippi's most renowned and capable cavalry commanders—General Tom Green. Only moments before the Federal barrage ended, this hero of San Jacinto, "who had behaved with great gallantry throughout the fight," suddenly disappeared in an explosion of smoke and flying shrapnel. Private A. R. Danchy, one of Woods' rangers "standing within a few yards of the general," wrote that Green was sitting on his horse "talking to one of his staff . . . [when] a shell . . . exploded just above his head." Since the general was an old hand at cheating death, those who rushed to him dared hope that once again he might escape the Grim Reaper. But their blood ran cold at the sight of Green's headless body crumpled in a tattered heap between an injured staff officer and the general's dead horse.[31]

When Parsons learned of Green's death about fifteen minutes later, he assumed that he was in command, since Green had placed him in charge of "the forces in the field." But Major, who outranked Parsons, correctly assumed that the burden of command was his and began directing the troops in his vicinity, giving orders that were tentative, confusing, and often contradictory. It is apparent that Major, who later displayed sterling qualities as a commander, was severely shaken.[32]

Perhaps he had reason to be. The horrible demise of his brother-in-law, the unexpected burden of command, the almost unbelievable destructiveness of naval guns, and perhaps the embarrassment of his own inactivity up to this point simply overwhelmed him. Although it was too late to make any difference, Major ordered Dave and the rest of the reserves waiting in the fields behind the ravine to occupy positions abandoned by Gould's and Woods' troops. Then minutes later he ordered a general retreat.[33]

Dave and his comrades, who had been mere spectators of the battle, rushed to the levee. But the battle was over. Little remained to suggest the fury of the contest except a dissipating blanket of smoke, a thin pallet of debris floating in the river, and the mutilated bodies of horses and men lying in the shallows and strewn along the levee.

Many of Woods' and Gould's troops already had fled to the fields in the rear, but Parsons, learning of Major's order to retreat, refused to budge. For several minutes he considered pursuit of the enemy, but after firing a few ineffective volleys at the retreating vessels below the bend, he also decided the battle was lost and recalled his men. His reasons for doing so must have been similar to Major's—the exhaustion of his troops, gaping holes in his ranks, poor visibility because of darkness, the superior firepower of the enemy, and the discovery that pursuit on the west bank would be halted anyway once Smith's column passed the Pierre's junction with the Red.[34]

As Parsons and his boys started for the rear to join the rest of their comrades, they almost collided with fresh Confederate troops pouring into the valley shrieking the Rebel yell. It was Bagby's troops arriving too late to participate in the fighting but in time to help care for the dead and wounded. Leaving medical teams to do what they could, Major and Parsons led their battered troops back to their camp on the west bank of the Pierre. Confederate surgeons worked the rest of the night and through the next morning in an old church patching up wounded soldiers, and burial details spent most of April 13 collecting bodies. According to an observer on one of the Federal vessels, both banks of the Red were "strewn with wounded and dead . . . [for] two miles." Some of the wounded were unshipped Federals abandoned by their commander. "[Since] my responsibilities . . . [to] the fleet were great," Kilby Smith explained in his report, "I did not deem it proper to gather up the wounded but left them with the dead in the care of the enemy."[35]

Although each side claimed minimal casualties for itself and heavy losses for the other, the total in killed, wounded, and missing was small considering the fury of the two-hour battle. Including West's gunners and riflemen whose ranks were decimated, Confederate losses numbered thirty-four killed, sixty-two wounded, and twelve missing. Federal losses, though comparable, included fewer killed but more than twice as many wounded. Nevertheless, this battle represents one of the most spectacular and perhaps foolhardy exploits of the Western war—a largely small arms attack on a partially ironclad, heavily armed, naval flotilla.[36]

Years later when veterans got together at old soldiers' reunions to relive the war in loving detail, this struggle became the classic example of Rebel courage west of the Mississippi. Although the Federals preferred to explain these claims of Southern bravery in terms of mass befuddlement produced by too much green Louisiana rum, the story of Blair's Landing deserves an honored place in the history of the war in the West.[37]

Whatever the source of their courage, Green's troops, especially those of the Twelfth, Nineteenth, and Twenty-first, fought like wild animals against incredible odds. And with the timely assistance of the river, they almost won. Premature discovery before they were in position, poor marksmanship by West's gunners, and a shameful lack of coordination in the use and movement of the troops on hand contributed to their defeat.

And there is another Confederate miscue that becomes discernible in the light of historical hindsight—Major's failure to commit his reserves after it became apparent that Federal troops were not going to attempt a landing from the transports. Since some of these reserves carried Enfields, the additional weight of their firepower could have delayed or perhaps prevented Smith's gunners from getting their naval pieces into action. The explosion of a single magazine or boiler at the head of the Federal column could have blocked the river and thwarted Smith's escape. Instead Major kept his reserves in the rear, watching as their comrades engaged in a life-or-death struggle with Federal gunboats. By the time Major ordered Dave and his comrades to move up, Green was dead and the battle lost.

Dave's views on all this largely went unrecorded. Sticking to his practice of either ignoring or minimizing events in which he did not play a major role, he wrote practically nothing about the battle. It seems likely, however, that since he hoped to keep his vow, he probably was secretly pleased with his passive role. At any rate it is doubtful that his comrades on the battle line missed the deafening, air-polluting discharge of his ineffective old scattergun. Certainly its presence on the levee would not have changed the course of the battle.

CHAPTER 10

The Race for the River

After the battle at Blair's Landing, Dave and Little Will joined a sizable honor guard that accompanied General Tom Green's body back to Pleasant Hill. The normally sleepy little town, swollen to three times its normal size, now served as an assembly point for prisoners bound for Camp Ford, a staging area for reinforcements on their way to the front, a hospital for hurt and broken soldiers, and a morgue for bodies awaiting burial.[1]

As the ambulance and its escort wound through the wreckage-strewn streets, Dave and his companions tried to close their nostrils to the smell of death. The suffocating stench, which caused many travelers to go miles out of their way to avoid the town, came from decomposing bodies of horses, mules, and soldiers not yet buried. Most lay where they had fallen, and five days after the battle, little had been done to dispose of the rotting flesh. "In riding over the battlefield I see a great quantity of dead men piled up in the head of a deep hollow and brush only thrown over them," one soldier wrote. "Whatever officer is in charge of this ought to be cashiered."[2]

For Dave and the other members of the escort, these evidences simply served as a reminder of battles yet to come. Taylor was massing his army for an attack on Banks, who with Porter's fleet was holed up in Natchitoches and Grand Ecore. Dave and Little Will expected to be part of this onslaught, for Parsons' Brigade already was on its way from Blair's Landing to Natchitoches, following "the high land west of the Red River bottom."[3]

And other cavalry units also were en route. "The cavalry have been ordered to join General [Hamilton P.] Bee before Grand Ecore and Natchitoches," a Texas cavalry officer wrote. "The Yankees, who started to Shreveport by the river have all passed down, and the whole Federal force now seems to be at Grand Ecore with a fleet of gunboats, and a place well fortified by nature."[4]

After turning over Green's body to the provost in Pleasant Hill for shipment to Texas for burial, Dave and Little Will spent the next three days in Mansfield and Keatchie. Parsons' baggage and ordinance depot had arrived at Keatchie, and the two boys exchanged their shotguns for powerful Enfields and shiny new sabers. Dave must have accepted his new weapons with misgivings, for he knew that more would be expected of him now that he was better armed, but since he had not been able to replace his Whitney handgun which was lost at Cache River, these were his only weapons.[5]

The next day Dave and Little Will rode south from Mansfield through a "hilly country, rather poor, consisting of places of ancient settlement." The war had driven local residents from their homes, and the landscape consisted of a checkerboard of old fallow fields that bore not a vestige of the "marks of human hands except for the old ridges thrown up by the plow" months before.[6]

As usual, Dave and Little Will shared the road with columns of infantry, bands of prisoners, and hundreds of refugees fleeing the war zone. Smashed wagons and wrecked equipment cluttered the roadsides, and occasionally the road itself was blocked by fallen trees, intended to slow Banks' retreat. Smouldering farms and outbuildings, destroyed by Federal arson squads, dotted the landscape and marked the path of the enemy's flight.

Three miles north of Natchitoches, Dave and Little Will found their brigade camped along a little creek which was lined with trees, vines, and creepers. A large playground nearby was situated behind a "small, neat, one-story log" schoolhouse, "newly built and well seated with plank benches," now occupied by men from the Twenty-first. Although the schoolhouse had escaped the torch of arsonists, it contained some obscene graffiti, no doubt left there by some dirty-minded Yankee soldier. "I believe that the blackguard who wrote that was killed in the next battle in which he fought," one of Carter's rangers wrote, "for I don't believe that God would let so vile a man live."[7]

As Dave and Little Will joined their messmates, they were surprised to find Joseph P. Weir of the Hill County Volunteers temporarily commanding their regiment. The command of both the Twelfth and the brigade was for the moment in a state of flux. Burleson, wounded slightly at Blair's Landing, had returned to Texas. William Steele, a division commander from the Indian Territory with no division to command, was in charge as the ranking officer. Although Parsons technically retained command of his diminutive brigade, Steele had assumed command of the troops in camp, only about twelve hundred mounted soldiers, which consisted largely of Parsons' boys (the Twelfth, Nineteenth, and Morgan's Battalion) and Carter's Twenty-first. When Dave and Little Will arrived, Parsons was in Keatchie arranging for the delivery of ammunition, and Carter, still insisting that he was the legitimate commander of the brigade, was said to be in Shreveport arguing his case. During Carter's absence DeWitt Giddings had assumed command of the Twenty-first, which, though part of Parsons' Brigade, had combined with remnants of some independent companies to form a command that Carter's boys chose to consider separate from Parsons'. But the major concern at the moment was participation in Taylor's offensive against Natchitoches and Grand Ecore.[8]

As the days passed, however, the offensive did not materialize. The reason was revealed when Parsons returned. He reported that Kirby Smith had detached Walker's division from Taylor's army for service in Arkansas where U.S. General Frederick Steele was en route to Shreveport from Little Rock. But by reinforcing Sterling Price in Arkansas, Smith had left Taylor with only about six thousand effectives, including William Steele's cavalry, with which to try to crush Banks' twenty-five-thousand-man army and Porter's flotilla.[9]

Therefore, Taylor had no choice but to scale down his operations to mere harassment. He ordered William Steele to keep pressure on Banks, to "picket the lower Natchitoch[es] Road, as near Natchitoch[es] as possible," but to avoid "a general engagement" with the enemy. Since Banks kept vedettes stationed in the northern outskirts of the city, Dave and Parsons' boys under Steele's command spent the next two weeks skirmishing with Banks' patrols.[10]

By stripping Taylor of the bulk of his infantry, Kirby Smith had reduced the war in Louisiana to little more than a sideshow, with the main performance in Arkansas. Taylor's howls of protest could be heard all across the department. Smith, who had joined Price in person to supervise Confederate operations in Arkansas, sought to justify his actions by arguing that Frederick Steele's troops posed a genuine threat to Shreveport while Banks' forces in Louisiana did not. But in reality Steele's Federals, having to depend largely on the country for subsistence, had little chance of reaching Shreveport anyway, much less of conquering it. Both the Confederates and the Federals failed to take into account the utter destitution of southwestern Arkansas, and although Smith and Price eventually defeated the Federals near Camden and at Jenkins' Ferry, it largely was Frederick Steele's logistical dilemma that caused him to return to Little Rock.[11]

Meanwhile, Taylor, outnumbered about five to one but determined to do what he could with what he had, reorganized and regrouped his forces. He appointed a newcomer, General J. A. Wharton, a transfer from General Joseph E. Johnston's command east of the Mississippi, to replace Hamilton P. Bee as commander of cavalry. He moved Prince

C. A. J. Polignac's division, his primary remaining infantry unit, to a position directly behind Wharton's cavalry. Taylor then strengthened Arthur Bagby's, X. B. DeBray's, and W. P. Hardeman's brigades; distributed eight artillery batteries among Polignac's, Bee's, and Wharton's troops; stepped up John R. Liddell's harassment of Federals on the east bank of the Red; and dispatched Major's and Bee's brigades downriver to prevent Federal forces below from coming to Banks' assistance.[12]

Not all these changes were welcomed by Parsons' boys in William Steele's command. For one thing Dave and his comrades did not readily accept Wharton as their commander of cavalry. Although a Texan, he had little knowledge of the Red and was believed to know little about the type of fighting its rugged banks required. Convinced that Natchitoches could be taken by direct assault, although the Confederates were outnumbered, Wharton persuaded Taylor to launch simultaneous attacks on opposite ends of the town hoping to catch the Federals by surprise. Steele's troops, including Dave and the rest of Parsons' boys, considered this suicide, but they had no choice but to spearhead one of Wharton's attacking columns.[13]

But unknown to the Confederates, Banks already had begun his evacuation of Natchitoches and was headed for Alexandria, about fifty miles downstream as the crow flies. Therefore, when Dave and his comrades stormed into Natchitoches, they found the town largely abandoned and had little to do except to extinguish fires recently set by Banks' arson squads. As a result of the Confederates' quick action, Natchitoches was not burned.[14]

But Dave, Little Will, and the rest of Parsons' boys in Steele's vanguard did not remain long in the liberated city. Instead they rushed in pursuit of Banks' retreating columns. Since the Federals were delayed by their baggage wagons, Dave and his comrades overtook them easily, only to be held at bay by the superior firepower of Banks' rear guard.

The country between Natchitoches and Alexandria was a veritable jungle of burning houses, barns, slave quarters, gins, and cotton in various stages of harvest, a reminder that Federal torch squads still were at work. One Texas soldier noted that the entire Valley of the Red was "a perfect forest of blackened chimneys," adding that "ruin and desolation is stamped upon the whole face of the country."[15]

Skirmishing between Banks' rear guard and Steele's vanguard near Cloutierville the next few days took the form of long-range exchanges, a condition that favored the Federals. Although Dave, Little Will, and a few other members of the Confederate advance guard carried Enfields, many were armed only with Mississippi rifles, antique Mexican

War muskets, and old shotguns. Therefore, the Federals, armed with Enfields and breech-loading carbines, had no trouble making Parsons' boys keep their distance. "Our men were not frightened, but, knowing that the enemy's guns ranged a thousand yards, while ours ranged only four hundred yards," a member of the Twenty-first noted, "we prudently left the field." [16]

Under these conditions it was easy for Dave to keep his vow. He wrote that he and his messmates kept constant pressure on the rear guard of Banks' army while maintaining a safe distance. Since skirmishing was at long range, seldom was anyone on either side seriously hurt. "I knew our rifles would not bear up to the enemy," a soldier in Giddings' regiment wrote, "[for] at great distances, the balls would wobble and hit wide of their mark while their force would become so spent as not to enter what they hit." And a member of the Ellis County Rangers noted that the "firing was very heavy but [at] so great a distance that only a few were wounded." [17]

Since Banks' chief objective was escape, he sought to avoid pitched battles. But there was a troublesome bottleneck separating his columns from Alexandria—a deep-water crossing on the Cane some thirty-five miles south of Natchitoches. The crossing, known as Monett's Ferry and already occupied by Bee's troops, presented the Confederates with their best chance of stopping Banks.

Indeed, it appeared that Banks might be forced to give up. With over sixteen hundred of Bee's boys with four batteries occupying the Cane, Wharton and Steele in his rear, Liddell covering the Red on his left, Polignac's infantry bearing down on him from the north, and Porter's fleet too far away to lend assistance, Banks was trapped—as one of Giddings' boys put it—"like a bird in a cage." The high banks of the river above the crossing formed "natural barriers" that made it impossible for the Federals to retreat laterally, and a jubilant Taylor wrote that he was certain that he could "make Banks unhappy on the morrow." [18]

But Banks had no intention of giving up. He pulled back his mounted troops, burned several dozen loaded wagons to prevent their falling into Confederate hands, divided his infantry into contingents "to protect . . . [his] front and rear," pounded Bee's positions on the Cane with his artillery, and launched exploratory assaults in three directions searching for an avenue of escape. [19]

Parsons' boys, dogging the heels of Banks' rear guard, moved to the attack on April 21. "We turned down the Old Cane River and . . . came after them in force," one of them wrote, and Dave noted that he and his messmates spent the next three days following "after . . . Banks' army fighting almost every day." On April 22 Giddings' and

Burford's regiments pressed the enemy farther downriver, "picking up almost forty [enemy] stragglers," while Morgan's Battalion and Parsons' Twelfth dug in along the west bank of the Cane near Cloutierville to slam the trap shut along Banks' right rear.[20]

The Cane at this point curved to the south and generally ran parallel with the Red, slicing through steep banks and rugged cliffs. Once Dave and his comrades occupied the high elevations along the river, they found it relatively easy to hold their ground. "From . . . Cloutierville, the Old Cane River flows south," one of Giddings' Texans wrote, "its channel . . . bounded on either side by an almost perpendicular bluff about seventy feet high, which no army could ascend."[21]

But on the afternoon of April 23, Banks was given a way out of the Confederate trap. Bee, holding the river positions along the Cane in Banks' front, was led to believe that Federal reinforcements from transports on the Red were on their way to strike his rear. Thinking he was avoiding encirclement, he ordered his boys to pull back from the Cane, leaving a section of the river above Monett's Ferry undefended. Banks' troops did not hesitate. Using a swiftly constructed pontoon bridge and some shallows pointed out by a Negro, they swarmed across the undefended section of the Cane and by noon the next day were pouring into Alexandria.[22]

With Banks' army on the loose, Confederate pursuit began all over again, but this time with less enthusiasm. As one of Giddings' rangers put it, "[Why] chase the bird after letting it out of the cage?"[23]

Shortly after dawn on April 24, Dave and his comrades abandoned their positions on the bluffs, mounted their horses, and joined the chase. Two companies of Parsons' Brigade, one from the Twelfth and one from the Twenty-first, overtook the enemy, shot their way through a flimsy line of skirmishers, swooped down on an enemy position, and routed a Federal force more than twice the size of their own.[24]

Late that day, however, the tables were turned as a segment of the Twelfth, including Dave, Little Will, and two of the Ellis County companies, became the unwilling targets for field artillery and snipers from a ridge about a mile beyond the enemy's pontoon bridge. Dave and his companions scattered in all directions and took refuge in a deserted plantation, but Federal cannoneers and sharpshooters blasted the dwellings and outbuildings to bits. Were it not for superb horsemanship, approaching darkness, and the protection provided by trees, fences, and the ruins of old buildings, the entire Confederate squadron might have been wiped out. As it was, Dave and his friends escaped with only minor casualties. "[Federal] infantry, cavalry, and battery sent thousands of missiles around us," one of them wrote, "and had it not been for the protection afforded by trees in the yard, posts of same, and garden, and some walls of brick houses, many of us would have been killed." [25]

The fighting on April 24 was the heaviest Dave had experienced so far in the campaign, but he seems to have thought more about preserving his life and those of his comrades than of keeping his vow. In desperation he charged enemy positions, firing indiscriminately into the blinding smoke, not knowing whether he killed anyone or not. Later he preferred to believe that he had not. "I . . . constantly tried to keep my vow," he wrote after the war, "and I think I . . . succeeded fairly well." [26]

The engagements on April 22, 23, and 24, which involved practically all of Parsons' effectives, did not escape the notice of Confederate brass. A special commendation by Wharton dated May 24 contained glowing praise for Parsons' troops, who, despite stubborn enemy resistance, repeatedly charged Federal positions. A soldier in the Twelfth noted that Wharton called his regiment's attack on April 24 unequaled even "on the other side of the . . . [Mississippi] River," and Taylor, after praising his cavalry's valiant efforts during the three-day encounter, paid special tribute to his cavalry commanders: "It is difficult to estimate the importance of the service rendered by Wharton, Steele, and Parsons. The gallantry and pluck they exhibited in fighting such odds for three days is beyond praise. Parsons displayed great courage and has the confidence of his brigade. He should be promoted at once." [27]

On April 25 sporadic fighting continued all along the Alexandria post road, in the forests and swamps along its route, and throughout the valleys of the upper Rapides and lower Red. Again constituting the vanguard of Wharton's cavalry, Dave and the men of Parsons' Brigade grappled with the enemy all day, skirmishing most of the afternoon and well into the night, fighting after dark by the light of "a conflagration of burning buildings burnt by [Union] stragglers." Giddings' and Burford's boys, covering the flanks and rear of Steele's vanguard, complained more about scorching heat, blinding smoke, and choking dust than about enemy resistance. A ranger in the Twenty-first wrote: "Along most of our route our road lay on high land near the west edge of the Red River bottom. The Yankees had previously burned nearly all dwellings and now . . . amused themselves by burning all the cornhouses. Our front ranks skirmished with their rear guard every day, but my regiment, being in the middle, did not participate in the skirmishes." [28]

Then on April 26, after three weeks of almost constant skirmishing, Parsons' Brigade was pulled from its forward position and replaced by

William Hardeman's command. Dave and his comrades bivouacked eighteen miles above Alexandria to catch their breath. Corn from one of Taylor's subsistence stations arrived the next day, and Parsons' boys spent the next three days tending their horses, binding their wounds, and enjoying a period of leisure. "Our brigade is resting today," a member of the Twelfth wrote on April 27, "the first one since the 8th." [29]

Meanwhile, as Dave and his comrades relaxed, Banks and Porter prepared to defend Alexandria. Thousands of U.S. soldiers and run-away slaves used hundreds of wagons to construct elaborate fortifications while Porter tried to patch up his sievelike riverboats. Some transports, "their sides . . . half shot away" and their smokestacks looking like "huge pepper boxes," bore mute testimony of the intense Confederate fire encountered during their voyage from Grand Bayou. [30]

But Porter's fleet posed a problem for Banks. The unexpected spring drought had plunged the river to rock-bottom levels, creating a large, riverwide, low-water cataract that local residents called "the falls." The rushing shallows, laced with treacherous limestone outcroppings, blocked the river and stranded ten of Porter's vessels in the upper channel. They also halted Banks' downriver flight, since the army could hardly abandon the navy. At first the only solution seemed to be to burn the vessels and let the sailors join the army in walking downstream to the Mississippi River. [31]

An engineering genius on William Franklin's staff, however, Lieutenant Colonel Joseph Bailey of Wisconsin, advanced a plan to extricate the entrapped vessels. He suggested the building of a large dam with a central spillway to boost the level of the river to float the boats into the lower channel. Although at first skeptical, Banks finally gave his approval, and the army went to work unloading transports, removing metal plating from the gunboats to reduce their draft, and constructing Bailey's dam. A resident of Alexandria later described the project: "Bailey began construction . . . on the Pineville side, constructing a wing dam of large trees cut from the riverside, the butts tied to cross logs, the tops pointing toward the current, kept in place by stones, bricks, and brush. From the Alexandria side, where large trees were scarce, he made a crib of logs and lumber, filled in with stones . . . and heavy pieces of machinery from the sugar houses and cotton gins, and lumber from homes in the vicinity." [32]

Meanwhile, Taylor, believing that Banks was "utterly demoralized and ripe for destruction," proceeded to step up harassment of the Federals. Denied outright assault because of his numerical disadvantage, he ordered his skirmishers, snipers, and artillery to pour a steady fire into Union breastworks, deployed his cavalry to discourage Fed-

eral foraging, and tried to convince Banks that he had received reinforcements by putting squads to work beating drum "calls, blowing
bugles, and rolling empty wagons over fence rails."[33]

But the spectre of starvation haunted both sides. At this point at
least, Banks' supply of rations for his men was adequate; but his cavalry and draft animals were starving. And if he failed to reach the
Mississippi in three weeks, so would his men. Taylor, on the other
hand, was in even worse shape. Since the supply of corn in Taylor's
prearranged subsistence stations was depleted and his river connec-
tion with Shreveport blocked by a sunken steamer (the *New Falls City*),
both his men and horses were going hungry. On April 25 Taylor informed Kirby Smith's adjutant that some kind of subsistence must "be
sent . . . from above," or he and his troops would "have to eat . . .
[their] boots." Although the *New Falls City* was removed at the end of
April, severe shortages in Shreveport limited both the quantity and
quality of rations reaching Taylor during the month of May.[34]

Dave and his comrades, part of a column composed largely of Parsons' Brigade but commanded by William Steele, scouted the Bayou
Rapides in search of Federal patrols and food. Irreplaceable cavalry
mounts, too weak to stand, occasionally had to be shot; and dozens of
Parsons' boys deserted, considering the possibility of a firing squad
preferable to the certainty of starvation. A ranger in Dave's company
wrote:

> While on the raid from Mansfield to . . . [Yellow Bayou], we did not
> have much to eat; both armies had been over the ground twice and
> Banks on his retreat destroyed everything after taking what he could
> use for his army.
>
>   So for thirty days we had practically nothing to eat. I remember that
> one of our mess slipped off to find something to eat and I gave him
> five dollars and he paid it for a pone of cornbread, and it had a thin
> crust on it, but nevertheless it was good.[35]

But Dave noted that just as the Lord provided the children of Israel
with manna during their wilderness wanderings, so He supplied the
men of Parsons' Brigade with sustenance during the Red River campaign. On May 3 Dave and some of his friends dashed into a burning
sugarhouse torched by retreating Federals and salvaged "160 hogs-
heads of molasses and much sugar." The next day they found some
dead Union soldiers with knapsacks full of hardtack. These items,
along with farm animals and grain taken from plantations along the
lower Red, helped Parsons and his boys survive.[36]

It would seem that the shortage of rainfall during the spring of
1864 should have reduced the mosquito population in the region, but

such was not the case. Swarms of the bloodsucking insects followed Steele's troops during the day and feasted on them at night. Dave and his companions soon were suffering from multitudes of bites, some causing extensive swelling and high fever. One of Dave's companions wrote: "While marching and fighting in Louisiana, we also had to fight black swamp mosquitoes all the time, day and night. The only way we could possibly get sleep was to . . . lie in a circle with our heads pointing in and take turns fighting off the mosquitoes. In shifts of an hour, we passed the brush around and got a fairly good night's sleep."[37]

And there were times when the Federals seemed as numerous as the mosquitoes. On May 5 Dave and the men of Steele's column were ambushed on a tributary of the Bayou des Glaize by "some 3,000 or 4,000 infantry." Steele, whose quick thinking prevented many of his boys from being killed, formed his troops into a battle formation and charged the entrenched Federals, only to be thrown back. Hopelessly outnumbered, Steele signaled his boys to retreat. In reporting the skirmish, he wrote that the enemy's lines were "more than three times the length of . . . [his] single-rank cavalry formations" and that he and his men simply were overwhelmed.[38]

But the overall picture of the Red River war seemed to favor the Confederates. Taylor's snipers hampered construction on Bailey's dam, and Confederate reinforcements from Arkansas were reported on their way to Louisiana. Although Taylor knew he could not keep Banks bottled up in Alexandria indefinitely, he concentrated on controlling the Red below the city. "I am . . . massing everything on the Boeuf and river below Alexandria," Taylor wrote on May 8. "The main struggle is for the river—vital for the enemy."[39]

Although spread thin, Taylor's troops performed well. Wharton's cavalry patrolled roads north and west of Alexandria, sniped at vessels on the river, and stripped all farm animals and grain from nearby plantations to keep them out of Federal hands. While Dave and the rest of Steele's boys challenged enemy forces along the Rapides road and the Bayou des Glaize, Bagby's horsemen captured and burned a transport near Fort De Russy and dispersed a Federal squadron on the Bayou Robert road. Polignac's veterans, supported by squadrons from Bee's and Baylor's divisions, collided with enemy units in the valleys of the Bayous Boeuf, Robert, and des Glaize. Major's cavalry with two sections of artillery prowled the Red below Fort De Russy, destroyed or captured five Federal vessels in six days, and closed the river to enemy shipping. William Vincent's Louisiana regiment, operating in concert with Bagby's and DeBray's cavalry, burned bridges and felled trees to obstruct Federal movement around Fort De Russy and harried Banks' scouting parties as far south as the Atchafalaya.

Liddell's brigade, on the east bank of the Red, occupied Pineville, stymied all Federal efforts to dislodge it, and peppered Banks' breastworks on the west bank with howitzer shells.[40]

Of course, the question foremost in the minds of soldiers on both sides during these weeks was whether Bailey's dam would extricate Porter's stranded vessels. On May 8 they got a partial answer. Amid the cheers of Federal soldiers and sailors, three of the ten trapped riverboats splashed through the spillway and settled into the navigable waters of the lower channel. But before the seven remaining vessels could follow, a section of the dam collapsed, and the level of the upper channel again plunged to unnavigable depths.

Unperturbed by the setback, Banks' work crews mended the break, completed two so-called bracket dams above the main one, and flushed the remaining vessels through the spillway. By midmorning on May 13, Porter's entire flotilla rested in the deeper waters of the lower Red, ready to resume their race for the Mississippi.[41]

After putting Alexandria to the torch, Banks and Porter again started downriver, their eyes fixed on the Father of Waters, only forty miles away. The riddled Federal vessels, stripped of all armor and smeared with tar to conceal their bare timbers, moved easily through the murky waters, their passengers paying little heed to corpses that marked their passage. A Union soldier on one of the riverboats wrote that he saw "a great many bodies floating downstream . . . [with] some lodged near the river bank with buzzards picking at them."[42]

Meanwhile, on shore Banks' troops jammed the river roads south of Alexandria, heading for the Red's junction with the Mississippi. Everything that could not be transported was burned, thrown in the river, or otherwise destroyed. Hundreds of baggage wagons joined thousands of Federal soldiers and runaway slaves streaming from the burning city. Taylor wrote: "On yesterday [May 13] the enemy moved heavy masses down the river road from Alexandria, the head of his column reaching a point twenty miles below last night. Three hundred and thirteen wagons accompanied the column. Heavy explosions were heard at Alexandria during the day and dense clouds of smoke enveloped it. Twenty-three transports and two gunboats had up steam and the river was full of floating masses of cotton."[43]

Sickened by Banks' escape from Alexandria, Taylor still hoped that he might defeat his elusive foe. Although his ammunition was running low, his rations were practically nonexistent, and his troops were widely scattered, Taylor sent Polignac's, Major's, and Bagby's troops to slow the Federal retreat and ordered Wharton to press "the enemy's rear and flank on the river road below Alexandria."[44]

Dave and the men of the Twelfth again played a significant role in Confederate cavalry operations. Wharton sent Steele in pursuit, and Steele selected Parsons' Brigade, perhaps his most effective unit, to head his vanguard. Steele placed Parsons, who had the Twelfth and Nineteenth under his commmand, directly "in the rear of the enemy" and "placed the Twenty-First . . . and Morgan's battalion on his flank."[45]

During the next two days, May 14 and 15, Dave and his comrades were in almost constant contact with the enemy. They skirmished on May 14 until the Federals "opened a heavy fire of artillery" which forced them to fall back. On May 15, while the opposing sides engaged in an artillery duel on a plain as "smooth as a billiard table," Parsons' boys were dispatched to cover Polignac's right flank and pounced on an enemy baggage train near Cheneyville, dispersing its escort, capturing a wagon full of supplies, and taking thirty prisoners.[46]

After more than four hours of heavy bombardment, the artillery duel ended, and Banks resumed his withdrawal. Parsons' boys joined Steele's troops in hot pursuit, but their efforts were hampered by thousands of starving Negroes begging for food. Nevertheless, they captured dozens of stragglers from Banks' army who were too weak and exhausted to continue their flight.[47]

Dave and the rest of Steele's boys entered Moreauville the next day and bivouacked on a campground "where preachers once held their revivals." Scouts reported that the first columns of Banks' exhausted army had reached the burned out village of Simmesport, less than ten miles from the Mississippi. The final chapter of the campaign was about to begin.[48]

---•▸— ◂—

CHAPTER 11

The Final Charge at Yellow Bayou

The uncompleted and partially wrecked Fort Yellow Bayou, dubbed "Fort Humbug" by the soldiers who occupied it, lay on the west bank of Yellow Bayou between the bayou's junction with the Bayou des Glaize and its junction with the Atchafalaya. It was in the vicinity of this Confederate fort, now in Federal hands, that Banks determined to make his final stand, and he dug in along the stream, named for the beautiful yellow flowers that covered its banks.

But to cross the Yellow Bayou and the Atchafalaya, Banks again enlisted the aid of Lieutenant Colonel Joseph Bailey, the architect and builder of the dam at Alexandria, who erected a wagon bridge across Yellow Bayou and fashioned an ingenious floating bridge across the Atchafalaya by positioning vessels from Porter's fleet abreast to support perpendicular gangplanks across the riverboats. Once these bridges were in place on May 17, 1864, they provided Banks' soldiers with an effective avenue of escape. Like frightened rabbits, his hungry and exhausted troops swarmed across the bridges to board riverboats waiting in the entrance of the Old River Lock Channel to take them to New Orleans.[1]

But May 17 was a day of skyrocketing temperatures, intermittent skirmishing, and mass confusion. Banks' troops, harassed by Wharton's patrols and caked with dust and sweat, were widely scattered. Before they could take advantage of Bailey's bridges, they had to reach them. Banks' pathetic soldiers, therefore, streamed through the des Glaize swamps and stumbled along the roads leading to Yellow Bayou. Like walking scarecrows in a world of make-believe, they trudged along, trying to cover the last few steps that would put them beyond the reach of their pursuers.

Having been on the move for days without rest, many collapsed along the way. "I was so dead sleepy that twice I fell flat on the ground as I was walking along," one wrote in his diary. "The fall woke me up each time and I kept going someway. Men had given out and were sleeping all along beside the road like dead men."[2]

And since many of Banks' boys had not eaten in days, they suffered periodic blindness, dizziness, and blackouts. They ate whenever and whatever they could, often behaving more like wild animals than men. One wrote: "The cattle had been shot and were lying where they fell. It was everyone for himself. Chunks were cut out and were eaten before the animal was done kicking. A pack of wolves never acted more ravenous and bloodthirsty. I managed to get my hand between the ribs of one and [get] hold of the liver. I couldn't pull my hand out without straightening the fingers so got only shreds, but I kept it up until I had taken the edge off my appetite."[3]

On the Confederate side there was similar starvation and exhaustion, but the pursuer was less frenzied than the pursued. Except for a fleeting hope that they might yet prevent Banks' escape, Southern soldiers were less emotional and more resolute, methodical, and accustomed to privation.

Dave and the other men of the Twelfth spent most of May 17 skirmishing and rounding up stragglers. Their job, as part of Steele's vanguard, was to delay Banks' escape until the rest of Taylor's army could catch up. Operating in conjunction with squadrons from Major's and DeBray's divisions, Dave and his comrades approached to within two miles of Fort Yellow Bayou, only to be driven back by Federal artillery. "We skirmished until almost dark," Steele wrote, when the Federals "opened a heavy fire of artillery upon us from a position which became better known as the battlefield of the next day."[4]

That battlefield, known afterward as Yellow Bayou, encompassed about three square miles of dried up swampland, abandoned cane fields, and dead timber. The Federal battleline, bristling with artillery, centered on the bayou, with the wrecked fort anchoring the right flank. On May 18, however, a sizable Federal force (three brigades with artillery) commanded by A. J. Mower recrossed Yellow Bayou under orders to hold Wharton's vanguard at bay until Banks' troops could escape across the bridges installed by Bailey. A large field, divided into sections by a network of trenches dug earlier by Southerners, lay directly west of the fort and between two large swamps, but only one of the swamps, the one on the south, contained enough mud and water to hamper troop movements. An earthen levee, which protected the cane fields against high water during the rainy season, extended from the Bayou des Glaize almost to the fort, and dry underbrush and dead grass, needing only a spark to ignite it, infested the southern end of the field, near a belt of dead trees that bordered the mud-gumbo swamp.[5]

On May 18, the day of the battle, Wharton ordered his rangers (including Parsons' Brigade commanded by William Steele) into their saddles at first light. Since the swamp southwest of the fort on the Confederate right contained potholes of bottomless mud and since Bailey's bridge across the bayou less than three miles downstream was sure to be well protected, Wharton decided to move against Federal positions along the levee in the vicinity of the fort.

As Wharton and his boys approached the bayou about midmorning, they were attacked by Federal cavalry that seemed to come out of nowhere, and the Confederates scattered in all directions. Parsons, commanding his old regiment, tried to get his boys to stay and fight. His "fine, resonant voice" could be heard above the furor, admonishing them to hold their ground. "Halt! What! The gallant Twelfth behave this way," he cried, "with Federal cavalry on their heels?" Then after again calling on them to end their retreat, he added, "And if they charge you, wheel and empty their saddles, G—— d—— them."[6]

This engagement ended quickly as both sides fell back, and Wharton resumed his march in the direction of the fort. He had four 12-pound smoothbores and seven 3-inch, rifled guns, but was low on ammunition. The Confederates moved cautiously through the dead forest, not knowing when and where the enemy would make its next appearance. It seems that Wharton planned to try to neutralize the Federal artillery and long-range rifles entrenched along the levee by mounting a surprise all-out frontal assault. Although such an attack could be costly, it might, if successful, open an avenue of attack for the rest of Taylor's army when it arrived.[7]

It was almost noon by the time Dave and the rest of Wharton's vanguard reached the large, abandoned sugarcane field where the bloodiest fighting of the day was to take place. The fort was dead ahead, and the mud-gumbo swamp was off to the right. Standing between Wharton and the Federal battle line along the bayou was Mower and his three brigades with field artillery. The commanders on both sides believed they faced huge enemy forces, so after a brief engagement about midday, each fell back and ordered his troops to dig in and prepare for a grand conflagration.

Personally supervising his troops on his right, Wharton had to depend upon Major to manage the troops on the left. Fortunately for Wharton, Polignac's infantry arrived, and he used it to bolster his center. James Taylor's Seventeenth, now commanded by Robert Stone, and Trezevant Hawpe's Thirty-first were held in reserve on the right while the Nineteenth and Twelfth were assigned reserve positions in the left rear. Thomas Harrison's and Warren Stone's brigades formed the main line of Polignac's right, almost directly in front of the fort, and the rest of William Steele's boys, along with Major's troops, constituted Wharton's left flank, strung out among the trees west of the large cane field in the vicinity of the dried-up swamp.[8]

Time passed slowly as Dave and the men of the Twelfth waited for Wharton's bugler to sound the charge. As tension mounted they worked off their anxiety by building "a breastwork of a fence and some logs" in "a skirt of timber" on the edge of the cane field. The Confederates, from common soldier to division commander, realized that their only chance of success rested upon split-second timing so that the full weight of their attack fell upon the enemy lines at the same time.[9]

But things went wrong from the beginning. One major miscue occurred on the left, where Dave and his comrades waited in reserve. Without consulting Wharton and overriding Steele's objections, Major ordered the Twelfth, Nineteenth, and a section of William G. Moseley's artillery to new positions on Polignac's left, leaving a gap between Polignac's troops in the trenches and the rest of Major's boys near the dry swamp. Therefore, when the first charge was sounded shortly after one o'clock, a large part of Parsons' Brigade, including Dave and about two hundred of the Twelfth, was caught out of position; and the left side of Wharton's line, where the rest of Steele's troops were situated, was stopped in its tracks by "double charges of canister shot."[10]

The Federal gunners in Mower's battle line had a flanking position on the advancing Confederates and ripped them apart. The horror created by canister fired at close range has been described by the great Civil War historian, Bruce Catton: "Canister was the gunner's close-range ammunition; a charge of canister consisted simply of a tin can full of lead slugs somewhat smaller than golf balls. When the gun was fired, the tin can disintegrated and the slugs went out in an expanding cloud, like a charge fired from a monstrously over-sized sawed-off shotgun. Within two hundred yards this weapon was murderous beyond belief."[11]

Once the left end of the Confederate line was dispersed by the canister broadside, the Federals poured a deadly musket fire into Steele's broken ranks and moved forward into the open field where Polignac's boys fought like wild men. Curling around what remained of Steele's left flank, two regiments of Federal sharpshooters caught the rest of Major's troops in a withering crossfire and forced them back, leaving scores of Confederate dead and wounded strewn across the northern end of the field. Federal success in stopping Wharton's first charge can be explained almost entirely in terms of Mower's adroit use of canister and Major's untimely attempt to move part of Steele's command to a new position. Since Dave and Little Will were part of the errant detachment, they missed most of the action generated by Wharton's first charge, but they later complained that they almost were run over by the Twenty-first and Morgan's Battalion during the retreat.[12]

The Federals, merely interested in defending their emplacements along the bayou, did not press their advantage but returned to their original positions among the trees about a half mile west of the levee. Steele, of course, was enraged with Major for tampering with his troop dispositions. He wrote: "I . . . state that my force on my left was weakened and I [was] prevented from strengthening it by the removal of a portion of my brigade by Brigadier General Major, by whose order, I am informed by the regimental commander, they were placed on the extreme right, in consequence of which disposition they were not found when needed on the left."[13]

Since both sides occupied essentially their original positions and more than half of Banks' troops already were across the Atchafalaya, many soldiers thought the battle was over. But Wharton, in pursuit of Taylor's edict to inflict as much punishment as possible on the escaping Federals, ordered his commanders to regroup for a second charge.[14]

But Wharton's order fell on deaf ears. Wharton's commanders knew that nothing worthwhile could be accomplished by another charge. Even Parsons, whose bravery was never questioned, at first did not respond. Concern for his men, the dearth of cover in the open field, and the heavier fire power of the entrenched Federals help explain his hesitation. Wharton repeated his order. According to one of Dave's comrades, Parsons delayed as long as he dared and then reluctantly ordered his men forward, saying, "If I must, I must."[15]

By now Dave and the men of the Twelfth and Nineteenth were in their new position on Polignac's left, occupying part of the field where some of the heaviest fighting had taken place only minutes before. In response to buglers sounding the second and final charge, they cautiously moved out onto the corpse-strewn field. Bitter fighting again erupted on both of their flanks, but there was no enemy movement among the trees directly in front of them. These Federal positions, occupied by two regiments of Missouri infantry and a Missouri battery, appeared to be abandoned. But when Dave and his comrades approached to within a hundred yards of the Federals, the Missourians opened fire. "[The Confederates] passed across the open field," one of the Missourians wrote, "apparently confident that they would meet no further resistance."[16]

But Dave and his comrades, commanded by Captain Weir of the Volunteers, were not caught completely off guard. Having seen the rays of the sun glisten from the Missourians' weapons before the shooting started, most of them dropped to the ground and escaped the flesh-tearing destruction of the first Federal volley. Then as the field filled with smoke, the men of the Twelfth and Nineteenth scattered, seeking what little cover the terrain had to offer.[17]

Dave felt the same gnawing sickness in his stomach that he had experienced at Cache River before the first shot was fired, but he crouched low and moved forward, firing through the smoke into the Federal positions. At this point his vow seems to have been forgotten.[18]

The Missouri battery in the trees to Dave's left made its presence known. Again canister ripped the Confederate front, but not having a flanking position as before, it did less damage.

After several minutes the artillery barrage lifted, and the Missourians moved forward from the timber to engage Parsons' boys in the open field. Seconds later another wave of Federal infantry bolted forward, screaming the Yankee's answer to the Rebel yell. The small arms fire swelled into a deafening tumult, and the battle became an infantry duel, plain and simple, as each side poured deadly musket fire into the ranks of the other.[19]

Dave fired his Enfield as rapidly as he could reload and moved forward through the dense smoke, often finding it difficult to distinguish friend from foe. Suddenly he was aware that Little Will no longer was at his side, and he felt strangely alone, as if he were the only Confederate soldier on the field.

Then it happened! There was a sharp, burning shock of pain in his chest as his Enfield seemed to explode in his hands. A minié ball had splintered the stock of his Enfield and ricocheted into his chest, lodging behind his shoulder blade. Dave later wrote that the wound was not as serious as he at first had thought, since the ball missed vital organs and major arteries. Nevertheless, the minié, "partially spent, buried itself just behind . . . [his] heart."[20]

His head spinning crazily, Dave fell to his knees. He was not sure of direction, but he was acutely aware of the close proximity of the enemy. "[At] least one hundred men shot at me at a distance of not more than fifty yards," he wrote.[21]

Partially disabled and now crawling on his hands and knees, Dave ignored the savage fighting that raged around him. Here, opposite the fort and less than a thousand yards from the bayou, the heaviest fighting of the battle took place. Polignac's boys, occupying the center of the Confederate line south of the fort, fought like tigers.

Farther to the south, the gunfire ignited the dry brush in the open field, and the fire quickly spread to the dead timber that lined the south end of the cane field. Searing heat and flying embers added to the debacle of horror.[22]

Although it seemed much longer to Dave, about fifteen minutes passed. Some of Polignac's boys fought their way into the burning woods that lined the cane field and got to within a dozen yards of Federal artillery positions. But again things went wrong on the Confederate left, where Parsons' exhausted troops, fighting shoulder to shoulder with Polignac's men, struggled to hold their ground. Once more they were outflanked by "a very heavy column" whose "destructive fire" drove them toward the center and back into the ditches that Polignac's troops had occupied before the charge. Unaccustomed to fighting on foot and weak from hunger, many of Parsons' boys collapsed from heat prostration and exhaustion. By the time they had retreated to their original positions, they were, according to a member of the Ellis County Rangers, "so completely exhausted that some fainted."[23]

Although bleeding and disoriented, Dave determined the direction of the Confederate rear and began his retreat. Twice he fell, each time doubting that he had the strength to get up. He looked around for Little Will, but the figures moving around him in the smoke were indistinguishable. After what seemed an eternity, Dave took refuge in a deep trench filled with Polignac's boys, since it provided the only protection out in the open field.[24]

Dave must have passed out at this point, for the next thing he knew, the smoke had thinned, the firing was more intermittent, and he was alone in the trench. Peering over the edge of the embankment, he could see a long row of Federal soldiers moving toward him. Realizing that he was in "danger of being overtaken by the enemy," he crawled out of the trench and stumbled forward as fast as his rubbery legs would carry him. "Seeing I must either surrender or risk my life running before a solid line of . . . [enemy soldiers] at least seventy-five yards long," he wrote, "I chose the latter."[25]

Dave managed to run about a dozen yards before being hit again. This time the wound was more serious, since the enemy ball nicked an artery in his neck. It cut a deep furrow, bringing forth a burst of blood that splattered his clothing and streamed down his right arm. He later wrote:

> Only one ball struck me and first destroyed my gun, and then after being thus partially spent, buried itself just behind my heart. Now these last guns, the last ever fired at . . . [my] regiment, were fired at me—every one at me for I was far behind all the others. Thus it fol-

lows that not only the first balls fired in the . . . [battle of Cache River] hit me, but the last balls [at Yellow Bayou] also—or rather the first and last balls that hit anyone. This to me was exceedingly strange.[26]

As Dave went down with his second wound, the rattle of musketry virtually stopped. Except for the cries of the wounded, an unnatural hush fell over the battlefield.

Soon there was a scurry of activity as able-bodied and less seriously wounded soldiers attended their badly wounded comrades, some helping others from the field. The next thing Dave knew, he was in the arms of Little Will, who frantically bound his neck to stop the bleeding.

For Dave and the men of Parsons' Brigade the war was over. Although almost a year of fighting remained, and the brigade was not disbanded until the following May, never again would they engage the enemy in combat.[27]

Wharton's final charge at Yellow Bayou, like the first, had accomplished nothing except to increase the number of casualties on both sides. Mower's battle line in the timber between the field and the bayou remained intact, and there had been no serious threat to Banks' artillery emplacements that lined the bayou. With the Confederates' aggressive inclinations blunted, Federal soldiers now could complete their escape. About sunset the Confederates watched as the last of Banks' stragglers crossed the bayou and headed for Bailey's riverboat bridge across the Atchafalaya. The next morning the forest fire ignited by the battle burned itself out after consuming part of the fort. Although there was a brief artillery duel and some skirmishing that afternoon on the east bank of Yellow Bayou, Parsons' boys were not involved, and by noon the next day all of Banks' wagons and troops were safely situated on the east bank of the Atchafalaya. As the rest of Taylor's troops arrived in piecemeal fashion, they found that there was nothing more that they could do. The enemy no longer was within reach.[28]

The consequence of Parsons' final battle, the last of the Red River campaign, becomes clear only when the big picture is examined. The battle of Yellow Bayou cost Wharton about 608 men and Banks approximately 350. Most of the Confederate wounded belonged to Polignac's command, but Steele estimated that "the Twelfth, Nineteenth, and Twenty-First regiments and Morgan's Battalion" lost slightly "more than 200 . . . in killed and wounded."[29]

But whatever the brigade's losses, the number might have been much larger had it not been for many of its members being out of position during the first charge and for Parsons' hesitation prior to the second. One of Dave's companions in the Twelfth wrote: "Our regiment didn't suffer as greatly as some others, but we have to lament the loss of some fifteen killed—my messmate, Johnny Morgan, the ball entering the back portion of his head and coming out above his right eye. . . . Captain Weir was killed . . . ; Lieutenant [Edward] Gardner of Kyser's [company] also killed."[30]

At least three of Parsons' dead were from Dave's company, including Corporal Sanford Turner, who died during the night following the battle. One of Turner's buddies recounted a strange tale of his passing:

> On the morning of the battle of Yellow Bayou, Corporal . . . Turner remarked to me as we were taking up the line of march that if we had a battle that day he would get killed. I asked him why he spoke thus, and the reply was, "I dreamed a dog bit me on the thigh." I told him that I did not believe in . . . [omens]. In the afternoon we were ordered forward, and then the fight began in which we lost several killed and wounded.
>
> Turner and myself were both wounded. Turner's wound proved fatal, and he died during the night in the same ward in which I was located.[31]

But perhaps there should not have been any casualties at all, for there are indications that the battle was unnecessary and accomplished nothing. As long as Banks could protect his riverboat bridge across the Atchafalaya, the Federal avenue of escape was open. It was just a matter of time before Banks effected his final escape. Alwyn Barr, in his *Polignac's Texas Brigade,* wrote: "A consensus among Confederate troops engaged at Yellow Bayou held that the battle had been unnecessary, since the Federals were retreating across the Atchafalaya at the time, and placed the blame on General Wharton. It would appear actually to have been a rather poorly managed effort to punish the Union army one last time before it escaped completely."[32]

Taylor, still angry with Kirby Smith for transferring part of his army to Arkansas, described the Confederate effort in glowing terms, but complained: "Nothing but the withdrawal of Walker's division from me has prevented the capture of Banks' army and the destruction of Porter's fleet. I feel bitter about this because my army has been robbed of the just measure of its glory and the country [of] the most brilliant and complete success of the war."[33]

During the next several days the dead were "buried in an enclosed graveyard at a church" on the Coco Plantation, which, along with the Norwood Plantation, served as a hospital for the wounded. Slave quarters, barns, corncribs, smokehouses, and hastily erected shelters were filled with wounded soldiers wearing both the blue and the gray.[34]

Under the care of Little Will and several of his messmates, Dave was carried to a nearby farmhouse, where the next day an army surgeon dug the minié from his back. Dave, with Little Will serving as his nurse, spent the next ten days at the farm, paying the farmer and his wife four dollars a day for their room and board.

On the morning of May 28 Dave, complaining that there was no more corn for his horse, convinced Little Will that he was well enough to return to Texas. Like thousands of Confederate soldiers, Dave and Little Will got their meager possessions together and started home, making no effort to inform their commanders of their departure. Dave still was so weak that he had to be helped into the saddle, but soon the two friends were homeward bound.[35]

The unauthorized departure of soldiers following the battle did not go unnoticed by Confederate brass. Taylor, apparently appalled by his rapidly diminishing ranks, noted that even his most "reliable infantry commands . . . have dwindled to nothing."[36]

Dave and Little Will, happy to be going home, walked their horses down a narrow trail through the forest. They must have been marveling at their close brushes with the Grim Reaper when again they escaped death or serious injury by inches. Dave described the incident: "As we went along the road by the side of a field in the woods, Stuart riding in advance of me, we passed under a large dead tree. And without any warning at all, a fairly good two-horse load of wood fell in the road behind my horse so close it almost brushed his tail. We both stopped short, astonished again at our narrow escape."[37]

Dave added this nearly fatal accident to his growing list of miraculous escapes which he attributed to divine intervention. By now he considered the keeping of his vow an absolute necessity. He wrote: "Sometime not long after that, I resolved in my own mind I would never again fire another gun in battle. And while this resolve was easily kept because the regiment was never again in action, it might not have been so easy had the termination of the war come later. Still I meant to keep my resolve come what would."[38]

CHAPTER 12

The Last Encampment

*D*ave spent most of the last year of the war with his regiment. Except for the unauthorized sick leave after the battle of Yellow Bayou and a procurement furlough in the spring of 1865, his story is essentially that of his unit.

Dave's devotion to duty can be explained partially in terms of an honor bestowed upon him in August 1864, while the brigade was camped in Tensas Parish, Louisiana. While Parsons served briefly as acting commander of the "Sub-District of North Louisiana," Dave was chosen top sergeant (orderly) of his company. He wrote:

> [Perhaps] because of my numerous and unusual misfortunes, Company E made me their first sergeant in August following. It was considered, and rightly, too, the most difficult position to fill because the orderly had to look after the welfare of every man in the company as to both food and clothes for them and food for his horse. All issues were based on the orderly's report: he must keep track of every man so as to account for him and have him present on inspection day. Then too he must select every guard and every man for extra service of every kind.[1]

Dave's roster and account book, filled with personal notations and currently in the hands of his great-great-grandson, suggest that he took his duties seriously and assumed responsibilities which, according to his own admission, normally were "the business of the first lieutenant." Eager to learn, he seems to have welcomed duties that broadened his knowledge of commerce or sharpened his administrative skills. "Added to this in my case I had to keep the company rolls and accounts, make out its muster rolls, etc.," he explained, "but . . . I did not object for it taught me a little practical business at an early period in my life."[2]

Although Dave and his comrades did no fighting during the final year of the war, they had to struggle with two continuing problems that threatened their very existence—abject privation and confusion in the higher echelons of departmental command. Both kept them on the move searching for food and fodder or responding to conflicting and often senseless orders which reflected the frustration of the last days.[3]

After Yellow Bayou, Parsons' Brigade was in a devastated state. It bivouacked "near the . . . battlefield . . . four miles [from] Simmesport" until the last week in May, when it moved to a site on Bayou des Glaize below Alexandria for slightly better forage. Rumor had it that the brigade would assist Sterling Price in Missouri, but if based on fact, these plans were canceled, probably because of the unit's poor condition. Then late in the year Parsons was ordered to Houston, but en route, the destination of the brigade was changed to Arkansas.[4]

Gaunt, diseased, half-starved, and dressed in rags, Dave and his comrades were no different from most other soldiers of the western Confederacy. A few weeks after Yellow Bayou, Taylor complained that his troops were "without shoes," sick, and "utterly worn out with marching and fighting. [No] movement can be made," he wrote to Kirby Smith, "until an adequate supply is furnished. The Clothing Bureau is liberal in promise and utterly barren in performance."[5]

Smith responded by explaining that the Shreveport Clothing Bureau was "crippled in its resources and cut off from its supplies by the loss of the lower Rio Grande" and in general labored under great "difficulties and disadvantages." Clothing shortages became so critical among Parsons' boys that a special procurement furlough system was initiated to allow "one man from each company" to go home each month to seek suitable clothing. Even this practice, however, failed to solve the problem, since most items needed simply were not available in sufficient quantities.[6]

During the summer and fall of 1864, Kirby Smith's organizational charts became a hodgepodge of black lines, cross-marks, illegible figures, and confusing notations. But some significant changes emerged from his chaotic record keeping. Taylor, whose feud with Smith threatened to wreck the department, was shifted to a command east of the Mississippi, and Magruder was transferred from Texas to the subdistrict of Arkansas. William Steele, having commanded Parsons' Brigade during the Red River campaign, retained that position until early in 1865, when he was elevated to a corps command and Parsons again assumed command of the brigade that wore his name. Carter, who still considered himself the rightful commander of Parsons' Brigade, accepted a Texas assignment that eventually led to his commanding another brigade there. Carter's old regiment, the Twenty-first commanded by DeWitt Giddings, remained part of Parsons' Brigade until the spring of 1865, when it was transferred to Texas to serve in Carter's new brigade. Burford, the commander of the Nineteenth, was absent much of the time because of ill health. Therefore, in May 1864 he claimed his longevity exemption and went home, leaving his regiment in the hands of a capable lieutenant named Benjamin Watson.[7]

Once Magruder was installed as commander of Arkansas, he wasted no time introducing a rigid program to try to end desertion, bolster the size and number of his units, and prepare his troops for a last-ditch stand. Establishing his headquarters in Camden, he demanded the immediate execution of soldiers convicted of desertion and flooded Shreveport with exaggerated reports of Federal troop strength in Arkansas. Magruder's endless cries for reinforcements made him almost as unpopular in Shreveport as his antidesertion program did among his troops in Arkansas, but Kirby Smith finally responded to his calls for help and transferred several brigades of cavalry from Texas and Louisiana to Arkansas.[8]

Parsons' Brigade, one of those transferred, spent the winter of 1864–65 in southeastern Arkansas, patrolling the Arkansas, Saline, Ouachita, and Mississippi rivers. During these months, orders arrived almost daily from Camden, keeping Parsons and his boys on the move, shifting them aimlessly around the state, and completely destroying their confidence in Magruder. "It is supposed we will go to the Mississippi," one of Dave's comrades wrote in November 1864, "if Magruder in his intoxication does not order us in some other direction. We can't keep pace with his orders of late."[9]

In addition to the blitzkrieg of marching orders, Parsons' boys had to contend with pneumonia, "third-day chills," disintegrating clothing, starvation, and a devastating mortality rate among their horses. The shortage of food and fodder, of course, made all other problems more acute, and the brigade's constant movement during these weeks can be explained mostly in terms of its quest for subsistence. Some regions became totally destitute of forage. "We are compelled to abandon the country east of the Ouachita," a soldier in the Twelfth wrote shortly before Christmas, "on account of the scarcity of forage and breadstuffs."[10]

It is not surprising that units facing starvation increasingly ignored regulations and moral standards when foraging. And Parsons' Brigade was no exception. William Steele, before his elevation to a higher command, urged Parsons to control his troops to prevent indiscriminate looting and to keep them from becoming "a terror to the citizens . . . as has been too frequently the case." In another communication written by one of Dave's comrades a few weeks later, the fear was expressed that Parsons' entire command might be dismounted as punishment for its "notorious conduct" in dealing with civilians.[11]

Just when Parsons' boys concluded that starvation or desertion was their only recourse, their brigade was ordered to the Mississippi Valley to police government-sanctioned cotton trade with Yankee cotton buyers. This unusual trade, born of the western Confederacy's desperation and the North's cotton famine, allowed Southern planters to sell part of their produce to the enemy if a significant portion was given to the Confederate government. An Arkansas civilian described how it worked: "The trade is carried on, as I understand, in the following manner: Each planter or individual who has cotton to sell is first required to give . . . one half of his cotton to the government of the Confederate States without any compensation, the remaining half he then has the privilege of selling to whom he pleases under the permit and protection of General Smith. . . . The wagons are guarded and escorted to the river by our soldiers."[12]

Parsons' new assignment, which he received shortly after Christmas, was to escort the cotton trains and police the trade, making certain all cotton traders had permits and that the government got its share of the profits. Trade in arms and munitions was expressly forbidden, but thousands of pounds of Trans-Mississippi cotton was exchanged for food, "clothing for the army, cotton cards, medicines, etc." Parsons was required to submit regular reports to the Confederate Cotton Bureau concerning the volume of the trade and the number of violators arrested.[13]

But instead of apprehending violators, many of Parsons' boys stole cotton themselves and exchanged it for coffee, guncaps, powder, and bolts of dyed cloth. By dealing in stolen cotton and receiving contraband items, Dave and his comrades managed to violate almost all of the decrees levied by both governments trying to regulate the trade. Of course, their illegal participation in the trade did not last long, since Parsons soon was ordered out of the Mississippi Valley, but for about six weeks it became a bountiful source of supply and helps explain the health and hardiness of Parsons' Brigade during this period. The underground cotton trade seldom was mentioned in polite society, and because of its illegal and unpatriotic aspects, it became a source of embarrassment to both sides. Parsons' boys had little to say about the trade either at the time or later.[14]

Certainly letters written by Dave and his comrades ignored the subject. Not many letters were written anyway because of the scarcity of writing materials, but those which have survived tell of loneliness, boredom, privation, and youthful hopes for the future. Some rangers made plans for marriage after the war while others sought to tie the knot more quickly. "It seemed that all of Parsons' Brigade would get married," one of Dave's companions wrote, "if they could only get furloughs." [15]

But in February 1865 Parsons' stay in the Mississippi Valley ended abruptly as Kirby Smith ordered the brigade, along with other mounted units stationed in eastern Arkansas and Louisiana, to proceed to more bountiful campsites in Texas.

This move seems to have been prompted by the disturbing mortality rate among cavalry horses along the eastern border of the department. Letters written by both Confederate and Union soldiers allude to this fact. "All Texas cavalry except [William] Scurry's division has gone to Texas," a Union observer in western Mississippi reported in February. "Want of forage is the cause." [16]

So Dave with his unit returned to his "own . . . [be]loved, adopted state," first setting up housekeeping near Waverly in Walker County near the San Jacinto line and then "in a thicket of timber . . . [on] a high rolling plain" in Grimes County. Parsons' boys were delighted with their new surroundings, happy to be far removed from the desolation and blood-soaked battlefields of Louisiana and Arkansas. "I don't know when we have enjoyed so quiet and pleasant times," a soldier in Dave's regiment wrote while in Walker County, "as since we have been at this place." [17]

Parsons drilled his boys incessantly in both the Waverly and Grimes County sites, probably hoping to keep their minds off their pitiful plight and the dismal state of the war. All reports from the East were bad, and everyone wondered how much longer the war could last. "Then word came," Dave wrote, "that our army in Virginia under Lee and another in Georgia under [Joseph E.] Johnston and [John] Hood were being hard pressed." [18]

Perhaps the worst news of all, however, was the unhappy report that Lincoln had been reelected president of the United States. With Old Abe in the White House, there was little hope that the South could secure an honorable peace.

Confederate morale, noted for its tenacity and resilience, finally began to crumble. "The Northern armies are pressing on all sides and our people are depressed in spirits," one of Parsons' rangers wrote, ". . . but if no foreign aid comes in three months we must fall ere the first of July next. This has been my conviction since last June. The future is dark." [19]

As the spring of 1865 approached, Kirby Smith again reworked his organizational charts, and as heretofore, Parsons' boys disliked some of the consequences. Hamilton P. Bee was given another division command, and Parsons' Brigade was designated part of Bee's division. Having lost confidence in Bee during the Red River campaign, Parsons' rangers did not relish being in Bee's command, but since they had so many other things to worry about, they accepted their new status without undue complaint.[20]

One major problem was the increasing breakdown of communications between Kirby Smith and his commanders in the field. Some commanders waited for weeks for messages from Shreveport and frequently were ill equipped to make tactical decisions. As the war wound down, Smith not only communicated less but his adjutants seem to have become more careless and less reliable, causing field commanders to complain bitterly about Shreveport's failure to respond to their requests.

Parsons was no exception. Unable to obtain orders to the contrary, he moved his brigade to Camp Groce, south of Hempstead to be near Houston, where, according to rumor, Kirby Smith planned to relocate his headquarters. But before leaving Grimes County, he learned that he had been given a new regiment to replace the Twenty-first, which had been taken from him. The new regiment, the Thirtieth Texas Cavalry, was a grossly undersized but still mounted unit commanded by an irate and hot-tempered colonel named Edward Gurley, but it was not until Parsons arrived at Camp Groce in early April that the bulk of Gurley's boys caught up with him.[21]

The addition of the new regiment made little difference but was treated as good news, the first Dave and his comrades had received in a long time, but bad news overshadowed the good. One week after their arrival at Camp Groce, Parsons' boys were shocked to receive orders from Shreveport dismounting and disbanding their brigade. The various diminutive regiments of the brigade, now designated dismounted cavalry, were to become part of General J. H. Forney's (formerly Walker's) infantry division.[22]

But the war ended before Parsons and his boys could respond. "At . . . length," Dave wrote, "word came of Lee's surrender at Appomattox." With the subsequent surrender of Joe Johnston in North Carolina, Dick Taylor in Alabama, and finally Kirby Smith in Louisiana, the Confederate States of America passed into history.[23]

At first Kirby Smith refused to accept defeat and urged his officers and men to stand by their colors. But while preparing to move his headquarters from Shreveport to Houston, he learned of mutiny in his officers' corps, disloyalty among members of his staff, and wholesale desertion in his armies. Having no other alternative, Smith affixed his signature to a preliminary instrument of surrender on board a Federal steamer in Galveston harbor on June 2, 1865.[24]

Meanwhile, Dave and the men of Parsons' Brigade, dejected by their orders to dismount, maintained their camp near Hempstead until the second week in May. Then on May 12 Parsons, fearing epidemic illness and hoping for better forage, moved his brigade north to the Brazos, where he established his final bivouac on a broad prairie in the southwestern corner of Robertson County. Dave and his comrades spent the next week camped near "a nice clear branch" that transected the Houston and Texas Central Railroad. Unable to get Smith to respond and anxious for orders of any kind, Parsons sent inquiries to Generals Forney and S. B. Buckner, giving his location and asking for instructions. Again he received no reply.[25]

Then shortly after nine o'clock on the morning of May 20, Dave and his comrades were drilling when "a courier on a fast horse" raced into camp, hit the ground running, and asked for the brigade commander. Parsons came out of his tent, conferred briefly with the courier, and asked his sergeant major to assemble his troops. Lacking his usual sparkle and charm, he addressed his boys for the last time.

"Soldiers," Parsons began, "from all the information I can gather, the Trans-Mississippi Department has been surrendered." Then he spoke briefly, thanking his officers and men for their loyalty and confidence in him. Dave and the men of the brigade, with tears in their eyes, listened in disbelief. The moment was not unexpected, but now that it was here it somehow seemed unreal, as if it were part of a bad dream. Parsons asked his officers "to divide the teams and wagons" among the men. "Go home," he concluded, "the war is over!" Then he turned and disappeared into his tent.[26]

"[So] on May 20, 1865, while camped in Robertson County, Texas," Dave wrote, "we broke camp for the last time." He was concerned for the health and welfare of many of his comrades, some of whom were sick, without transportation, and penniless. "We were miles from home," he lamented, "and not one in a hundred had any money to pay his way home."[27]

Dave, however, was not without funds or transportation. He had forty dollars which he had carried through most of the war. His horse and those of most of his messmates were in pretty good condition considering their exposure to gunfire, starvation, and disease.[28]

Dave lashed his poncho and bedding behind his saddle, shoved his saber (his only remaining weapon) into its rigging, swung onto the back of his horse, and bade farewell to the drumbeats, bugle calls, muster inspections, and drill sessions of army life. He also said goodbye to the constant irritations and endless responsibilities of a top sergeant, resigning them to the dark recesses of his memory.[29]

The scattering of Parsons' rangers began shortly before noon, and by the middle of the afternoon the campsite was almost empty. Dave,

Little Will, and Lonesome John were among the last to leave, delaying their departure until the cool of the evening. Once on the road, they found themselves alone, their comrades having turned in different directions.

The three friends camped the first night on the outskirts of Owenville, the county seat of Robertson County, a pleasant village of recent birth, which was surrounded by a beautiful grove and situated upon a high, rolling prairie over which were scattered a few trees.[30]

Two days later the three horsemen rode into Waxahachie and drifted easily down the main street. Several men who were pitching horseshoes in front of the Rogers' House turned to stare but said nothing. Earlier, at the beginning of the war, soldiers passing through a town attracted a lot of attention, and patriotic citizens regaled them with flags, food, and beverages. But now soldiers were regarded at best with indifference, sadness, and perhaps a little embarrassment. For weeks returning soldiers had drifted through Waxahachie, and their presence had become commonplace, serving merely as an unpleasant reminder of the hardships of war and the humiliation of defeat.

Dave, Little Will, and Lonesome John rode past the ruins of the burned-out powdermill where Dave had almost lost his life two years earlier and took the road to Red Oak. First, Lonesome John and then Little Will, each in his turn, left Dave's side to head for his home, John near Red Oak and Will taking the road to his family farm nine miles north of Waxahachie.[31]

Dave rode alone the rest of the way home. When he reached Pleasant Run River, he turned northwest and entered the familiar forest beyond which lay his beloved Heath Branch. Here, within a couple of miles from home, Dave's horse showed signs of lameness, so the young veteran dismounted and, leading his mount, walked the rest of the way.

Soon the farmhouse on the hilltop came into view. Quill was seated on the gallery smoking his pipe and recognized his son a considerable distance away. He shouted the alarm, and several members of the Nance family appeared. Only Dave's mother, holding her daughter born the previous November, did not rush to meet him. It must have been a joyous reunion and a memorable occasion, but Dave wrote nothing about it, perhaps considering it too personal and too private to put on paper.

The next day Dave, in some of his father's work clothes, went out in the field across the branch to "finish the crop already planted." It seemed as if he had never been away. But somehow things were not the same. For one thing, he was not the same. He was not the same person who had ridden off to war forty-four months before. His faith in God was greater, and he felt that he better understood the divine forces operating in human lives. Dave was convinced that he owed his life to God, that he had a debt to pay, and he determined to pay that debt by devoting the rest of his life to Christian service. Of all the persons on earth, he sincerely believed, none appreciated and understood the value of God's mercy more than he.[32]

Dave also knew the horror and heartbreak of war. At last he knew what Quill had tried to tell him when he had first expressed an interest in becoming a soldier. Toward the end of his life, possibly with his sons and grandsons in mind, Dave denounced the war and his participation in it: "But like all boys in early life, I loved adventure, so that when the first call came for volunteer troops, I was crazy to go—yes, *crazy*, for that is the only way to describe a boy's sentiment when he is anxious to go to war. He is crazy, and if he goes he will see for himself—if he lives that long."[33]

Then in 1908, only seventeen years before his death, Dave recorded his chief regrets, accumulated during a lifetime, and all related to the war. The old soldier wrote: "And if there is any one act of his whole life which he regrets more than another, it is his entering the army. He regrets it, first, because he wishes he had never assisted in the protection of an institution so fraught with evil as that of human slavery; second, because war is murder, and murder has no mercy in it. Then, he entered the army against his father's will, and he regrets it for that too."[34]

But the great adventure had left invisible marks on Dave to match the visible ones. From his earliest beginnings, he had been troubled by the mysteries of life's inner meaning and humanity's reason for being. Now, armed with his vow and wartime experiences, he felt better prepared to combat meaninglessness and despair, determine the direction of his life, and understand the nature of the universe. The young farmer working in the fields at Heath Branch in the spring of 1865 had gone to war a confused, idealistic, and slightly rebellious youth. He had returned a mature, responsible adult.

The Later Years

Like all veterans returning home from war, David C. Nance found that his restless spirit complicated his transition to civilian life. Perhaps hoping that grueling, backbreaking labor would erase disturbing wartime memories, he spent the next three years working harder than ever before. In addition to running the Heath Branch Farm, he used income from land his father had given him to purchase an additional 122 acres of Dallas County prairie which he turned into a successful and lucrative enterprise. By planting all the new acreage in oats and wheat, he took advantage of skyrocketing postwar demands for grain and, in his words, became "fairly prosperous."

But despite his rigorous work schedule, Dave found time to seek fulfillment to his vow to "try earnestly to learn Heaven's truth." He spent months searching for a contemporary church that he felt most closely resembled the one established in Jerusalem in the first century and in June 1868 became a member of a small "Christian Church" near Lancaster. Although satisfied with his choice, his penchant for independent thinking eventually embroiled him in bitter disputes with church leaders, and after being branded a troublemaker, he decided "to sever the bonds of fellowship." For the rest of his days he seems to have been ostracized by church leaders and many other members of the Christian faith. "So under these conditions there was nothing left for me to do but renounce my fellowship with them and stand alone," Dave wrote in his theological treatise in 1924. "Well I did that and am still alone, having done the best I could, and I think God sees that too, and doesn't expect me to attend their meetings, for [by] doing this I am keeping the peace."

But Dave concluded as a young man that he needed to go to school in order to "become a competent thinker" and fully understand the illusive mysteries of the Holy Scriptures. So in the fall of 1868 he enrolled in Carlton College, a private Christian school in Bonham,

Texas, where he excelled in English composition and mathematics. Dave left college in the spring of 1870, married former classmate Sallie M. Hackley, purchased a small farm in Fannin County, where he built a house for his young bride, and spent the next decade teaching, farming, buying and selling land in Fannin and Dallas counties, carpentering, and operating a reaper for the public. It was during this time that all four of Dave's children were born—Charles Carlton in 1871, James Allen in 1873 (the year of Dave's father's death), Quilla in 1875, and Annie Laura (who married Byram P. Morris and became the mother of Don H. Morris) in 1877.

In July 1879 Dave was stricken with rheumatoid arthritis and was confined to his bed for almost eight months. While incapacitated, he wrote in his recollections that he "got a young man to run the reaper with . . . [his] team, giving him half of all he could make cutting at seventy-five cents an acre." Since his illness persisted, Dave and his wife left their children with their grandmother at Heath Branch and went to Hot Springs, Arkansas, where mineral water baths seemed to improve his condition.

Returning home in 1880, Dave spent the next nine years teaching during the winters and doing construction work during the summers. Then in 1889 Dave sold his farm near Bonham and returned to Dallas County, where, after his mother's death (1893), he purchased from his brother and sisters three-fourths of the wonderful old Heath Branch Farm. That spring he also purchased a general merchandise store in DeSoto, as the community around Heath Branch now was called, which he operated until December 1896. The next year he built a gristmill on the Heath Branch Farm but four years later moved it to Duncanville. After leasing part of the Heath Branch farm, Dave moved with his family to Duncanville, built another home, and operated the mill with only moderate financial success. He then sold his house in Duncanville, leased the gristmill, and on December 31, 1903, moved with his family back to the Heath Branch Farm. Soon thereafter at the foot of the hill on which the old Civil War home had rested, he built a new two-story home with a double gallery.

Dave's attention during the next few years centered upon experimenting with drought-resistant crops. Working closely with his youngest son, Quill, he seems to have enjoyed a measure of success. But Dave's rheumatism again temporarily confined him to his bed, and with the approach of World War I, he discontinued arduous physical labor and divided the Heath Branch farm among his four children. Although semiretired, partially disabled by rheumatism, and increasingly dependent upon his wife to perform mundane tasks around the house, Dave sold the gristmill in Duncanville, continued his experimentation with drought-resistant grains, attended occasional reunions of his old brigade, and sought to satisfy his "intense craving to'understand inspiration" revealed in the pages of the Bible.

Although Dave claimed to see visions and was convinced that from the beginning God had performed miracles for his benefit and that of his children, he never attended church services and seems never to have found answers to all the religious questions that troubled him. "Yes, I am alone," wrote the old man of Heath Branch in 1924, "but still learning and still trusting God."

So Dave spent his final weeks on this earth studying his Bible, entertaining his children and friends who dropped by to visit, and enjoying his grandchildren who evidently spent as much time as possible with the old soldier. "He had a doting attitude toward his grandchildren," Don H. Morris wrote in 1969. "I was his oldest grandson [and] . . . lived in his home and that of my grandmother a good part of . . . [my first] several years, so I had an opportunity to be his spoiled grandson."

A few days before his death, Dave applied for a Confederate pension from the State of Texas and described his health as "poor." Finally, in the summer of 1925, the eighty-two-year-old David C. Nance died peacefully in his sleep at "the old sweet home" on Heath Branch. He was laid to rest in the William Rawlings Cemetery near Lancaster.

Notes

1. FRONTIER ORIGINS

1. David Carey Nance, recollections of "Personal History," labeled "For Annie," July 23, 1912 (hereafter cited as Nance, recollections), pp. 1–2. See also G. W. Nance, comp., *The Nance Memorial: A History of the Nance Family in General* (hereafter cited as the *Nance Family Memorial*), pp. 274–76; David Carey Nance, "D. C. Nance," in Philip Lindsley, comp., *The History of Greater Dallas and Vicinity*, I, 402–05; and David Carey Nance, theological treatise with autobiographical sketch, chap. 2, "Early Life: Military," January 1924 (hereafter cited as Nance, theological treatise), p. 1.

2. Nance, recollections, pp. 1–3; and *Nance Family Memorial*, p. 275.

3. Nance, recollections, pp. 8–9.

4. Ibid., pp. 3–8; and Annie Nance Morris, interview by Jackie Morris Warmsley, n.d., p. 1.

5. Nance, theological treatise, pp. 1–2. See also Nance, recollections, pp. 8–9; and *Nance Family Memorial*, p. 274.

6. Nance, theological treatise, pp. 1–2. See also Nance, recollections, pp. 8–10; and Annie Nance Morris, interview, pp. 2–4.

7. Nance, recollections, pp. 9–10. Although A. Q. Nance's farm in present-day DeSoto was sold after his death in 1873, Dave Nance repurchased most of the original acreage in 1899 and spent his last years among the old farm's "everlasting hills" and "crystal streams." Dave and his sons converted the original house on the hill into a hay barn and blacksmith shop. About the same time a two-story house with a large front porch (owned and occupied in the spring of 1974 by Mrs. L. L. McNair) was built at the foot of the hill near one of the artesian springs on the property. It was here during his final years that Dave wrote his recollections, theological treatise, and most of the poems, sermons, and essays preserved among his papers. "O what joy it was," he wrote after reacquiring the old farm property, "to visit again the winding paths, the rippling streams, and bright waterfalls [where] . . . in years gone by I bathed my little feet and built my tiny fluttermills" (Nance, in Lindsley, comp., *History of Greater Dallas*, I, 402–03, 405).

8. Nance, theological treatise, pp. 1–2.

9. Ibid., p. 2.

10. Nance, recollections, p. 10. Killing snakes became one of young Dave's primary chores, and killing four or five a day was not unusual. Normally he used sticks and stones for this purpose, but one giant rattlesnake—said to be as "big around as a stove pipe" and having "fifteen rattles and a button"—had to be killed with a shotgun (Annie Nance Morris, interview, p. 3).

11. Nance, recollections, p. 10. See also Nance, theological treatise, p. 3.

12. On March 20, 1974, the author found the long-neglected Nance family burial plot which consisted of four graves marked by old, broken, moss-covered headstones. Located on private property in the 700 block of Spinner Road in DeSoto, it contained the graves of John, the male infant who died on July 4, 1860; a seven-year-old girl, Lee, who died in 1872; Quill, who died in 1873; and Elizabeth, who died in 1893. Dave, writing in 1908, referred to the gravestones of his parents, calling them "lone sentinels of those who bore me," which were clearly visible from the front porch of the new house built after the war at the foot of the hill. See Nance, in Lindsley, comp., *History of Greater Dallas*, I, 405.

13. Nance, "Allen Q. Nance—Limb Fourteen," in *Nance Family Memorial*, pp. 274–76; Nance, in Lindsley, comp., *History of Greater Dallas*, I, 402–05; and "David C. Nance," in *Memorial and Biographical History of Dallas County, Texas*, pp. 807–08.

14. Nance, "Allan Q. Nance—Limb Fourteen," in *Nance Family Memorial*, p. 274; and Nance, in Lindsley, comp., *History of Greater Dallas*, I, 403.

15. Ibid.

16. Annie Nance Morris, interview, pp. 3–5; Don H. Morris, personal interview; and Nance, in Lindsley, comp., *History of Greater Dallas*, I, 403.

17. Nance, recollections, p. 2; and Nance, in Lindsley, comp., *History of Greater Dallas*, I, 403.

18. Nance, "Allen Q. Nance—Limb Fourteen," in *Nance Family Memorial*, pp. 274–76; and Nance, recollections, p. 2.

19. Ibid.; and "David C. Nance," in *Memorial and Biographical History of Dallas County*, pp. 807–08.

20. Nance, theological treatise, p. 3.

21. D. C. Nance, quoted in "Mary J. Nance—Branch Two," in *Nance Family Memorial*, pp. 278–79.

22. Annie Nance Morris, interview, pp. 3–5.

23. Don H. Morris, personal interview.

24. Nance, recollections, p. 11. For a brief analysis of John Brown's raid, see David Herbert Donald, *Liberty and Union*, pp. 73–75.

25. Nance, "Allen Q. Nance—Limb Fourteen," in *Nance Family Memorial*, p. 274; and Nance, in Lindsley, comp., *History of Greater Dallas*, I, 403.

26. Terry G. Jordan, "Population Origins in Texas, 1850," *Geographical Review* 59 (1969): 91; Rupert N. Richardson, *The Frontier of Northwest Texas, 1846 to 1876*, pp. 225–26; Ernest Wallace, *Texas in Turmoil*, pp. 51–57; and Walter L. Buenger, *Secession and the Union in Texas*, pp. 45–46, 68–70, 76–79.

27. Nance, recollections, p. 11. For accounts of incendiarism in Texas in 1860, see William W. White, "The Texas Slave Insurrection of 1860," *Southwestern Historical Quarterly* 52 (1949), 259–83.

28. Nance, in Lindsley, comp., *History of Greater Dallas*, I, 403–04. See also *Dallas Herald*, June 25, 1860.

29. Nance, in Lindsley, comp., *History of Greater Dallas*, I, 404.

30. Don H. Morris, personal interview.

31. Ibid.

2. MAN ON A DARK MORGAN

1. Nance, theological treatise, p. 1; Nance, recollections, pp. 8–11; Nance, in Lindsley, comp., *History of Greater Dallas*, I, 402–03; and Annie Nance Morris, interview, pp. 6–8.

2. Ibid.; and Don H. Morris, personal interview.

3. Ibid.; and Nance, recollections, p. 16.

4. Members of the Stuart family evidently spelled their last name differently in different accounts (A. B. Morris, personal interview; and *History of Ellis County*, pp. 688–89). Dave's spelling of Little Will Stuart's last name also is inconsistent (see Nance, recollections, p. 25).

5. *History of Ellis County*, pp. 688–89; Don H. Morris, personal interview; and Nance, recollections, pp. 12–13. Late in May 1861, Governor Edward Clark of Texas bestowed a colonelcy upon W. H. Parsons and authorized him to organize a regiment of dragoons for state service. Parsons organized the first company himself and established a training bivouac four miles northwest of Waco. Soon the bivouac was moved to a new site, known as Camp Moss, located in Limestone County. During the weeks that followed, Parsons' company was joined by other companies from Freestone, Limestone, Hill, and Johnson counties. Then in June 1861, Parsons moved his bivouac to Red Oak Creek in Ellis County. This site, known as Camp McCullough, remained the seat of Parsons' training and recruiting activities until his regiment was formally organized at Rocket Springs near Waxahachie on September 11, 1861. See M. L. Hickey, "Parsons' Brigade," in *A Memorial and Biographical History of Johnson and Hill Counties, Texas*, pp. 259–60; W. H. Getzendaner, J. Fred Cox, and A. M. Dechman, "Report of Committee—1883," in Parsons' Brigade Association, *A Brief and Condensed History of Parsons' Texas Cavalry Brigade* (hereafter cited as *Brief History of Parsons' Brigade*), pp. 7–8; H. Orr, introduction to Henry Orr's journal, September–October 1861, in John Q. Anderson, ed., *Campaigning with Parsons' Brigade: The War Journal and Letters of the Four Orr Brothers, Twelfth Texas Cavalry Regiment*, pp. 1–4; P. O. Hébert to E. Clark, October 16, 1861, War Department, *War of the Rebellion: A Compilation of the Official Records of the Union and Confederate Armies* (hereafter cited as *Official Records*), Series I, vol. IV, pp. 121–22. All references hereafter will be Series I unless otherwise indicated. See also Special Orders No. 18, July 25, 1861, ibid., pp. 95–96; Special Orders to R. S. Hamilton, September 28, 1861, ibid., Series II, pp. 1385–86.

6. Nance, recollections, p. 13.

7. Ibid., p. 12; and *Brief History of Parsons' Brigade*, pp. 7–8.

8. Ibid.; and *Dallas Herald*, October 9, 1861.

9. *Brief History of Parsons' Brigade*, pp. 7–8.

10. Nance, recollections, p. 12; Nance, theological treatise, p. 4; and Nance, in Lindsley, comp., *History of Greater Dallas*, I, 404.

11. Nance, recollections, p. 12.

12. Ibid., p. 13.

13. Ibid.; H. Orr, introduction, journal of Henry Orr, September 1861, in Anderson, ed., *Campaigning with Parsons' Brigade*, pp. 1–4; Hickey, "Parsons' Brigade," in *History of Johnson and Hill Counties*, p. 259; letter to R. S. Hamilton, September 28, 1861, in *Official Records*, Series II, vol. II, 1385–87; *Tri-Weekly Telegraph* (Houston), November 7, 20, 1861; and *Dallas Herald*, October 9, 1861.

14. Nance, recollections, pp. 13–14.

15. Ibid.; and Don H. Morris, personal interview.

16. Ibid.

17. Nance, recollections, p. 14.

18. Ibid.

19. Ibid., p. 13; and H. Orr, journal, November 20, 1861, in Anderson, ed., *Campaigning with Parsons' Brigade*, p. 13.

20. Nance, recollections, pp. 13–14. One reason soldiers stationed around Houston were unhappy with their location during the winter of 1861–62 was the unusually heavy rainfall during that period. See *Brief History of Parsons' Brigade*, p. 9; and Robert Orr to "Brother Sam," January 10, 1862, and H. Orr to "Dear Mother," January 22, 1862, in Anderson, ed., *Campaigning with Parsons' Brigade*, pp. 20–24.

21. Nance, recollections, pp. 13–14; and Don H. Morris, personal interview.

22. Ibid.

23. Muster Roll RP 739315, Company E, Twelfth Regiment, Texas Cavalry. In D. C. Nance's application for a Confederate pension in 1925, just a few weeks before his death, he gave October 28, 1861, as the date of his enlistment, since this was the date his regiment was transferred to Confederate service (Nance, Soldier's Application for a Confederate Pension, June 16, 1925).

24. William Zuber (*My Eighty Years in Texas*, p. 211) mistakenly referred to William J. Neal's company as the Methodist Bulls. Since Neal had been killed in the battle of Cache River by that time, he could not possibly have been in command of a company wearing that name. Actually the Methodist Bulls were the men of Company F, commanded by William G. Veal. Since Veal's name was similar to Neal's, this probably explains Zuber's mistake. There seems to be no doubt that Veal's Ellis County Rangers was the Bulls (see Nance, recollections, p. 15; H. Orr to "Friends at Home," April 10, 1862, in Anderson, ed., *Campaigning with Parsons' Brigade*, pp. 35–36; H. Orr to "My Dear Brothers," August 26, 1864, ibid., p. 146; *Brief History of Parsons' Brigade*, pp. 8–9; and Hickey, "Parsons' Brigade," in *History of Johnson and Hill Counties*, p. 259.

25. Nance, recollections, p. 15; and H. Orr to "Friends at Home," April 10, 1862, and H. Orr to "My Dear Sister," April 23, 1862, in Anderson, ed., *Campaigning with Parsons' Brigade*, pp. 35–36, 37–39.

26. Don H. Morris, personal interview.
27. Ibid.
28. Clement Eaton, *A History of the Southern Confederacy*, p. 107.
29. Nance, recollections, p. 15.
30. Ibid., pp. 14–15.
31. Ibid.; and H. Orr, journal, November 20, 1861, in Anderson, ed., *Campaigning with Parsons' Brigade*, p. 13.

3. STORM CLOUDS OVER SIMS BAYOU

1. Nance, recollections, p. 12; Nance, in Lindsley, comp., *History of Greater Dallas*, I, 404; Nance, theological treatise, p. 4; Don H. Morris, "Some Things I Remember about My Grandfather," p. 3; and idem, personal interview. See also H. Orr to "Sister Mary," December 5, 1861, in Anderson, ed., *Campaigning with Parsons' Brigade*, p. 14; and W. H. Parsons, *Inside History and Heretofore Unwritten Chapters on the Red River Campaign of 1864 and the Participation Therein of Parsons' Texas Cavalry Brigade: The Policy and Motives of the Then Proposed Federal Invasion of the Line of the Red River* (hereafter cited as *Inside History*), pp. 105–06.

2. L. T. Wheeler, Introduction, in W. H. Parsons, *Condensed History of Parsons' Texas Cavalry Brigade, 1861–1865, Together with Inside History and Heretofore Unwritten Chapters of the Red River Campaign of 1864* (hereafter cited as *Condensed History of Parsons' Brigade*), pp. 3–4.

3. Some of Parsons' troops were not impressed with their commander with the white plume in his hat and complained that he was "too haughty" and that he "strutted around" too much (see H. Orr to "Dear Mother and Father," November 4, 1862, and H. Orr to "Dear Sister Mollie," November 10, 1862, in Anderson, ed., *Campaigning with Parsons' Brigade*, pp. 74, 80–81). See also Wheeler, Introduction, in Parsons, *Condensed History of Parsons' Brigade*, p. 4.

4. H. Orr to "Brother Lafayette," December 21, 1861, in Anderson, ed., *Campaigning with Parsons' Brigade*, p. 16; H. Orr, journal, December 24, 1861, ibid., pp. 18–19; H. Orr to "My Dear Sister," February 23, 1862, ibid., p. 29; H. Orr to "Dear Brother and Family," February 25, 1862, ibid., p. 31; and H. Orr, journal, February 28, 1862, p. 32.

5. X. B. DeBray to H. P. Walker, August 28, 1861, *Official Records*, IV, 98; W. Byrd to H. E. McCulloch, September 9, 1861, ibid., pp. 103–04; H. E. McCulloch to P. O. Hébert, September 20, 1861, ibid., p. 107; E. Clark to P. O. Hébert, October 3, 1861, ibid., pp. 113–14; P. O. Hébert to E. Clark, October 16, 1861, ibid., pp. 121–22; E. Clark to P. O. Hébert, October 22, 1861, ibid., p. 125; P. O. Hébert to J. P. Benjamin, October 24, 1861, ibid., pp. 126–27; D. M. Stapp to W. Byrd, extract, in W. Byrd to P. O. Hébert, October 28, 1861, ibid., pp. 129–30; W. C. Young to J. P. Benjamin, November 3, 1861, ibid., p. 145; P. O. Hébert to J. P. Benjamin, November 15, 1861, ibid., pp. 139–40; and the *Tri-Weekly Telegraph* (Houston), November 20, 1861.

6. S. Maclin to P. O. Hébert, October 19, 1861, *Official Records*, IV, 125; and S. B. Davis to H. E. McCulloch, December 3, 1861, ibid., p. 152.

7. Charles S. Potts, "Railroad Transportation in Texas," *Bulletin of the University of Texas* 119 (1909): 29; Nance, recollections, p. 15; and H. Orr, journal, November 20, 1861, in Anderson, ed., *Campaigning with Parsons' Brigade,* p. 13.

8. H. Orr to "Brother Lafayette," December 21, 1861, in Anderson, ed., *Campaigning with Parsons' Brigade,* pp. 14–17.

9. Ibid., pp. 16–17; H. Orr to "Sister Mary," December 5, 1861, ibid., p. 14; and Don H. Morris, personal interview.

10. H. Orr to "Brother Lafayette," December 21, 1861, in Anderson, ed., *Campaigning with Parsons' Brigade,* p. 15.

11. Ibid.

12. Don H. Morris, personal interview; and Nance, recollections, p. 16.

13. Ibid.

14. Don H. Morris, personal interview.

15. Nance, recollections, p. 16; Roster and Record Book of the Thirty-Fifth Annual Reunion of Parsons' Brigade and the United Confederate Veterans, Midlothian, Texas, August 4–5, 1915; and Don H. Morris, "Some Things I Remember about My Grandfather," p. 3.

16. Nance, recollections, pp. 16–17.

17. H. Orr to "Dear Mother," January 22, 1862, in Anderson, ed., *Campaigning with Parsons' Brigade,* p. 23.

18. Robert Orr to "Brother Sam," January 10, 1862, ibid., p. 20.

19. H. Orr to "Dear Mother," January 22, 1862, ibid., p. 23.

20. H. Orr to "Sister Mary," December 5, 1861, ibid., p. 14. See also H. Orr, journal, November 20–23, 1861, ibid., p. 13.

21. Don H. Morris, "Some Things I Remember about My Grandfather," p. 3; and H. Orr to "Brother Lafayette," December 21, 1861, in Anderson, ed., *Campaigning with Parsons' Brigade,* p. 15.

22. Ibid.

23. H. Orr, journal, December 25, 1861, ibid., p. 19.

24. Nance, recollections, p. 18.

25. H. Orr, journal, December 25, 1861, in Anderson, ed., *Campaigning with Parsons' Brigade,* p. 191.

26. H. Orr to "Brother Lafayette," December 21, 1861, ibid., pp. 14–15.

27. Nance, recollections, p. 16.

28. H. Orr to "Dear Mother," January 22, 1862, in Anderson, ed., *Campaigning with Parsons' Brigade,* p. 22.

29. Robert Orr to "Dear Sam," January 10, 1862, ibid., p. 20; and H. Orr to "Dear Lafayette," December 21, 1861, ibid., p. 17.

30. H. Orr to "Dear Mother," January 22, 1862, ibid., pp. 21–23.

31. P. O. Hébert to J. P. Benjamin, October 31, 1861, *Official Records,* IV, 130. The description of P. O. Hébert is based upon Thomas North's flamboyant but sometimes questionable *Five Years in Texas,* p. 105.

32. H. Orr, journal, January 31, 1861, in Anderson, ed., *Campaigning with Parsons' Brigade,* p. 24.

33. H. Orr to "Dear Mother," January 22, 1862, ibid., pp. 21–24.

34. H. Orr to "My Dear Mother," February 9, 1862, ibid., p. 26.

35. H. Orr to "Dear Parents," February 13, 1862, ibid., p. 27.
36. Nance, recollections, p. 16; and H. Orr to "Dear Brother and Family," February 25, 1862, in Anderson, ed., *Campaigning with Parsons' Brigade*, p. 31.
37. Nance, recollections, p. 12.
38. H. Orr to "Dear Brother and Family," February 25, 1862, in Anderson, ed., *Campaigning with Parsons' Brigade*, p. 31.
39. Ibid.; and George H. Hogan, "Parsons' Brigade of Texas Cavalry," *Confederate Veteran* 33 (1925): 17.
40. Nance, recollections, p. 16.
41. H. Orr, journal, February 27, 1862, in Anderson, ed., *Campaigning with Parsons' Brigade*, p. 32; see also, p. 31.
42. Ibid., February 28, 1862.
43. Ibid., March 1, 1862, p. 33.
44. Nance, recollections, p. 16. On July 11, 1974, the author found Billy Parsons' grave in the Shiloh Cemetery in the country churchyard of the Cumberland Presbyterian Church near Ovilla, Texas. The weatherbeaten headstone bore the following inscription:

Wm. P. Parsons
Died Feb. 24, 1862
Aged 24 years, 3 ms.,
    5 days.

4. THE ROAD TO CACHE RIVER

1. Nance, recollections, p. 17; H. Orr, journal, April 4, 1862, and H. Orr to "Friends at Home," April 10, 1862, in Anderson, ed., *Campaigning with Parsons' Brigade*, pp. 34–36.
2. Nance, recollections, p. 17.
3. H. Orr to "Friends at Home," April 10, 1862, in Anderson, ed., *Campaigning with Parsons' Brigade*, pp. 35–36; Hickey, "Parsons' Brigade," in *History of Johnson and Hill Counties*, pp. 259–60; and John W. Truss to "My Dear Wife," in Johnette Highsmith Ray, ed., "Civil War Letters from Parsons' Texas Cavalry Brigade," *Southwestern Historical Quarterly* 69 (1965): 213.
4. See Nance, theological treatise, pp. 29–30.
5. Nance, miscellaneous papers, undated fragment.
6. Flavius W. Perry, in Joe R. Wise, ed., "Letters of Lieutenant Flavius W. Perry, Seventeenth Texas Cavalry, 1862–1863," *Military History of Texas and the Southwest* 13.2 (1976): 12.
7. H. Orr to "Dear Parents, Sister, and Brothers," May 26, 1863, in Anderson, ed., *Campaigning with Parsons' Brigade*, pp. 103–04. See also Nance, recollections, p. 17; report of Thomas C. Hindman, May 31–November 3, 1862, *Official Records*, XIII, 29; J. P. Blessington, *The Campaigns of Walker's Texas Division*, pp. 38–41; and Michael B. Dougan, "Life in Confederate Arkansas," *Arkansas Historical Quarterly* 30 (1972): 17.
8. Letter from a military encampment near Little Rock, May 23, 1862, quoted in the *Tri-Weekly Telegraph* (Houston), June 9, 1862. See also Nance,

recollections, pp. 17–18. For additional insight into conditions in Arkansas during the spring of 1862, see report of Thomas C. Hindman, May 31–November 3, 1862, *Official Records*, XIII, 33; Blessington, *Campaigns of Walker's Texas Division*, pp. 38–39; William Baxter, *Pea Ridge and Prairie Grove*, p. 45; and *Arkansas Gazette* (Little Rock), June 14, 1862.

9. John Schofield, report of Union operations in Missouri and north-western Arkansas, April 10–November 20, 1862, *Official Records*, XIII, 8–16; report of Thomas C. Hindman, May 31–November 3, 1862, ibid., pp. 30–31; Parsons, quoted in Hogan, "Parsons' Brigade of Texas Cavalry," p. 18; and David Y. Thomas, *Arkansas in War and Reconstruction*, p. 139.

10. Writing in the summer of 1912, Nance (recollections, p. 18) explained that the camp was situated "on the north bank of the river . . . where Argenta [North Little Rock] is now located."

11. Ibid., pp. 17–18.

12. The Searcy Lane fight was a total Confederate victory resulting in the wiping out of a Federal patrol of about 180 men. Parsons first learned of the Federal presence from one of his spies in the town of Searcy and dispatched Major Rogers with "175 men and officers to go north till the enemy was lo-cated." The Federal patrol, made up largely of German troops, was looting Searcy when a Union scout reported the approach of Rogers' squadron. As the Federals attempted to escape, Rogers' rangers caught them "at a dis-advantage . . . in the aforesaid lane" south of town and opened fire "with double-barreled shotguns at close range." Within minutes the lane was strewn with dead and wounded. After the battle townspeople from Searcy, who had locked themselves in their houses, came out to view the carnage (see George N. Hogan and Finas A. Stone, reminiscences, in Mamie Yeary, comp., *Reminis-cences of the Boys in Gray, 1861–1865*, pp. 338–39, 725–29). See also Nance, recollections, pp. 17–18; F. M. Christman's account in Raymond L. Muncy, *Searcy, Arkansas: A Frontier Town Grows Up in America*, pp. 46–48; E. W. Rogers' report, *Arkansas Gazette* (Little Rock), State Centennial Edition, June 15, 1936; "Report of Committee—1883" and "One of the Twelfth," August 3, 1862, in *Brief History of Parsons' Brigade*, pp. 10, 27; and *Tri-Weekly Telegraph* (Houston), June 9, 1862.

13. Nance, recollections, pp. 17–18.

14. Ibid.

15. Ibid., p. 19; "Report of Committee—1883," in *Brief History of Par-sons' Brigade*, pp. 9–10; and Hogan, "Parsons' Brigade of Texas Cavalry," pp. 17–18.

16. H. Orr to "Father and Mother," June 6, 1862, in Anderson, ed., *Cam-paigning with Parsons' Brigade*, pp. 47–49; and Hickey, "Parsons' Brigade," in *History of Johnson and Hill Counties*, pp. 259–60.

17. H. Orr to "Brother James," June 8, 1862, in Anderson, ed., *Campaigning with Parsons' Brigade*, pp. 49–52; Zuber, *My Eighty Years in Texas*, pp. 142–45; Perry, in Wise, ed., "Letters of Lieutenant Flavius W. Perry," p. 26; Hickey, "Parsons' Brigade," in *History of Johnson and Hill Counties*, pp. 259–60; Marshall S. Pierson, in Norman C. Delaney, ed., "The Diary and Memoirs of Marshall Samuel Pierson, Company C, Seventeenth Regiment, Texas Cavalry,

1862–1865," *Military History of Texas and the Southwest* 13.3 (1976): 25–26; Blessington, *Campaigns of Walker's Texas Division,* pp. 39–41; and *Tri-Weekly Telegraph* (Houston), June 9, 21, 27, 1862.

18. T. H. Holmes to S. Cooper, October 26, 1862, *Official Records,* XIII, 899; report of Thomas C. Hindman, May 31–November 3, 1862, ibid., pp. 28–39; Bobby L. Roberts, "General T. C. Hindman and the Trans-Mississippi District," *Arkansas Historical Quarterly* 32 (1973): 301; Thomas, *Arkansas in War and Reconstruction,* pp. 153–54; and *Arkansas Gazette* (Little Rock), June 14, 1862.

19. John Schofield, report of Union operations in Missouri and northeastern Arkansas, April 10–November 20, 1862, *Official Records,* XIII, 7–16; report of Thomas C. Hindman, May 31–November 3, 1862, ibid., pp. 28–46; address by Thomas C. Hindman to soldiers and citizens of the district, May 31, 1862, ibid., p. 830; Roberts, "General T. C. Hindman and the Trans-Mississippi District," pp. 308–09; *Arkansas Gazette* (Little Rock), June 28, 1862; Thomas, *Arkansas in War and Reconstruction,* pp. 139–42; and Thomas L. Snead, "The Conquest of Arkansas," in Robert V. Johnson and Clarence C. Buel, eds., *Battles and Leaders of the Civil War,* III, 443–45.

20. H. Orr to "Dear Sister," May 16, 1862, and H. Orr to "Brother James," June 8, 1862, in Anderson, ed., *Campaigning with Parsons' Brigade,* pp. 43–46, 49–52; report of Thomas C. Hindman, May 31–November 3, 1862, *Official Records,* XIII, 30–31, 35–37; Nance, recollections, pp. 19–20; Thomas, *Arkansas in War and Reconstruction,* pp. 142–43; and *Arkansas Gazette* (Little Rock), June 28, 1862.

21. Report of Thomas C. Hindman, May 31–November 3, 1862, *Official Records,* XIII, 37.

22. H. Orr to "Brother James," June 9, 1862, in Anderson, ed., *Campaigning with Parsons' Brigade,* pp. 52–53. See also Roberts, "General T. C. Hindman and the Trans-Mississippi District," p. 301.

23. H. Orr to "Father and Mother," June 6, 1862, and H. Orr to "Brother James," June 8, 9, 1862, in Anderson, ed., *Campaigning with Parsons' Brigade,* pp. 47–49, 49–53. Perhaps understandably, Federal commanders found it difficult to control their raiding parties. Contrary to specific orders prohibiting the destruction and theft of personal property and family heirlooms, some Federal soldiers broke "into the private apartments of ladies, . . . [opened] their trunks and drawers, and . . . [took] what they wanted" (General Eugene A. Carr, quoted in Thomas, *Arkansas in War and Reconstruction,* pp. 138–39).

24. H. Orr, letter, June 9, 1862, in Anderson, ed., *Campaigning with Parsons' Brigade,* p. 53; H. Orr to "Father and Mother," June 6, 1862, ibid., p. 48; and report of Thomas C. Hindman, May 31–November 3, 1862, *Official Records,* XIII, 30.

25. H. Orr to "Father, Mother, Sister, and Brother," July 15, 1862, in Anderson, ed., *Campaigning with Parsons' Brigade,* pp. 55–58.

26. Robert L. Kerby, *Kirby Smith's Confederacy: The Trans-Mississippi South, 1863–1865,* pp. 32–33.

27. Report of Thomas C. Hindman, May 31–November 3, 1862, *Official Records*, XIII, 33, 37; and *Arkansas Gazette* (Little Rock), June 28, 1862.

28. H. Orr, undated fragment of a missing letter, in Anderson, ed., *Campaigning with Parsons' Brigade*, pp. 54–55. The editor of the Orr brothers' papers (published under the title, *Campaigning with Parsons' Brigade*) concluded that this fragment was written near Napoleon, Arkansas. It is my belief, however, that it was part of a letter written at Camp Searcy.

29. Report of Thomas C. Hindman, May 31–November 3, 1862, *Official Records*, XIII, 36–37.

30. H. Orr to "Father, Mother, Sister, and Brother," July 15, 1862, in Anderson, ed., *Campaigning with Parsons' Brigade*, pp. 55–56.

31. Ibid.

32. Nance, recollections, p. 25.

5. DRIED BLOOD AND SWAMP WATER

1. H. Orr to "Father, Mother, Sister, and Brother," July 15, 1862, in Anderson, ed., *Campaigning with Parsons' Brigade*, p. 56; and Pierson, in Delaney, ed., "Diary of Samuel Pierson," pp. 26–27.

2. Nance, recollections, p. 21.

3. Ibid.; and H. Orr to "Father, Mother, Sister, and Brother," July 15, 1862, in Anderson, ed., *Campaigning with Parsons' Brigade*, pp. 55–56.

4. Nance, recollections, p. 21; and Nance, "Military Record of David Carey Nance," in *Nance Family Memorial*, p. 277.

5. Nance, recollections, pp. 21–22; and H. Orr to "Father, Mother, Sister, and Brother," July 15, 1862, in Anderson, ed., *Campaigning with Parsons' Brigade*, pp. 55–56.

6. Nance, recollections, p. 22.

7. Pierson, in Delaney, ed., "Diary of Samuel Pierson," pp. 25–26; Perry to "My Dear Mother," July 30, 1862, in Wise, ed., "Letters of Lieutenant Flavius W. Perry," p. 14; H. Orr to "Father, Mother, Sister, and Brother," July 15, 1862, in Anderson, ed., *Campaigning with Parsons' Brigade*, pp. 56–57; John W. Truss to "My Dear Wife," July 14, 1862, in Ray, ed., "Civil War Letters from Parsons' Texas Cavalry Brigade," p. 214; Parsons, quoted in Hogan, "Parsons' Brigade of Texas Cavalry," p. 18; Roberts, "General T. C. Hindman and the Trans-Mississippi District," p. 308; and Frederick H. Dyer, *Compendium of the War of the Rebellion*, II, 672.

8. Nance, recollections, pp. 21–22; H. Orr to "Father, Mother, Sister, and Brother," July 15, 1862, in Anderson, ed., *Campaigning with Parsons' Brigade*, pp. 55–56; and Hickey, "Parsons' Brigade," in *History of Johnson and Hill Counties*, p. 260.

9. Nance, recollections, p. 21; and Nance, "Military Record of David Carey Nance," in *Nance Family Memorial*, p. 277.

10. Nance, recollections, p. 22; Nance, theological treatise, p. 4; Nance, "Military Record of David Carey Nance," in *Nance Family Memorial*, p. 277; and "David C. Nance," in *History of Dallas County*, p. 808.

11. Parsons to "Comrades of the Twelfth and Nineteenth Regiments of the

Old Cavalry Brigade of the Trans-Mississippi Army," June 24, 1878, in *Brief History of Parsons' Brigade,* p. 19.

12. Perry to "My Dear Mother," July 30, 1862, in Wise, ed., "Letters of Lieutenant Flavius W. Perry," p. 15.

13. Ibid.

14. Nance, recollections, p. 23; Nance, theological treatise, p. 4; and Nance, "Military Record of David Carey Nance," in *Nance Family Memorial,* p. 277.

15. Ibid. "The enemy turned loose their artillery upon us, firing some forty or fifty times," a Confederate soldier wrote, "but it was not well directed and went tearing through the tree tops." Parsons' artillery never fired a shot, since Confederate gunners could never get their piece into position (H. Orr to "Dear Father, Mother, Sister, and Brother," July 15, 1862, in Anderson, ed., *Campaigning with Parsons' Brigade,* p. 57). See also Truss to "My Dear Wife," July 14, 1862, in Ray, ed., "Civil War Letters from Parsons' Texas Cavalry Brigade," p. 214.

16. Nance, "Military Record of David Carey Nance," in *Nance Family Memorial,* p. 277.

17. Nance, recollections, p. 23.

18. Ibid., pp. 23–24. See also Nance, "Military Record of David Carey Nance," in *Nance Family Memorial,* p. 277.

19. Nance, recollections, pp. 23–24.

20. Nance, "Military Record of David Carey Nance," in *Nance Family Memorial,* p. 277; Nance, recollections, p. 23–24; Nance, theological treatise, p. 4; and "David C. Nance," *History of Dallas County,* p. 808.

21. Nance, "Military Record of David Carey Nance," in *Nance Family Memorial,* p. 277.

22. Nance, recollections, p. 25; and Nance, theological treatise, p. 4.

23. Nance, "Military Record of David Carey Nance," in *Nance Family Memorial,* p. 277.

24. Nance, recollections, p. 25.

25. Stone, reminiscences, in Yeary, comp., *Reminiscences of the Boys in Gray,* p. 729; Hogan, ibid., p. 339; John M. Wright, ibid., p. 823; Pierson, in Delaney, ed., "Diary of Samuel Pierson," p. 27; Perry, in Wise, ed., "Letters of Lieutenant Flavius W. Perry," p. 14; Truss to "My Dear Wife," July 14, 1862, in Ray, ed., "Civil War Letters from Parsons' Texas Cavalry Brigade," p. 214; Parsons to "Comrades of the Twelfth and Nineteenth Regiments of the Old Cavalry Brigade of the Trans-Mississippi Army," June 24, 1878, in *Brief History of Parsons' Brigade,* pp. 20–21; and Thomas, *Arkansas in War and Reconstruction,* pp. 145–47.

26. Parsons to "Comrades of the Twelfth and Nineteenth Regiments of the Old Cavalry Brigade," June 24, 1878, in *Brief History of Parsons' Brigade,* pp. 19–20; report of Thomas C. Hindman, May 31–November 3, 1862, *Official Records,* XIII, 37–38; and Thomas, *Arkansas in War and Reconstruction,* pp. 145–48.

27. Nance, recollections, p. 20; report of Thomas C. Hindman, May 31–November 3, 1862, *Official Records,* XIII, 37–38; Parsons to "Comrades of the Twelfth and Nineteenth Regiments of the Old Cavalry Brigade," June 24,

1878, in *Brief History of Parsons' Brigade*, p. 20; Thomas, *Arkansas in War and Reconstruction*, pp. 145–48; Hickey, "Parsons' Brigade," in *History of Johnson and Hill Counties*, pp. 119–21; Hogan, "Parsons' Brigade of Texas Cavalry," pp. 17–18; H. Orr to "Dear Parents," August 21, 1862, in Anderson, ed., *Campaigning with Parsons' Brigade*, pp. 62–64; and Dyer, *Compendium of the War of the Rebellion*, II, 676.

28. Nance, theological treatise, p. 5; and Nance, recollections, p. 25.

29. Nance, recollections, pp. 25–26; and H. Orr to "Father and Mother," October 6, 1862, in Anderson, ed., *Campaigning with Parsons' Brigade*, p. 54.

30. Nance, recollections, p. 26.

31. Ibid.

32. Ibid., pp. 26–27. See also Nance, theological treatise, p. 5; and Nance, "Military Record of David Carey Nance," in *Nance Family Memorial*, p. 277.

33. Nance, recollections, p. 27.

34. Ibid., pp. 28–29. When Walker's Texas Infantry arrived in Little Rock the following September, one of its members wrote that "the college was used as a hospital" and was "distant from town about two miles" (Blessington, *Campaigns of Walker's Texas Division*, p. 39).

35. Nance, recollections, p. 27.

36. Nance, theological treatise, p. 5.

37. Ibid., pp. 9–10.

38. Ibid.

39. Ibid., p. 7.

40. Nance, recollections, p. 24. This light blue, faded, homespun shirt with a patched sleeve was one of several treasured mementos D. C. Nance brought home from the war. It was shown to the author in the fall of 1972 by D. C. Nance's great-granddaughter, Jackie Morris Warmsley.

41. Nance, theological treatise, pp. 6–7; and Nance, recollections, pp. 26–27.

42. Ibid., pp. 27–28; and Nance, "Military Record of David Carey Nance," in *Nance Family Memorial*, p. 277.

43. Nance, recollections, p. 30.

44. Ibid., p. 28; and Nance, "Military Record of David Carey Nance," in *Nance Family Memorial*, p. 277.

45. Nance, recollections, p. 28. The death rate in the erysipelas ward must have been staggering. Although the accuracy of Nance's memory is open to question, he reported in the *Nance Family Memorial* that he was the only one of twenty patients in that ward to survive the deadly infestations of erysipelas, boils, "dysentary, and . . . flux" (Nance, "Military Record of David Carey Nance," in *Nance Family Memorial*, p. 277).

46. Nance, recollections, p. 28.

47. Nance, theological treatise, pp. 10–12.

48. Nance, recollections, p. 29.

49. Ibid.

50. H. Orr to "Dear Brothers," August 21, 1862, in Anderson, ed., *Campaigning with Parsons' Brigade*, p. 67.

51. Ibid., p. 66.

52. After the war Parsons explained his unit's retention of its mounted status in terms of its unparalleled proficiency. "The Twelfth . . . won . . . [this] high honor a month after reaching the theatre of war in Arkansas," he wrote, "when all other cavalry commands then on the front were [being] dismounted" (Parsons to "Comrades of the Twelfth and Nineteenth Regiments of the Old Cavalry Brigade of the Trans-Mississippi Army," June 24, 1878, in *Brief History of Parsons' Brigade*, p. 16). For information on the reorganization of Confederate command structure west of the Mississippi during the summer and winter of 1862, see Special Order 164, July 16, 1862, *Official Records*, XIII, 855; General Order 5, August 20, 1862, ibid., p. 887; General Order 39, September 28, 1862, ibid., p. 811; Special Order 42, September 30, 1862, ibid., p. 987; "Organization of the Army of the Trans-Mississippi Department," December 12, 1862, ibid., XXI, 902–04; Special Order 18, in B. F. Marchbank, comp., "Sacred Record: Special Orders Issued by Colonel W. H. Parsons, Commanding, Parsons' Cavalry Brigade, Texas, Confederate Army," pp. 15–16; John M. Harrell, "Arkansas," in Clements A. Evans, ed., *Confederate Military History*, X, 154; and Roberts, "General T. C. Hindman and the Trans-Mississippi District," p. 301.

53. Nance, recollections, p. 29.

54. Ibid. Nance still had part of this money during the summer of 1912. He wrote: "I have . . . one $1.00 Missouri bill, two Texas Treasury warrants, two Ellis County bills (shinplasters), and one Guadalupe County bill—these I remember were among the bills hidden and found."

55. Ibid., p. 30.

6. INFERNO IN A CONFEDERATE POWDERMILL

1. Nance, recollections, pp. 30–31.

2. Ibid., pp. 30–31, 33–34; Charles C. Cumberland, "The Confederate Loss and Recapture of Galveston, 1862–1863," *Southwestern Historical Quarterly* 51 (1947): 109–30.

3. Nance, recollections, pp. 30–31; Special Order 49, in Marchbank, comp., "Sacred Record: Special Orders Issued by Colonel W. H. Parsons," pp. 15–16; and H. Orr to "Mother," September ?, 1862, in Anderson, ed., *Campaigning with Parsons' Brigade*, pp. 71–72. The Twelfth Texas Cavalry had spent the final months of 1862 "moving and scouting continually" within a geographic triangle formed by Helena, Little Rock, and Batesville. During this time the Federals clashed frequently with Parsons' boys and contrived a couple of new names for them. A member of the Ellis County Rangers wrote: "They call us murderers, the 'Swamp Fox' Regiment—the latter I think tolerable appropriate for we lie in the swamps in the daylight and travel at night" (H. Orr to "Lieutenant Payne, Dear Friend," August 12, 1862, in ibid., p. 61).

4. Nance, recollections, pp. 30–31.

5. Ibid.

6. Ibid., p. 31.

7. Ibid., pp. 30–31.

8. Helen G. Goodlett, "Settlement and Development of Ellis County, Texas," Master's thesis, University of Colorado, 1933, pp. 2–16.

9. Ibid., pp. 48–61, 68–78. For advertisements heralding the accommodations of the Rogers' House, see *Dallas Herald*, February 1, 1860; April 24, 1861.

10. Goodlett, "Settlement and Development of Ellis County," pp. 70–78.

11. Nance, recollections, pp. 30–31; Nance, "Military Record of David Carey Nance," in *Nance Family Memorial*, p. 278; and *Waxahachie Daily Light*, clipping labeled "April 1936."

12. Nance, recollections, pp. 30–31.

13. Ibid.; Nance, "Military Record of David Carey Nance," in *Nance Family Memorial*, p. 278; and Nance, theological treatise, p. 7.

14. Nance, recollections, pp. 18–19; *Dallas Herald*, May 6, 1863; and *Waxahachie Daily Light*, clipping labeled "April 1936" and August 29, 1957.

15. Nance, recollections, pp. 18–19. For another account of the same incident, see H. Orr to "Dear Parents, Sister, and Brothers," May 26, 1863, in Anderson, ed., *Campaigning with Parsons' Brigade*, p. 103.

16. *Dallas Herald*, May 6, 1863; and *Waxahachie Daily Light*, clipping labeled "April 1936" and August 29, 1957.

17. Ibid., June 28, 1932, and April 17, 1973; and Goodlett, "Settlement and Development of Ellis County," p. 70.

18. Nance, recollections, p. 31; and *Dallas Herald*, May 6, 1863. The mid-nineteenth-century methods of manufacturing gunpowder along with the dangers involved are explained in detail in Fane G. Austin, "Highly Explosive," *Atlantic Monthly* 26 (November 1870): 529–33.

19. Nance, recollections, p. 31; and *Dallas Herald*, May 6, 1863.

20. Nance, recollections, p. 31.

21. Ibid., pp. 31–32; *Waxahachie Daily Light*, clipping labeled "April 1936" and August 29, 1957. The standard powdermill architecture during the nineteenth century was perfected in Europe. The Waxahachie mill probably resembled the European model (see Austin, "Highly Explosive," p. 535).

22. Nance, recollections, p. 31.

23. The formula for gunpowder was fifteen parts charcoal to ten parts sulfur and seventy-five parts saltpeter. Essentially the saltpeter was the gunpowder, and the charcoal was added to make it burn. The sulfur merely made the mixture (mill cake) more reliable. These three ingredients were harmless as long as they were kept separate, but together they became highly explosive (see Austin, "Highly Explosive," pp. 530, 533–36).

24. The blistering phase of the operation was designed to remove all particles of moisture from the powder, fuse the sulfur and saltpeter, and make the mixture more moisture resistant (ibid.). Since the Confederates lacked sophisticated equipment to heat their powder to extreme temperatures, some of it either retained or absorbed particles of moisture and occasionally failed to fire in battle.

25. *Dallas Herald*, May 6, 1863.

26. Nance, recollections, p. 32.

27. *Dallas Herald*, May 6, 1863.

28. Nance, theological treatise, p. 8; Nance, "Military Record of David

Carey Nance," in *Nance Family Memorial*, p. 277; and Nance, in Lindsley, comp., *History of Greater Dallas*, I, 404.

29. *Dallas Herald*, May 6, 1863.

30. Ibid.; and *Waxahachie Daily Light*, clipping labeled "April 1936" and August 29, 1957.

31. Nance, recollections, p. 32; *Dallas Herald*, May 6, 1863; and *Waxahachie Daily Light*, clipping labeled "April 1936."

32. *Dallas Herald*, May 6, 1863.

33. Nance, theological treatise, p. 8; and Nance, recollections, p. 32.

34. *Waxahachie Daily Light*, clipping labeled "April 1936," and August 29, 1957.

35. Nance, recollections, p. 31; Nance, theological treatise, pp. 7–8; and Nance, "Military Record of David Carey Nance," in *Nance Family Memorial*, p. 278.

36. Nance, theological treatise, p. 8; and Nance, recollections, pp. 31–32.

37. Ibid.

38. Ibid., p. 36; and Nance, in Lindsley, comp., *History of Greater Dallas*, I, 404.

39. Nance, recollections, p. 33.

40. Ibid.; and Annie Nance Morris, interview, pp. 4–5.

41. Nance, recollections, p. 33.

42. H. Orr to "Father," August 12, 1863, in Anderson, ed., *Campaigning with Parsons' Brigade*, p. 115.

7. SHADOWS OF IMPENDING DEFEAT

1. Nance, recollections, p. 33; E. K. Smith to J. Davis, September 28, 1863, *Official Records*, XXII, pt. 2, pp. 1028–29; and Allan Ashcraft, *Texas in the Civil War: A Résumé History*, pp. 24–25.

2. Nance, recollections, 33; Felix Pierre Poché, diary, December 26, 1863, in Edwin C. Bearss, ed., *A Louisiana Confederate: Diary of Felix Pierre Poché*, pp. 66–67; H. Orr to "Dear Mother and Father," November 4, 1862, in Anderson, ed., *Campaigning with Parsons' Brigade*, p. 77; and Ashcraft, *Texas in the Civil War*, pp. 24–25.

3. N. P. Banks to H. W. Halleck, December 12, 1863, *Official Records*, XXVI, pt. 1, p. 847; Richard Taylor, *Destruction and Reconstruction*, pp. 132–34; Stephen B. Oates, *Confederate Cavalry West of the River*, pp. 88–112; and *Red River Journal* (Alexandria, La.), July 30, 1975.

4. E. K. Smith to J. Davis, September 28, 1863, *Official Records*, XXII, pt. 2, p. 1028; E. K. Smith to J. Seddon, September 11, 1863, ibid., p. 1010; Robert S. Weddle, *Plow-Horse Cavalry: The Caney Creek Boys of the Thirty-Fourth Texas*, p. 113; and Kerby, *Kirby Smith's Confederacy*, pp. 221–43, 253–60.

5. E. K. Smith to J. Seddon, September 11, 1863, *Official Records*, XXII, pt. 2, pp. 1010–111; and E. K. Smith to J. G. Walker, July 11, 1863, ibid., XXVI, pt. 2, p. 108.

6. E. K. Smith to J. Davis, September 28, 1863, ibid., XXII, pt. 2, p. 1028.

7. Nance, recollections, p. 33; H. Orr to "Dear Father," August 30, 1863, in

Anderson, ed., *Campaigning with Parsons' Brigade,* p. 117; and J. P. Hawkins to J. B. McPherson, November 9, 1863, *Official Records,* XXVI, pt. 1, p. 791.

8. Nance, recollections, p. 33; and H. Orr to "Dear Father," August 30, 1863, in Anderson, ed., *Campaigning with Parsons' Brigade,* p. 117.

9. Nance, recollections, p. 33; S. S. Anderson to P. O. Hébert, September 1, 1863, *Official Records,* XXVI, pt. 2, p. 194; G. M. Bryan to A. B. Burleson, ibid., p. 195; and H. Orr to "Dear Sister," April 30, 1863, in Anderson, ed., *Campaigning with Parsons' Brigade,* p. 96.

10. Parsons to "Comrades of the Twelfth and Nineteenth Regiments of the Old Cavalry Brigade," June 24, 1878, and G. W. Carter to H. Erving, May 5, 1863, in *Brief History of Parsons' Brigade,* pp. 16, 41–42; H. Orr to "Dear Sister," July 2, 1863, in Anderson, ed., *Campaigning with Parsons' Brigade,* pp. 111–13; John D. Winters, *The Civil War in Louisiana,* pp. 203–04; Zuber, *My Eighty Years in Texas,* p. 166; Buck Walton, *An Epitome of My Life: Civil War Reminiscences,* pp. 61–76; and Harrell, "Arkansas," in Evans, ed., *Confederate Military History,* X, 153–54.

11. Organization of J. A. Wharton's Cavalry, March 1865, *Official Records,* XLVIII, pt. 1, p. 1458; W. Steele to S. S. Anderson, June 5, 1864, ibid., XXXIV, pt. 1, p. 628; Marchbank, comp., "Sacred Record: Special Orders Issued by Colonel W. H. Parsons," p. 21; H. Orr to "Dear Father and Mother," February 18, 1863, in Anderson, ed., *Campaigning with Parsons' Brigade,* p. 91; H. Orr to "Dear Father and Mother," May 30, 1863, in ibid., p. 105; H. Orr to "Father," July 10, 1864, in ibid., p. 142; Walton, *Epitome of My Life,* pp. 58–61; Lester N. Fitzhugh, "Texas Forces in the Red River Campaign, March–May, 1864," *Texas Military History* 30 (1963), p. 21 n. 18; Zuber, *My Eighty Years in Texas,* pp. 145–46; and Oates, *Confederate Cavalry West of the River,* pp. 123–29.

12. H. Orr to "Dear Father," July 7, 1863, in Anderson, ed., *Campaigning with Parsons' Brigade,* p. 113; J. G. Walker to E. Surget, July 10, 1863, *Official Records,* XXIV, pt. 2, p. 466; and Winters, *Civil War in Louisiana,* p. 202.

13. H. Orr to "Dear Father," August 30, 1863, in Anderson, ed., *Campaigning with Parsons' Brigade,* p. 117.

14. Ibid.

15. Walton, *Epitome of My Life,* pp. 73–74.

16. Ibid.

17. S. S. Anderson to P. O. Hébert, September 1, 1863, *Official Records,* XXVI, pt. 2, p. 194; G. M. Bryan to A. B. Burleson, September 1, 1863, ibid., p. 195; and H. Orr to "Dear Mother," October 28, 1863, in Anderson, ed., *Campaigning with Parsons' Brigade,* p. 123.

18. Nance, recollections, p. 33; and One of the Twelfth, "Sketches from a Diary of an Officer of the Twelfth Texas Cavalry," August 3, 1862, in *Brief History of Parsons' Brigade,* p. 28.

19. S. S. Anderson to P. O. Hébert, October 28, 1863, *Official Records,* XXVI, pt. 2, p. 368.

20. S. S. Anderson to P. O. Hébert, October 31, 1863, ibid., p. 375; E. K. Smith to J. Seddon, September 11, 1863, ibid., XXII, pt. 2, pp. 1010–11.

21. S. S. Anderson to P. O. Hébert, October 29, 1863, ibid., XXVI, pt. 2, p. 368.

22. E. K. Smith to R. Taylor, January 4, 1864, ibid., XXXIV, pt. 2, p. 819; E. Cunningham to T. H. Holmes, January 8, 1864, ibid., p. 843; H. Orr to "Dear Father," October 5, 1863, in Anderson, ed., *Campaigning with Parsons' Brigade*, p. 120; and Parsons to "Comrades of the Twelfth and Nineteenth Regiments of the Old Cavalry Brigade of the Trans-Mississippi Army," June 24, 1878, in *Brief History of Parsons' Brigade*, p. 16.

23. C. S. West to R. Taylor, *Official Records*, XXVI, pt. 2, p. 426. See also W. R. Boggs to T. Holmes, January 17, 1864, ibid., XXXIV, pt. 2, p. 885.

24. L. Merrill to F. Steele, December 11, 1863, ibid., XXI, p. 773; L. Merrill to F. H. Master, ibid., pp. 775–76; E. Cunningham to S. B. Maxey, January 4, 1864, ibid., XXXIV, pt. 2, p. 819; Walton, *Epitome of My Life*, p. 72; and One of the Twelfth, "Sketches from a Diary of an Officer of the Twelfth Texas Cavalry," December 31, 1863, January 1, 1864, in *Brief History of Parsons' Brigade*, p. 28.

25. E. K. Smith to "His Excellency, the President," January 20, 1864, *Official Records*, XXXIV, pt. 2, pp. 895–96; and Kerby, *Kirby Smith's Confederacy*, p. 240.

26. E. K. Smith, "Red River Campaign, March 10 to May 22, 1864," in Ben LaBree, ed., *The Confederate Soldier in the Civil War*, p. 330.

27. E. K. Smith to "His Excellency, the President," January 20, 1864, *Official Records*, XXXIV, pt. 2, pp. 895–96.

28. E. K. Smith, "Red River Campaign," in LaBree, ed., *Confederate Soldier in the Civil War*, p. 330; and Kerby, *Kirby Smith's Confederacy*, pp. 238–51.

29. E. K. Smith to R. Taylor, January 4, 1864, *Official Records*, XXXIV, pt. 2, p. 819; E. K. Smith to "His Excellency, the President," January 20, 1864, ibid., pp. 895–96; and Taylor, *Destruction and Reconstruction*, pp. 149–50.

30. Zuber, *My Eighty Years in Texas*, p. 196; and L. Merrill to F. H. Master, *Official Records*, XXI, 775–76.

31. Ibid.; and L. Merrill to F. Steele, December 11, 1863, ibid., p. 773.

32. One of the Twelfth, "Sketches from a Diary of an Officer of the Twelfth Texas Cavalry," January 1, 1864, in *Brief History of Parsons' Brigade*, p. 28. See also B. C. Lancaster, reminiscences, in Yeary, comp., *Reminiscences of the Boys in Gray*, p. 418; W. Steele to R. C. Newton, January 15, 1864, *Official Records*, XXII, pt. 2, p. 773; Alfred T. Howell to his brother, January 11, 1866, in William E. Sawyer and Neal A. Baker, eds., "A Texan in the Civil War," *Texas Military History* 2 (1962): 276; *Dallas Herald*, February 4, 1864; and Alwyn Barr, *Polignac's Texas Brigade*, pp. 15–16.

33. Lancaster, reminiscences, in Yeary, comp., *Reminiscences of the Boys in Gray*, p. 48; One of the Twelfth, "Sketches from a Diary of an Officer of the Twelfth Texas Cavalry," January 1, 1864, in *Brief History of Parsons' Brigade*, p. 28; and Barr, *Polignac's Texas Brigade*, p. 35.

34. W. R. Boggs to T. H. Holmes, January 14, 1864, *Official Records*, XXXIV, pt. 2, p. 868; W. R. Boggs to T. H. Holmes, January 17, 1864, ibid., p. 885; E. K. Smith to "His Excellency, the President," January 20, 1864, ibid., pp. 895–96; H. Orr to "Good morning, Sister," February 8, 1864, in Anderson, ed., *Campaigning with Parsons' Brigade*, p. 129; and Zuber, *My Eighty Years in Texas*, p. 197.

35. H. Orr to "Good morning, Sister," February 8, 1864, in Anderson, ed., *Campaigning with Parsons' Brigade*, p. 129; and E. K. Smith to "His Excellency, the President," January 20, 1864, *Official Records*, XXXIV, pt. 2, p. 895.

36. E. K. Smith to S. B. Maxey, January 19, 1864, *Official Records*, XXXIV, pt. 2, p. 1030; and E. K. Smith to R. Taylor, January 14, 1864, ibid., p. 895.

37. H. Orr to "Good morning, Sister," February 8, 1864, in Anderson, ed., *Campaigning with Parsons' Brigade*, p. 129; Zuber, *My Eighty Years in Texas*, pp. 197–99; and Nance, recollections, p. 33.

38. Ibid.

8. RED RIVER BATTLEGROUND

1. Nance, recollections, p. 33. See also Nance, theological treatise, p. 9; and Nance, "Military Record of David Carey Nance," in *Nance Family Memorial*, p. 278.

2. Kerby, *Kirby Smith's Confederacy*, pp. 294–301; Ludwell H. Johnson, *Red River Campaign: Politics and Cotton in the Civil War*, pp. 79–100; E. K. Smith to R. Taylor, April 1, 1864, in Joseph H. Landry, comp., "Military Records of the Civil War in Louisiana, 1861–1865, Consisting of All Documents in the *War of the Rebellion: A Compilation of the Official Records of the Union and Confederate Armies* Which Relate to Louisiana," p. 513; Taylor, *Destruction and Reconstruction*, pp. 153–54; and Harrell, "Arkansas," in Evans, ed., *Confederate Military History*, X, 237.

3. Kerby, *Kirby Smith's Confederacy*, pp. 284–85.

4. S. M. Eaton to C. T. Christensen, February 2, 1865, *Official Records*, XLVIII, pt. 1, pp. 720–21.

5. Johnson, *Red River Campaign*, p. 94.

6. Nance, "Allen Q. Nance—Limb Fourteen," in *Nance Family Memorial*, p. 275.

7. Nance, recollections, pp. 11–12, 33; Nance, in Lindsley, comp., *History of Greater Dallas*, I, 405; Nance, theological treatise, pp. 4–13; and "David C. Nance," in *History of Dallas County*, p. 808.

8. H. C. Medford, in Rebecca W. Smith and Marion Mullins, eds., "Diary of H. C. Medford, Confederate Soldier, 1864," *Southwestern Historical Quarterly* 34 (1930): 133; R. Taylor to W. R. Boggs, *Official Records*, XXXIV, pt. 1, p. 495; and Circular 24, March 19, 1864, ibid., pt. 2, pp. 1059–60.

9. E. K. Smith to R. Taylor, April 1, 1864, in Landry, comp., "Military Records of the Civil War in Louisiana, 1861–1865," p. 513.

10. S. S. Anderson to W. H. Parsons, March 7, 1864, *Official Records*, XXXIV, pt. 2, pp. 1024–25.

11. Ibid.; E. Cunningham to S. B. Maxey, March 8, 1864, ibid., p. 1030; and E. Cunningham to E. Greer, March 24, 1864, ibid., pp. 1077–78. See also John Dimitry, "Louisiana," in Evans, ed., *Confederate Military History*, X, 126–34.

12. William W. Heartsill, *Fourteen Hundred and Ninety-One Days in the Confederate Army; or, Camp Life, Day by Day, of the W. P. Lane Rangers from April 19,*

1861, to May 20, 1865, pp. 195–96; and Bill Winsor, *Texas in the Confederacy: Military Installations, Economy, and People*, p. 16.

13. Zuber, *My Eighty Years in Texas*, pp. 145–46; E. K. Smith to R. Taylor, April 8, 1864, in Landry, comp., "Military Records of the Civil War in Louisiana," p. 523; E. P. Turner to "His Excellency, P. Murrah," March 23, 1864, *Official Records*, XXXIV, pt. 2, pp. 1074–75; and Thomas A. Elgin, reminiscences, in Yeary, comp., *Reminiscences of the Boys in Gray*, pp. 212–13.

14. Heartsill, *Fourteen Hundred and Ninety-One Days in the Confederate Army*, p. 198.

15. Ibid., p. 193.

16. Ibid., p. 198; Truss to "Rebecca My Affectionate Friend," February 21, 1864, in Ray, ed., "Civil War Letters from Parsons' Texas Cavalry Brigade," pp. 222–23; Richard G. Walker, reminiscences, in Yeary, comp., *Reminiscences of the Boys in Gray*, p. 772; and Daniel C. and John M. Wright, ibid., p. 823.

17. Robert Wright, reminiscences, in Yeary, comp., *Reminiscences of the Boys in Gray*, p. 824.

18. J. G. Meem to W. H. Parsons, April 9, 1864, *Official Records*, XXXIV, pt. 3, p. 754.

19. Zuber, *My Eighty Years in Texas*, p. 199. See also Kerby, *Kirby Smith's Confederacy*, p. 304.

20. E. K. Smith to R. Taylor, April 8, 1864, *Official Records*, XXXIV, pt. 1, p. 528; and J. G. Meem to W. H. Parsons, April 9, 1864, ibid., pt. 3, p. 754.

21. Confederate soldier, quoted in Kerby, *Kirby Smith's Confederacy*, p. 319.

22. Medford, in Smith and Mullins, eds., "Diary of H. C. Medford," p. 220; A. L. Nelms to "My Dear Companion and Parents," April 13, 1864, in Weddle, *Plow-Horse Cavalry*, p. 117; and *Charleston (S.C.) Daily Courier*, May 9, 1864.

23. Medford, in Smith and Mullins, eds., "Diary of H. C. Medford," p. 220. See also Pierson, in Delaney, ed., "Diary of Samuel Pierson," pp. 34–35.

24. Thomas Crutchers Smith, reminiscences, in Yeary, comp., *Reminiscences of the Boys in Gray*, pp. 705–06. See also W. G. Vincent to A. H. May, March 28, 1864, *Official Records*, XXXIV, pt. 1, p. 511; R. Taylor to W. R. Boggs, April 11, 1864, in Landry, comp., "Military Records of the Civil War in Louisiana," p. 527; Medford, in Smith and Mullins, eds., "Diary of H. C. Medford," pp. 219–20; Alonzo Plummer, *Confederate Victory at Mansfield Including the Federal Advance from and Retreat to Natchitoches*, p. 27; and A. L. Nelms to "My Dear Companion and Parents," April 13, 1864, in Weddle, *Plow-Horse Cavalry*, p. 117.

25. Frank Rainey, reminiscences, in Yeary, comp., *Reminiscences of the Boys in Gray*, p. 627.

26. Medford, in Smith and Mullins, eds., "Diary of H. C. Medford," p. 223.

27. Iowa soldier, quoted in Johnson, *Red River Campaign*, p. 153. See also Medford, in Smith and Mullins, eds., "Diary of H. C. Medford," pp. 222–24; and Plummer, *Confederate Victory at Mansfield*, p. 37.

28. Medford, in Smith and Mullins, eds., "Diary of H. C. Medford," p. 221. See also R. Taylor to W. R. Boggs, April 9, 1864, in Landry, comp., "Military Records of the Civil War in Louisiana," p. 524.

29. John H. King, reminiscences, in Yeary, comp., *Reminiscences of the Boys in Gray,* pp. 405–06. See also the report of R. Taylor, April 18, 1864, *Official Records,* XXXIV, pt. 1, p. 570; Medford, in Smith and Mullins, eds., "Diary of H. C. Medford," pp. 222–24; and Johnson, *Red River Campaign,* p. 151.

30. Report of R. Taylor, April 18, 1864, *Official Records,* XXXIV, pt. 1, pp. 570–71; report of T. Kilby Smith, March 16, 1864, ibid., p. 383; report of E. P. Davis, April 12, 1864, ibid., p. 425; report of John C. Chadwick, June 13, 1864, ibid., p. 444; A. L. Lee to G. B. Drake, April 13, 1864, ibid., p. 450; H. Orr to "Father, Mother, and Family," April 27, 1864, in Anderson, ed., *Campaigning with Parsons' Brigade,* p. 133; R. Taylor to W. R. Boggs, April 8, 1864, in Landry, comp., "Military Records of the Civil War in Louisiana," pp. 522–23; Medford, in Smith and Mullins, eds., "Diary of H. C. Medford," p. 220; Taylor, *Destruction and Reconstruction,* p. 171; and Richard B. Irwin, "The Red River Campaign," in Johnson and Buel, eds., *Battles and Leaders of the Civil War,* IV, 357.

31. R. Taylor, quoted in Parsons, *Inside History,* p. 87. See also Kerby, *Kirby Smith's Confederacy,* pp. 306–08.

32. Nance, recollections, p. 34; and Rainey, reminiscences, in Yeary, comp., *Reminiscences of the Boys in Gray,* p. 627.

33. H. Orr to "Father, Mother, and Family," April 27, 1864, in Anderson, ed., *Campaigning with Parsons' Brigade,* p. 133.

34. Report of T. Kilby Smith, March 16, 1864, *Official Records,* XXXIV, pt. 1, p. 571.

35. R. Taylor to W. R. Boggs, April 11, 1864, in Landry, comp., "Military Records of the Civil War in Louisiana," p. 527; T. K. Smith to G. B. Drake, April 10, 1864, *Official Records,* XXXIV, pt. 1, pp. 380–81; W. G. Boggs to R. Taylor, April 11, 1864, ibid., p. 530; Plummer, *Confederate Victory at Mansfield,* p. 38; and Johnson, *Red River Campaign,* p. 211.

36. Parsons, *Inside History,* pp. 83–84.

37. R. Taylor to S. S. Anderson, April 18, 1864, *Official Records,* XXXIV, pt. 1, pp. 570–71; and Taylor, *Destruction and Reconstruction,* p. 175.

9. AMBUSH AT BLAIR'S LANDING

1. Nance, theological treatise, p. 8; R. Taylor to S. S. Anderson, April 18, 1864, *Official Records,* XXXIV, pt. 1, p. 571; D. Porter to W. T. Sherman, April 6, 1864, *Official Records of the Union and Confederate Navies in the War of the Rebellion* (hereafter cited as *Official Records of the Navies*), Series I, vol. XXVI, p. 60. All references hereafter will be to Series I unless otherwise indicated. See also Lester N. Fitzhugh, "Texas Forces in the Red River Campaign, March–May, 1864," *Texas Military History* 3 (1963): 20; Johnson, *Red River Campaign,* pp. 207–10; and Kerby, *Kirby Smith's Confederacy,* p. 309.

2. R. Taylor to S. S. Anderson, April 18, 1864, *Official Records,* XXXIV, pt. 1, pp. 570–71; N. P. Banks to E. Stanton, April 18, 1864, ibid., p. 204; G. M. Bache, abstract log of the *U.S.S. Lexington,* March 1–June 28, 1864, *Official Records of the Navies,* XXVI, 788–91; Taylor, *Destruction and Reconstruction,* pp. 175–76; Alwyn Barr, "The Battle of Blair's Landing," *Louisiana Stud-*

ies 2 (1963): 204; and J. H. McLeary, "History of Green's Brigade," in Dudley G. Wooten, ed., *A Comprehensive History of Texas, 1685–1897*, II, 730.

3. Barr, "Battle of Blair's Landing," p. 206.

4. Report of T. Kilby Smith, April 16, 1864, *Official Records*, XXXIV, pt. 1, pp. 381–82; N. P. Banks to E. Stanton, April 6, 1865, ibid., p. 204.

5. N. P. Banks to U. S. Grant, April 13, 1864, ibid., p. 185; and Irwin, "The Red River Campaign," in Johnson and Buel, eds., *Battles and Leaders of the Civil War*, IV, 357.

6. Report of T. Kilby Smith, April 16, 1864, *Official Records*, XXXIV, pt. 1, pp. 381–82; Federal historians, in *Harper's Pictorial History of the Civil War*, quoted by Parsons, *Inside History*, p. 84; and D. Porter to T. K. Smith, May 4, 1864, *Official Records of the Navies*, XXVI, p. 55.

7. Barr, "Battle of Blair's Landing," p. 205.

8. Parsons, quoted in Hogan, "Parsons' Brigade of Texas Cavalry," p. 19; Parsons to "Comrades of the Twelfth and Nineteenth Regiments," June 24, 1878, in Parsons, *Condensed History of Parsons' Brigade*, p. 19; J. A. Wharton, General Order 7, May 24, 1864, in ibid., p. 37; and Parsons, *Inside History*, p. 83.

9. Parsons, *Inside History*, p. 87.

10. Ibid.

11. Ibid., p. 88.

12. B. T. Sevies, reminiscences, in Yeary, comp., *Reminiscences of the Boys in Gray*, p. 677.

13. Parsons, *Inside History*, p. 88.

14. D. Porter to T. K. Smith, May 4, 1864, *Official Records of the Navies*, XXVI, 55; and D. Porter to W. T. Sherman, April 16, 1864, ibid., p. 62.

15. Barr, "Battle of Blair's Landing," p. 206.

16. T. O. Selfridge, "The Navy in the Red River," in Johnson and Buel, eds., *Battles and Leaders of the Civil War*, IV, 363; and report of T. Kilby Smith, April 16, 1864, *Official Records*, XXXIV, pt. 1, p. 381.

17. Ibid.; and Selfridge, "The Navy in the Red River," in Johnson and Buel, eds., *Battles and Leaders of the Civil War*, IV, 363.

18. Ibid.; and report of T. Kilby Smith, April 16, 1864, *Official Records*, XXXIV, pt. 1, p. 381.

19. Selfridge, "The Navy in the Red River," in Johnson and Buel, eds., *Battles and Leaders of the Civil War*, IV, 363.

20. Report of T. Kilby Smith, April 16, 1864, *Official Records*, XXXIV, pt. 1, pp. 381–82; Plummer, *Confederate Victory at Mansfield*, pp. 42–43; and McLeary, "History of Green's Brigade," in Wooten, ed., *Comprehensive History of Texas*, II, 731.

21. Selfridge, "The Navy in the Red River," in Johnson and Buel, eds., *Battles and Leaders of the Civil War*, IV, 363; McLeary, "History of Green's Brigade," in Wooten, ed., *Comprehensive History of Texas*, II, 730–31.

22. Report of T. Kilby Smith, April 16, 1864, *Official Records*, XXXIV, pt. 1, p. 381; R. Taylor to S. S. Anderson, April 18, 1864, ibid., pp. 570–71; D. Porter to T. K. Smith, May 4, 1864, *Official Records of the Navies*, XXVI, 55; D. Porter to W. T. Sherman, April 16, 1864, ibid., p. 61; J. P. Couthouy, abstract

log of the *U.S.S. Chillicothe*, March 7–June 8, 1864, ibid., p. 778; H. H. Gorringe, abstract of the *U.S.S. Cricket*, March 1–May 7, 1864, ibid., p. 781; and G. M. Bache, abstract of the *U.S.S. Lexington*, March 1–June 28, 1864, ibid., p. 789.

23. Selfridge, "The Navy in the Red River," in Johnson and Buel, eds., *Battles and Leaders of the Civil War*, IV, 363; R. Taylor to S. S. Anderson, April 18, 1864, *Official Records*, XXXIV, pt. 1, p. 571; J. P. Couthouy, abstract log of the *U.S.S. Chillicothe*, March 7–June 8, 1864, *Official Records of the Navies*, XXVI, 778; and Barr, "Battle of Blair's Landing," p. 207.

24. D. Porter to G. Welles, April 14, 1864, in Parsons, *Inside History*, pp. 91–92; report of T. Kilby Smith, April 16, 1864, *Official Records*, XXXIV, pt. 1, p. 382; and R. Taylor to W. R. Boggs, April 18, 1864, ibid., p. 571.

25. Selfridge, "The Navy in the Red River," in Johnson and Buel, eds., *Battles and Leaders of the Civil War*, IV, 363; Kerby, *Kirby Smith's Confederacy*, p. 309; report of T. Kilby Smith, April 16, 1864, *Official Records*, XXXIV, pt. 1, p. 382.

26. D. Porter to G. Welles, April 14, 1864, in Parsons, *Inside History*, pp. 91–92; report of T. Kilby Smith, April 16, 1864, *Official Records*, XXXIV, pt. 1, p. 382; report of T. O. Selfridge, April 16, 1864, *Official Records of the Navies*, XXVI, 49; and G. M. Bache, abstract log of the *U.S.S. Lexington*, March 1–June 28, 1864, ibid., pp. 787–90.

27. Report of T. Kilby Smith, April 16, 1864, *Official Records*, XXXIV, pt. 1, pp. 381–82; D. Porter to G. Welles, April 14, 1864, in Parsons, *Inside History*, p. 91.

28. Lancaster, reminiscences, in Yeary, comp., *Reminiscences of the Boys in Gray*, pp. 417–18; report of T. Kilby Smith, April 16, 1864, *Official Records*, XXXIV, pt. 1, pp. 370–71, 381; N. P. Banks to E. Stanton, April 6, 1865, ibid., p. 204; and G. M. Bache, abstract log of the *U.S.S. Lexington*, March 1–June 28, 1864, *Official Records of the Navies*, XXVI, 789.

29. Report of T. Kilby Smith, April 16, 1864, *Official Records*, XXXIV, pt. 1, p. 382; R. Taylor to W. R. Boggs, April 18, 1864, ibid., p. 571; and Barr, "Battle of Blair's Landing," p. 208.

30. Ibid.; and R. Taylor to W. R. Boggs, April 18, 1864, *Official Records*, XXXIV, pt. 1, p. 571.

31. A. R. Danchy, reminiscences, in Yeary, comp., *Reminiscences of the Boys in Gray*, pp. 171–72; report of T. Kilby Smith, April 16, 1864, *Official Records*, XXXIV, pt. 1, p. 382; A. L. Lee to W. Franklin, April 14, 1864, ibid., p. 453; R. Taylor to S. S. Anderson, April 18, 1864, ibid., p. 571; D. Porter to T. K. Smith, May 4, 1864, *Official Records of the Navies*, XXVI, 55; D. Porter to W. T. Sherman, April 16, 1864, ibid., p. 62; Taylor, *Destruction and Reconstruction*, p. 176; McLeary, "History of Green's Brigade," in Wooten, ed., *Comprehensive History of Texas*, II, 731; Parsons, *Inside History*, p. 89; R. Taylor, General Orders, April 13, 1864, in ibid., p. 93; and Fitzhugh, "Texas Forces in the Red River Campaign," p. 20.

32. Barr, "Battle of Blair's Landing," p. 208; Parsons, *Inside History*, p. 88; and W. T. Mechling, in Alwyn Barr, ed., "William T. Mechling's Journal of the Red River Campaign," *Texana* 1 (1963): 369.

33. Barr, "Battle of Blair's Landing," p. 208; and Parsons, *Inside History,* p. 90.

34. Ibid., p. 97; R. Taylor to W. R. Boggs, April 18, 1864, *Official Records,* XXXIV, pt. 1, p. 571; report of T. O. Selfridge, April 6, 1864, *Official Records of the Navies,* XXVI, 49; and D. Porter to T. K. Smith, May 4, 1864, ibid., pp. 54–55.

35. Report of T. Kilby Smith, April 16, 1864, *Official Records,* XXXIV, pt. 1, p. 382; report of Nathaniel P. Banks, March 18, 1864, ibid., p. 204; Barr, "Battle of Blair's Landing," pp. 208–09; and Medford, in Smith and Mullins, eds., "Diary of H. C. Medford," p. 226.

36. Report of T. O. Selfridge, April 16, 1864, *Official Records of the Navies,* XXVI, 49; D. Porter to T. K. Smith, May 4, 1864, ibid., p. 55; D. Porter to W. T. Sherman, April 16, 1864, ibid., p. 62; Taylor, *Destruction and Reconstruction,* pp. 176–77; and Selfridge, "The Navy in the Red River," in Johnson and Buel, eds., *Battles and Leaders of the Civil War,* IV, 363–64.

37. Parsons, *Inside History,* p. 95.

10. THE RACE FOR THE RIVER

1. Nance, theological treatise, p. 8; T. F. Clark, reminiscences, in Yeary, comp., *Reminiscences of the Boys in Gray,* p. 137; E. C. Askey, ibid., p. 28; Poché, in Bearss, ed., *Louisiana Confederate,* p. 112; R. Taylor to W. R. Boggs, April 11, 1864, in Landry, comp., "Military Records of the Civil War in Louisiana," p. 527; R. Taylor to W. R. Boggs, April 14, 1864, in ibid., p. 531; Medford, in Smith and Mullins, eds., "Diary of H. C. Medford," pp. 223–25; and A. L. Nelms to "My Dear Companion and Parents," April 13, 1864, in Weddle, *Plow-Horse Cavalry,* pp. 117–18.

2. Medford, in Smith and Mullins, eds., "Diary of H. C. Medford," p. 224. See also Pierson, in Delaney, ed., "Diary of Samuel Pierson," pp. 35–36.

3. Zuber, *My Eighty Years in Texas,* p. 202.

4. Medford, in Smith and Mullins, eds., "Diary of H. C. Medford," pp. 226–27.

5. Don H. Morris, "Some Things I Remember about My Grandfather," p. 3; Medford, in Smith and Mullins, eds., "Diary of H. C. Medford," p. 266; R. Taylor to W. R. Boggs, April 5, 1864, in Landry, comp., "Military Records of the Civil War in Louisiana," p. 521; and H. Orr to "My Dear Sister," May 17, 1864, in Anderson, ed., *Campaigning with Parsons' Brigade,* p. 139.

6. Medford, in Smith and Mullins, eds., "Diary of H. C. Medford," p. 229.

7. Zuber, *My Eighty Years in Texas,* 203.

8. Reports of William Steele, June 5, 1864, *Official Records,* XXXIV, pt. 1, pp. 625, 628; E. K. Smith to R. Taylor, April 12, 1864, in Landry, comp., "Military Records of the Civil War in Louisiana," p. 529; R. Taylor to W. R. Boggs, April 14, 1864, ibid., p. 531; Zuber, *My Eighty Years in Texas,* pp. 145–46; Pierson, in Delaney, ed., "Diary of Samuel Pierson," pp. 36–37; and Medford, in Smith and Mullins, eds., "Diary of H. C. Medford," p. 226.

9. R. Taylor to W. R. Boggs, April 8, 1864, *Official Records,* XXXIV, pt. 1, p. 527; reports of J. S. Marmaduke, April 21, 1864, ibid., p. 819; S. S. Ander-

son to R. Taylor, April 20, 1864, ibid., p. 543; E. K. Smith to R. Taylor, April 22, 1864, ibid., p. 535; R. Taylor to E. K. Smith, April 28, 1864, in Landry, comp., "Military Records of the Civil War in Louisiana," p. 537; E. K. Smith, "Red River Campaign," in LaBree, ed., *Confederate Soldier in the Civil War,* p. 331; and Kerby, *Kirby Smith's Confederacy,* p. 310.

10. Mechling, in Barr, ed., "William T. Mechling's Journal," pp. 370–72.

11. Kerby, *Kirby Smith's Confederacy,* pp. 311–15; and Johnson, *Red River Campaign,* pp. 170–205.

12. Reports of William Steele, June 5, 1864, *Official Records,* XXXIV, pt. 1, pp. 625–27; H. P. Bee to W. R. Boggs, August 17, 1864, ibid., pp. 612–13; Mechling, in Barr, ed., "William T. Mechling's Journal," pp. 370–71; and H. Orr to "Father, Mother, and Family," April 27, 1864, in Anderson, ed., *Campaigning with Parsons' Brigade,* p. 133.

13. H. Orr to "Father, Mother, and Family," April 27, 1864, in Anderson, ed., *Campaigning with Parsons' Brigade,* p. 131; and H. Orr to "Dear Father," May 25, 1864, ibid., p. 140.

14. Reports of William Steele, June 5, 1864, *Official Records,* XXXIV, pt. 1, p. 625; R. Taylor to S. S. Anderson, April 24, 1864, ibid., p. 581; Francis R. Lubbock, *Six Decades in Texas: Memoirs of Francis Richard Lubbock,* ed. C. W. Raines, p. 540; Medford, in Smith and Mullins, eds., "Diary of H. C. Medford," p. 229; Kerby, *Kirby Smith's Confederacy,* p. 315; and Johnson, *Red River Campaign,* p. 221.

15. Federal soldier, quoted in Kerby, *Kirby Smith's Confederacy,* p. 318. See also R. Taylor to S. S. Anderson, *Official Records,* XXXIV, pt. 1, p. 581.

16. Zuber, *My Eighty Years in Texas,* p. 213; reports of William Steele, June 5, 1864, *Official Records,* XXXIV, pt. 1, p. 626.

17. H. Orr to "Father, Mother, and Family," April 27, 1864, in Anderson, ed., *Campaigning with Parsons' Brigade,* p. 131; Zuber, *My Eighty Years in Texas,* pp. 211–12; and Nance, recollections, p. 34.

18. Taylor, *Destruction and Reconstruction,* p. 180; Zuber, *My Eighty Years in Texas,* pp. 216, 244; H. Orr to "Father, Mother, and Family," April 27, 1864, in Anderson, ed., *Campaigning with Parsons' Brigade,* p. 131; and Johnson, *Red River Campaign,* p. 226.

19. R. Taylor to S. S. Anderson, April 24, 1864, *Official Records,* XXXIV, pt. 1, p. 580.

20. Ibid.; A. J. Smith to W. T. Sherman, September 26, 1865, ibid., p. 310; Nance, recollections, p. 34; H. Orr to "Father, Mother, and Family," April 27, 1864, in Anderson, ed., *Campaigning with Parsons' Brigade,* p. 131; and Parsons to "Comrades of the Twelfth and Nineteenth Regiments of the Old Cavalry Brigade of the Trans-Mississippi Army," June 24, 1878, in *Brief History of Parsons' Brigade,* p. 22.

21. Zuber, *My Eighty Years in Texas,* p. 244; and J. Bailey to W. Hoffman, April 23, 1864, *Official Records,* XXXIV, pt. 1, p. 402.

22. R. Taylor to S. S. Anderson, April 24, 1864, *Official Records,* XXXIV, pt. 1, pp. 580–81; R. Taylor to S. S. Anderson, May 10, 1864, ibid., p. 590; H. P. Bee to B. F. Weems, August 7, 1864, ibid., pp. 611–12; reports of N. P.

Banks, April 6, 1864, ibid., p. 207; Taylor, *Destruction and Reconstruction,* pp. 180–81; and Johnson, *Red River Campaign,* pp. 232–34.

23. Zuber, *My Eighty Years in Texas,* p. 216. See also R. Taylor to S. S. Anderson, April 24, 1864, *Official Records,* XXXIV, pt. 1, p. 580.

24. H. Orr to "Friends, Mother, and Family," April 27, 1864, in Anderson, ed., *Campaigning with Parsons' Brigade,* p. 134.

25. Ibid.

26. Nance, theological treatise, p. 10.

27. R. Taylor to S. S. Anderson, April 24, 1864, *Official Records,* XXXIV, pt. 1, p. 580; and H. Orr to "Father, Mother, and Family," April 27, 1864, in Anderson, ed., *Campaigning with Parsons' Brigade,* p. 134.

28. Zuber, *My Eighty Years in Texas,* p. 217. See also Johnson, *Red River Campaign,* p. 234.

29. H. Orr to "Father, Mother, and Family," April 27, 1864, in Anderson, ed., *Campaigning with Parsons' Brigade,* p. 133.

30. E. P. Pellet, quoted in Johnson, *Red River Campaign,* p. 214; and report of D. Porter, April 28, 1864, *Official Records of the Navies,* XXVI, 94.

31. J. Bailey to W. Hoffman, May 17, 1864, *Official Records,* XXXIV, pt. 1, p. 403; R. Taylor to S. S. Anderson, May 6, 1864, ibid., pp. 587–88; R. Taylor to S. S. Anderson, May 10, 1864, ibid., pp. 589–91; *Red River Journal* (Alexandria, La.), July 30, 1975; and report of D. Porter, May 16, 1864, *Official Records of the Navies,* XXVI, 130–35.

32. *Red River Journal* (Alexandria, La.), March 6, 1975. See also report of U. B. Pearsall, August 1, 1864, *Official Records,* XXXVI, pt. 1, p. 255; and Johnson, *Red River Campaign,* p. 249.

33. R. Taylor to S. S. Anderson, May 10, 1864, *Official Records,* XXXIV, pt. 1, p. 590; Kerby, *Kirby Smith's Confederacy,* pp. 316–17; and Johnson, *Red River Campaign,* pp. 254–55.

34. R. Taylor to W. R. Boggs, April 11, 1864, in Landry, comp., "Military Records of the Civil War in Louisiana," pp. 527–28; D. Porter to W. T. Sherman, April 16, 1864, *Official Records of the Navies,* XXVI, 60; and Johnson, *Red River Campaign,* pp. 209, 259.

35. W. R. Smith, reminiscences, in Yeary, comp., *Reminiscences of the Boys in Gray,* p. 708. See also Joseph Mosely, ibid., p. 548; and T. E. Palmer, ibid., p. 587.

36. R. Taylor's postscript to S. S. Anderson, May 2, 1864, in Landry, comp., "Military Records of the Civil War in Louisiana," pp. 539–40.

37. John T. Poe, reminiscences, in Yeary, comp., *Reminiscences of the Boys in Gray,* p. 613.

38. R. Taylor to S. S. Anderson, May 6, 1864, in Landry, comp., "Military Records of the Civil War in Louisiana," pp. 541–42; reports of William Steele, June 5, 1864, *Official Records,* XXXIV, pt. 1, pp. 626–27.

39. R. Taylor to S. S. Anderson, May 8, 1864, in Landry, comp., "Military Records of the Civil War in Louisiana," p. 543.

40. R. Taylor to S. S. Anderson, April 27, 1864, *Official Records,* XXXIV, pt. 1, pp. 583–84; ibid., May 2, 1864, p. 585; ibid., May 8, 1864, p. 589; ibid.,

May 10, 1864, p. 589; R. Taylor to S. S. Anderson, May 4, 1864, in Landry, comp., "Military Records of the Civil War in Louisiana," pp. 540–41; ibid., May 5, 1864, p. 541; and ibid., May 6, 1864, pp. 541–42.

41. N. P. Banks to E. Stanton, April 6, 1865, *Official Records*, XXXIV, pt. 1, p. 212. See also reports of N. P. Banks, May 21, 1864, ibid., p. 193; report of D. Porter, May 19, 1864, quoted in Taylor, *Destruction and Reconstruction*, p. 189; and Johnson, *Red River Campaign*, pp. 265–66.

42. S. C. Jones, *Reminiscences of the Twenty-Second Iowa Volunteer Infantry*, p. 68. See also R. Taylor to S. S. Anderson, May 14, 1864, *Official Records*, XXXIV, pt. 1, p. 591.

43. R. Taylor to S. S. Anderson, May 14, 1864, in Landry, comp., "Military Records of the Civil War in Louisiana," p. 546. See also report of D. Porter, May 16, 1864, *Official Records of the Navies*, XXVI, 130–35; D. Porter to G. Welles, May 16, 1864, ibid., p. 151; and Kerby, *Kirby Smith's Confederacy*, pp. 317–18.

44. R. Taylor to S. S. Anderson, May 16, 1864, in Landry, comp., "Military Records of the Civil War in Louisiana," p. 547.

45. Reports of William Steele, June 5, 1864, *Official Records*, XXXIV, pt. 1, p. 627.

46. Ibid.; R. Taylor to S. S. Anderson, May 16, 1864, ibid., pp. 529–93; report of G. W. Baylor, April 18, 1864, ibid., p. 621; and Johnson, *Red River Campaign*, p. 273.

47. Report of G. W. Baylor, April 18, 1864, *Official Records*, XXXIV, pt. 1, p. 621; and E. K. Smith to R. Taylor, May 17, 1864, in Landry, comp., "Military Records of the Civil War in Louisiana," p. 548.

48. Reports of N. P. Banks, April 6, 1865, *Official Records*, XXXIV, pt. 1, p. 212.

11. THE FINAL CHARGE AT YELLOW BAYOU

1. N. P. Banks to E. Stanton, May 21, 1864, *Official Records*, XXXIV, pt. 1, p. 193; R. S. Canby to W. H. Halleck, May 18, 1864, ibid., pt. 3, p. 644; N. P. Banks to E. Stanton, April 6, 1865, ibid., pt. 1, p. 212; R. Taylor to S. S. Anderson, May 18, 1864, in Landry, comp., "Military Records of the Civil War in Louisiana," p. 548; Ira S. Couvillon, personal interview; Irwin, "The Red River Campaign," in Johnson and Buel, eds., *Battles and Leaders of the Civil War*, IV, 360; Walton, *Epitome of My Life*, p. 83; Johnson, *Red River Campaign*, pp. 274–76; and Winters, *Civil War in Louisiana*, pp. 377–78.

2. Lawrence Van Alstyne, "Diary of an Enlisted Man," in Henry Steele Commager, ed., *The Blue and the Gray*, I, 399. See also Winters, *Civil War in Louisiana*, p. 379.

3. Van Alstyne, "Diary of an Enlisted Man," in Commager, ed., *Blue and the Gray*, I, 400.

4. W. Steele to S. S. Anderson, June 5, 1864, *Official Records*, XXXIV, pt. 1, p. 621. See also R. Taylor to S. S. Anderson, May 18, 1864, in Landry, comp., "Military Records of the Civil War in Louisiana," pp. 548–49; and H. Orr to

"Dear Father," May 25, 1864, in Anderson, ed., *Campaigning with Parsons' Brigade*, pp. 139–40.

5. Couvillon, personal interview; *Alexandria Morning Advocate*, May 18, 1975; report of S. G. Hill, May 28, 1864, *Official Records*, XXXIV, pt. 1, pp. 329–30; report of G. A. Eberhart, May 23, 1864, ibid., p. 367; report of S. G. Hill, May 28, 1864, ibid., p. 330; J. E. Harrison to "My Dear Daughter," May 18, 1864, and to "Dear Ballinger," May 22, 1864, quoted in Barr, *Polignac's Texas Brigade*, pp. 45–46; H. Orr to "Dear Father," May 25, 1864, in Anderson, ed., *Campaigning with Parsons' Brigade*, p. 140; Johnson, *Red River Campaign*, p. 275; and Winters, *Civil War in Louisiana*, p. 376.

6. Parsons, *Inside History*, p. 104; J. E. Harrison, quoted in Barr, *Polignac's Texas Brigade*, pp. 45–46; and report of S. G. Hill, May 28, 1864, *Official Records*, XXXIV, pt. 1, p. 330. See also R. Taylor to S. S. Anderson, May 16, 1864, ibid., p. 593; W. Steele to S. S. Anderson, June 5, 1864, ibid., pp. 627–28; and Johnson, *Red River Campaign*, p. 275.

7. Report of T. J. Ginn, May 24, 1864, *Official Records*, XXXIV, pt. 1, p. 372; R. Taylor to S. S. Anderson, May 16, 1864, ibid., p. 593; and Winters, *Civil War in Louisiana*, p. 376.

8. Parsons, *Inside History*, pp. 103–04; Barr, *Polignac's Texas Brigade*, p. 45; J. E. Harrison to "My Dear Daughter," May 18, 1864, and to "Dear Ballinger," May 22, 1864, quoted in ibid., pp. 45–46; report of R. Taylor, May 19, 1864, *Official Records*, XXXIV, pt. 1, p. 594; report of R. F. Fyan, May 21, 1864, ibid., p. 370; report of T. J. Ginn, May 24, 1864, ibid., p. 372; report of S. G. Hill, May 28, 1864, ibid., pp. 329–30; and Hogan, "Parsons' Brigade of Texas Cavalry," p. 19.

9. H. Orr to "Dear Father," May 25, 1864, in Anderson, ed., *Campaigning with Parsons' Brigade*, pp. 139–40; and Winters, *Civil War in Louisiana*, pp. 376–77.

10. Reports of William Steele, June 5, 1864, *Official Records*, XXXIV, pt. 1, p. 628; reports of N. P. Banks, May 21, 1864, ibid., p. 193; report of S. G. Hill, May 28, 1864, ibid., pp. 329–30; report of T. J. Ginn, May 24, 1864, ibid., p. 372; J. E. Harrison to "My Dear Daughter," May 18, 1864, and to "Dear Ballinger," May 22, 1864, quoted in Barr, *Polignac's Texas Brigade*, pp. 45–46; H. Orr to "Dear Father," May 25, 1864, in Anderson, ed., *Campaigning with Parsons' Brigade*, pp. 139–40; Nance, "Military Record of David Carey Nance," in *Nance Family Memorial*, p. 278; Parsons to "Comrades of the Twelfth and Nineteenth Regiments of the Old Cavalry Brigade of the Trans-Mississippi Army," June 24, 1878, in *Brief History of Parsons' Brigade*, p. 22; and Charles W. Squires, "My Artillery Fire Was Very Destructive," *Civil War Times Illustrated*, p. 25.

11. Bruce Catton, *Gettysburg: The Final Fury*, pp. 87–88. See also Squires, "My Artillery Fire Was Very Destructive," pp. 18–28.

12. Reports of N. P. Banks, May 21, 1864, *Official Records*, XXXIV, pt. 1, p. 193. See also report of S. G. Hill, May 28, 1864, ibid., pp. 329–30; report of J. C. Becht, May 25, 1864, ibid., p. 325; report of T. J. Ginn, May 24, 1864, ibid., p. 372; R. Taylor to S. S. Anderson, May 19, 1864, in Landry, comp.,

"Military Records of the Civil War in Louisiana," p. 549; J. A. Wharton, General Order 7, May 24, 1864, in *Brief History of Parsons' Brigade*, pp. 22, 44; J. E. Harrison to "My Dear Daughter," May 18, 1864, and to "Dear Ballinger," May 22, 1864, quoted in Barr, *Polignac's Texas Brigade*, pp. 45–46; and H. Orr to "Dear Father," May 25, 1864, in Anderson, ed., *Campaigning with Parsons' Brigade*, pp. 139–40.

13. Reports of William Steele, June 5, 1864, *Official Records*, XXXIV, pt. 1, p. 627.

14. Report of J. I. Gilbert, May 26, 1864, ibid., pp. 363–64.

15. H. Orr to "Dear Father," May 25, 1864, in Anderson, ed., *Campaigning with Parsons' Brigade*, p. 140.

16. R. F. Fyan to W. G. Donnan, May 21, 1864, *Official Records*, XXXIV, pt. 1, p. 370. See also the report of T. J. Ginn, May 24, 1864, ibid., p. 372; report of S. G. Hill, May 28, 1864, ibid., pp. 329–30; and H. Orr to "Dear Father," May 25, 1864, in Anderson, ed., *Campaigning with Parsons' Brigade*, p. 140.

17. H. Orr to "Dear Father," May 25, 1864, in Anderson, ed., *Campaigning with Parsons' Brigade*, p. 140. See also report of T. J. Ginn, May 24, 1864, *Official Records*, XXXIV, pt. 1, p. 372; report of W. C. Jones, April 12, 1864, ibid., p. 361; report of J. I. Gilbert, May 26, 1864, ibid., pp. 363–64; and R. F. Fyan to W. G. Donnan, May 21, 1864, ibid., p. 370.

18. Nance, recollections, pp. 34–35. See also Nance, "Military Record of David Carey Nance," in *Nance Family Memorial*, p. 278.

19. Report of T. J. Ginn, May 24, 1864, *Official Records*, XXXIV, pt. 1, p. 372; report of R. F. Fyan, May 21, 1864, ibid., p. 370; report of J. I. Gilbert, April 11, 1864, ibid., pp. 363–64; and report of L. A. Crane, May 22, 1864, ibid., p. 361.

20. Nance, recollections, p. 35. See also Nance, "Military Record of David Carey Nance," in *Nance Family Memorial*, p. 278.

21. Nance, recollections, p. 34.

22. R. F. Fyan to W. G. Donnan, May 21, 1864, *Official Records*, XXXIV, pt. 1, p. 370; Couvillon, personal interview; Johnson, *Red River Campaign*, p. 275; Barr, *Polignac's Texas Brigade*, pp. 45–46; and Winters, *Civil War in Louisiana*, p. 376.

23. H. Orr to "Dear Father," May 25, 1864, in Anderson, ed., *Campaigning with Parsons' Brigade*, p. 140; and report of T. J. Ginn, May 24, 1864, *Official Records*, XXXIV, pt. 1, p. 372.

24. Nance, recollections, p. 35.

25. Ibid.

26. Ibid. See also Nance, "Military Record of David Carey Nance," in *Nance Family Memorial*, p. 278.

27. Nance, recollections, p. 35; and Parsons to "Comrades of the Twelfth and Nineteenth Regiments of the Old Cavalry Brigade of the Trans-Mississippi Army," June 24, 1878, in *Brief History of Parsons' Brigade*, p. 22.

28. N. P. Banks to E. Stanton, April 6, 1865, *Official Records*, XXXIV, pt. 1, p. 212; report of S. G. Hill, May 28, 1864, ibid., pp. 329–30; report of N. P. Banks, May 21, 1864, ibid., p. 193; T. J. Kinney to J. B. Sample, May 20, 1864,

ibid., pp. 348–49; R. Taylor to S. S. Anderson, May 23, 1864, in Landry, comp., "Military Records of the Civil War in Louisiana," p. 550; and *Red River Journal* (Alexandria, La.), August 6, 1975.

29. Reports of William Steele, June 5, 1864, *Official Records*, XXXIV, pt. 1, p. 627. See also reports of N. P. Banks, May 21, 1864, ibid., p. 193; report of J. C. Becht, May 25, 1864, ibid., p. 325; report of A. J. Smith, September 26, 1865, ibid., p. 304; report of J. A. Mower, May 23, 1864, ibid., p. 320; S. G. Hill to J. B. Sample, May 28, 1864, ibid., p. 329; G. W. Van Beek to H. Hoover, May 29, 1864, ibid., p. 337; J. I. Gilbert to W. G. Donnan, May 26, 1864, ibid., p. 364; report of G. A. Eberhart, May 23, 1864, ibid., p. 367; R. F. Fyan to W. G. Donnan, May 21, 1864, ibid., p. 370; R. Taylor to S. S. Anderson, May 18, 1864, ibid., p. 594; report of E. H. Fordham, May 22, 1864, ibid., p. 467; report of G. W. Baylor, April 18, 1864, ibid., p. 467; Parsons to "Comrades of the Twelfth and Nineteenth Regiments of the Old Cavalry Brigade of the Trans-Mississippi Army," June 24, 1878, in *Brief History of Parsons' Brigade*, p. 22; Hogan, "Parsons' Brigade of Texas Cavalry," p. 17; Taylor, *Destruction and Reconstruction*, p. 190; and H. Orr to "Dear Father," May 25, 1864, in Anderson, ed., *Campaigning with Parsons' Brigade*, p. 140.

30. H. Orr to "Dear Father," May 25, 1864, in Anderson, ed., *Campaigning with Parsons' Brigade*, pp. 139–40.

31. Joseph Lafayette Estes, reminiscences, in Yeary, comp., *Reminiscences of the Boys in Gray*, p. 216.

32. Barr, *Polignac's Texas Brigade*, pp. 46–47. See also H. Orr to "Dear Father," May 25, 1864, in Anderson, ed., *Campaigning with Parsons' Brigade*, p. 140; Walton, *Epitome of My Life*, p. 83; A. L. Nelms to M. J. Nelms, June 1, 1864, in Weddle, *Plow-Horse Cavalry*, p. 125; and Taylor, *Destruction and Reconstruction*, pp. 189–90.

33. R. Taylor to S. S. Anderson, May 18, 1864, *Official Records*, XXXIV, pt. 1, p. 594.

34. Barr, *Polignac's Texas Brigade*, pp. 46–47.

35. Nance, recollections, p. 35.

36. R. Taylor to E. K. Smith, May 24, 1864, in Landry, comp., "Military Records of the Civil War in Louisiana," p. 550; and report of W. F. Lynch, March 18, 1864, *Official Records*, XXXIV, pt. 3, pp. 338–39.

37. Nance, recollections, pp. 35–36.

38. Ibid., p. 36.

12. THE LAST ENCAMPMENT

1. Nance, recollections, p. 36.

2. Ibid., p. 37; and Nance, Company E roster and personal account book.

3. R. Taylor to S. S. Anderson, May 23, 1864, in Landry, comp., "Military Records of the Civil War in Louisiana," p. 550; E. K. Smith to R. Taylor, June 5, 1864, ibid., p. 555; H. Orr to "Sister Mary," June 11, 1864, in Anderson, ed., *Campaigning with Parsons' Brigade*, pp. 141–42; and H. Orr to "My Dear Brothers," August 26, 1864, ibid., pp. 145–46.

4. W. Steele to W. H. Parsons, June 18, 1864, *Official Records*, XXXIV, pt. 4,

pp. 681–82; J. Wharton to J. Magruder, June 17, 1864, ibid., pp. 680–81; W. R. Boggs to J. Magruder, June 20, 1864, ibid., p. 684; W. R. Boggs to E. K. Smith, June 23, 1864, ibid., p. 691; P. H. Thompson to J. Walker, June 23, 1864, ibid., p. 691; J. Walker to E. K. Smith, August 13, 1864, ibid., XLI, pt. 1, p. 106; J. A. Wharton to E. K. Smith, August 9, 1864, ibid., pt. 2, pp. 1049–50; H. Orr to "My Dear Brothers," August 26, 1864, in Anderson, ed., *Campaigning with Parsons' Brigade*, p. 145; and J. A. Wharton to the "Officers and Soldiers of Parsons' Cavalry Brigade, Steele's Division," June 17, 1864, in *Brief History of Parsons' Brigade*, p. 46.

5. R. Taylor to E. K. Smith, May 24, 1864, in Landry, comp., "Military Records of the Civil War in Louisiana," p. 551.

6. H. Orr to "Sammie," August 4, 1864, in Anderson, ed., *Campaigning with Parsons' Brigade*, p. 144; and E. K. Smith to R. Taylor, June 5, 1864, in Landry, comp., "Military Records of the Civil War in Louisiana," p. 555.

7. Organization of J. A. Wharton's cavalry corps, March 1865, *Official Records*, XLVIII, pt. 1, p. 1458; organization of the Army of the Trans-Mississippi Department, December 31, 1864, ibid., XLI, pt. 4, p. 1143; J. A. Wharton to E. K. Smith, August 9, 1864, ibid., pt. 2, pp. 1050–51; organization of J. A. Wharton's cavalry corps, March 1865, ibid., XLVIII, pt. 1, p. 1458; H. Orr to "Dear Sister," November 12, 1864, in Anderson, ed., *Campaigning with Parsons' Brigade*, p. 149; and Fitzhugh, "Texas Forces in the Red River Campaign," p. 21.

8. J. G. Walker to E. K. Smith, August 13, 1864, *Official Records*, XLI, pt. 1, p. 106; J. A. Wharton to E. K. Smith, August 9, 1864, ibid., pt. 2, pp. 1049–50; W. Steele to W. H. Parsons, June 18, 1864, ibid., XXXIV, pt. 4, p. 681; R. Taylor to E. K. Smith, August 18, 1864, ibid., XLI, pt. 1, p. 111; W. R. Boggs to S. B. Buckner, August 25, 1864, ibid., p. 118; J. G. Walker to E. K. Smith, August 13, 1864, ibid., p. 106; and Joseph H. Parks, *General Edmund Kirby Smith*, pp. 437–38.

9. H. Orr to "Dear Sister," November 28, 1864, in Anderson, ed., *Campaigning with Parsons' Brigade*, p. 152. See also W. R. Boggs to E. K. Smith, June 23, 1864, *Official Records*, XXXIV, pt. 4, p. 691; J. A. Wharton to J. B. Magruder, June 17, 1864, ibid., pp. 680–81; W. Steele to W. H. Parsons, June 18, 1864, ibid., pp. 681–82; R. Taylor to E. K. Smith, August 18, 1864, ibid., XLI, pt. 1, p. 111; and J. A. Wharton to E. K. Smith, August 9, 1864, ibid., pt. 2, pp. 1049–50.

10. H. Orr to "Dear Sister," November 12, 1864, in Anderson, ed., *Campaigning with Parsons' Brigade*, p. 149; E. K. Smith to R. Taylor, June 5, 1864, in Landry, comp., "Military Records of the Civil War in Louisiana," p. 555; and Parks, *General Edmund Kirby Smith*, p. 440.

11. H. Orr to "Father," July 10, 1864, in Anderson, ed., *Campaigning with Parsons' Brigade*, p. 142; and W. Steele to W. H. Parsons, June 18, 1864, *Official Records*, XXXIV, pt. 4, p. 681.

12. R. W. McHenry to J. Davis, January 5, 1865, *Official Records*, XLVIII, pt. 1, p. 1316.

13. Ibid.; and I. N. Earl to C. T. Christensen, November 24, 1864, ibid., XLI, pt. 4, p. 663.

14. R. W. McHenry to J. Davis, January 5, 1865, ibid., XLVIII, pt. 1, p. 1316; C. C. Andrews to C. H. Dyer, November 25, 1864, ibid., XLI, pt. 4, p. 677; I. N. Earl to C. T. Christensen, November 24, 1864, ibid., p. 663; and H. Orr to "My Dear Brothers," August 26, 1864, in Anderson, ed., *Campaigning with Parsons' Brigade,* p. 145.

15. H. Orr, quoted in J. N. Orr to "Brother Sammie," January 26, 1865, in Anderson, ed., *Campaigning with Parsons' Brigade,* p. 156.

16. S. M. Eaton to C. T. Christensen, February 2, 1865, *Official Records,* XLVIII, pt. 1, p. 721; H. Orr to "My Dear Brother," March 13, 1865, in Anderson, ed., *Campaigning with Parsons' Brigade,* pp. 157–58.

17. H. Orr to "Sister," February 19, 1865, in Anderson, ed., *Campaigning with Parsons' Brigade,* p. 156; and H. Orr to "My Dear Brother," March 13, 1865, ibid., pp. 157–58.

18. Nance, recollections, p. 37.

19. One of the Twelfth, "Sketches from a Diary of an Officer of the Twelfth Texas Cavalry," January 1, 1865, *Brief History of Parsons' Brigade,* p. 29; and H. Orr to "Dear Sister," November 28, 1864, in Anderson, ed., *Campaigning with Parsons' Brigade,* p. 152.

20. Organization of J. A. Wharton's cavalry corps, March 1865, *Official Records,* XLVIII, pt. 1, pp. 1458–59.

21. H. Orr to "My Dear Mother," April 7, 1865, in Anderson, ed., *Campaigning with Parsons' Brigade,* p. 158; J. T. Witt, reminiscences, in Yeary, comp., *Reminiscences of the Boys in Gray,* pp. 812–13; and organization of J. A. Wharton's cavalry corps, March 1865, *Official Records,* XLIII, pt. 1, p. 1458.

22. A. M. Jackson to S. A. Hurlbut, April 14, 1865, *Official Records,* XLVIII, pt. 2, p. 92.

23. Nance, recollections, p. 37.

24. Weddle, *Plow-Horse Cavalry,* p. 158; and Kerby, *Kirby Smith's Confederacy,* pp. 428, 458–80.

25. Nance, recollections, p. 37; H. Orr to "My Dear Mother," April 7, 1865, in Anderson, ed., *Campaigning with Parsons' Brigade,* pp. 158–59; and Parsons, "Comrades of the Twelfth and Nineteenth Regiments of the Old Cavalry Brigade of the Trans-Mississippi Army," June 24, 1878, in *Brief History of Parsons' Brigade,* p. 24.

26. Nance, recollections, p. 37; and A. M. Dechman, "Brief History of the Nineteenth Regiment, Texas Cavalry, Confederate Army," and Parsons to "Comrades of the Twelfth and Nineteenth Regiments of the Old Cavalry Brigade," June 24, 1878, in *Brief History of Parsons' Brigade,* pp. 13, 24.

27. Nance, recollections, p. 37.

28. Ibid., p. 24; and Nance, "Military Record of David Carey Nance," in *Nance Family Memorial,* pp. 277–78.

29. Don H. Morris, "Some Things I Remember about My Grandfather," p. 3.

30. Nance, recollections, p. 37. Description of Owenville taken from the *Texas Almanac* for 1861, reproduced in B. P. Gallaway, ed., *The Dark Corner of the Confederacy: Accounts of Civil War Texas as Told by Contemporaries,* pp. 73–74.

31. Nance, recollections, p. 37.

32. Don H. Morris, "Some Things I Remember about My Grandfather," pp. 3–4.

33. Nance, theological treatise, p. 4.

34. Nance, in Lindsley, comp., *History of Greater Dallas*, I, 404.

Bibliography

Alexandria (La.) *Morning Advocate*, May 18, 1975.

Anderson, John Q., ed. *Brokenburn: The Journal of Kate Stone*. Baton Rouge, La.: Louisiana State University Press, 1955.

————. *Campaigning with Parsons' Texas Cavalry Brigade, CSA: The War Journals and Letters of the Four Orr Brothers, Twelfth Texas Cavalry Regiment*. Hillsboro, Tex.: Hill Junior College Press, 1967.

Arkansas Gazette (Little Rock), June 14–June 28, 1862; State Centennial Edition, June 15, 1936.

Ashcraft, Allan C. "Texas, 1860–1866: The Lone Star State in the Civil War." Ph.D. diss., Columbia University, 1960.

————. *Texas in the Civil War: A Résumé History*. Austin, Tex.: Texas Civil War Centennial Commission, 1962.

Austin, Fane G. "Highly Explosive." *Atlantic Monthly* 26 (November 1870): 529–33.

Barnes, James. *The Photographic History of the Civil War in Ten Volumes*. Vol. VI, *The Navies*. New York: Review of Reviews, 1912.

Barr, Alwyn. "The Battle of Blair's Landing." *Louisiana Studies* 2 (1963): 204–12.

————. "Confederate Artillery in the Trans-Mississippi." Master's thesis, University of Texas, Austin, 1961.

————. *Polignac's Texas Brigade*. Houston: Texas Gulf Coast Historical Association, 1964.

————. "Texas Losses in the Red River Campaign, 1864." *Texas Military History* 3 (1963): 104–10.

————, ed. "William T. Mechling's Journal of the Red River Campaign, April 7–May 10, 1864." *Texana* 1 (1963): 361–79.

Baxter, William. *Pea Ridge and Prairie Grove; or, Scenes and Incidents of the War in Arkansas*. Reprint. Van Buren, Ark.: Argus Press, 1957.

Bearss, Edwin C., ed. *A Louisiana Confederate: Diary of Felix Pierre Poché*. Natchitoches, La.: Louisiana Studies Institute, Northwestern State University, 1972.

Bee, Hamilton P. "Battle of Pleasant Hill—an Error Corrected." *Southern Historical Society Papers* 8 (1880): 184–86.

Black, Robert C., III. *The Railroads of the Confederacy.* Chapel Hill, N.C.: University of North Carolina Press, 1952.

Blackburn, J. K. P. "Reminiscences of the Terry Rangers." *Southwestern Historical Quarterly* 22 (1918): 38–78, 143–79.

Blessington, Joseph P. *The Campaigns of Walker's Texas Division.* Pemberton Reprint Series. Austin, Tex.: Pemberton Press, 1968.

Brown, Norman D., ed. *One of Cleburne's Command: The Civil War Reminiscences and Diary of Captain Samuel T. Foster, Granbury's Texas Brigade, CSA.* Austin, Tex.: University of Texas Press, 1980.

Buenger, Walter L. *Secession and the Union in Texas.* Austin, Tex.: University of Texas Press, 1984.

Catton, Bruce. *Gettysburg: The Final Fury.* New York: Berkley Books, 1974.

Charleston (S.C.) Daily Courier, May 9, 1864.

Cloyd, William C. "Waxahachie, a Progressive City," *Texas Magazine* (July 1910), pp. 67–69.

Cochran, John H. *Dallas County: A Record of Its Pioneers and Progress.* Dallas: Service Publishing, 1928.

Commager, Henry Steele, ed. *The Blue and the Gray.* Reprint. 2 vols. in 1. New York: Fairfax Press, 1982.

Connally, Roy. "Waxahachie, Texas Cotton Center." *Texas Magazine* (November 1912), pp. 85–87.

Couvillon, Ira S. Personal interview during tour of the Yellow Bayou battlefield, August 22, 1975.

———. "To Avoyelles with the Couvillons." Photocopy. Original typescript in the possession of Ira S. Couvillon, Simmesport, Louisiana 1966.

Cumberland, Charles C. "The Confederate Loss and Recapture of Galveston, 1862–1863." *Southwestern Historical Quarterly* 51 (1947): 109–30.

Dallas Herald, February 1, 1860–May 6, 1863.

DeBray, Xavier B. *A Sketch of the History of DeBray's Twenty-Sixth Regiment of Texas Cavalry.* Reprint. Waco, Tex.: Texian Press, 1961.

Delaney, Norman C., ed. "Diary and Memoirs of Marshall Samuel Pierson, Company C, Seventeenth Regiment, Texas Cavalry, 1862–1865." *Military History of Texas and the Southwest* 13.3 (1976): 23–38.

Dimitry, John. "Louisiana." In *Confederate Military History.* Vol. X. Edited by Clement A. Evans. Atlanta, Ga.: Confederate Publishing, 1899. Facsimile reprint. Secaucus, N.J.: Blue and Gray Press, 1974.

Donald, David Herbert. *Liberty and Union.* Lexington, Mass.: D. C. Heath, 1978.

Dougan, Michael B. "Life in Confederate Arkansas." *Arkansas Historical Quarterly* 30 (1972): 15–35.

Dupont, Albert L. "The Career of Paul Octave Hebért, Governor of Louisiana, 1835–1856." *Louisiana Historical Quarterly* 31 (1948): 528–29.

Dyer, Frederick H. *A Compendium of the War of the Rebellion.* 3 vols. New York: Thomas Yoseloff, 1959.

Eaton, Clement. *A History of the Southern Confederacy.* New York: Collier-MacMillan Free Press, 1954.

Efnor, Kate. "History of Ellis County, Texas." *American Sketch Book* 4 (1878): 366–75.

Ellis County History: The Basic 1892 Book with Additional Biographies. Fort Worth, Tex.: Ellis County Historical Museum and Art Gallery, 1972.

Felgar, Robert P. "Texas in the War for Southern Independence, 1861–1865." Ph.D. diss., University of Texas, Austin, 1935.

Fitzhugh, Lester N. "Texas Forces in the Red River Campaign, March–May, 1864." *Texas Military History* 3 (1963): 15–22.

Fremantle, A. J. L. *Three Months in the Southern States, April–June, 1863.* New York: John Bradburn, 1864.

Gallaway, B. P., ed. *The Dark Corner of the Confederacy: Accounts of Civil War Texas as Told by Contemporaries.* 2d ed. Dubuque, Iowa: Kendall-Hunt Publishing, 1972.

Galveston Daily News, Centennial Causeway Edition, August 15, 1939.

Gambrell, Herbert, ed. and comp. *Dallas: Guide and History.* Dallas: Writer's Project, 1940.

Geer, James K., ed. *A Texas Ranger and Frontiersman: The Days of Buck Barry in Texas.* Dallas: Southwest Press, 1932.

Goodlett, Helen G. "Settlement and Development of Ellis County, Texas." Master's thesis, University of Colorado, Boulder, 1933.

Harper's Weekly, April 16–May 21, 1864.

Harrell, John M. "Arkansas." In *Confederate Military History.* Vol. X. Edited by Clement A. Evans. Atlanta, Ga.: Confederate Publishing, 1899. Facsimile reprint. Secaucus, N.J.: Blue and Gray Press, 1974.

Heartsill, William W. *Fourteen Hundred and Ninety-One Days in the Confederate Army; or, Camp Life, Day by Day, of the W. P. Lane Rangers from April 19, 1861 to May 20, 1865.* 1876. Facsimile reprint. Edited by Bell I. Wiley. Jackson, Tenn.: McCowat-Mercer Press, 1954.

History of Ellis County, Texas. Ennis, Tex.: Ennis Chamber of Commerce, 1972.

Hogan, George H. "Parsons' Brigade of Texas Cavalry." *Confederate Veteran,* 33 (1925): 17–20.

Johnson, Ludwell H. *Red River Campaign: Politics and Cotton in the Civil War.* Baltimore: Johns Hopkins University Press, 1958.

Johnson, Robert V., and Clarence C. Buel, eds. *Battles and Leaders of the Civil War.* 1887–88. Facsimile reprint. 4 vols. New York: Thomas Yoseloff, 1956.

Jones, S. C. *Reminiscences of the Twenty-Second Iowa Volunteer Infantry: Giving Its Organization, Marches, Skirmishes, Battles, and Sieges As Taken from the Diary of Lieutenant S. C. Jones of Company A.* Iowa City, Iowa, 1907. Microfiche copy in Abilene Christian University Library.

Jordan, Terry G. "The Imprint of the Upper and Lower South on Mid-Nineteenth-Century Texas." *Annals of the Association of American Geographers* 57 (1967): 667–90.

———. "Population Origins in Texas, 1850." *Geographical Review* 59 (1969): 83–103.

Keith, Ruby. "Early History of Dallas." Master's thesis, University of Texas, Austin, 1930.

Kerby, Robert L. *Kirby Smith's Confederacy: The Trans-Mississippi South, 1863–1865.* New York: Columbia University Press, 1972.

Landry, Joseph H., comp. "Military Records of the Civil War in Louisiana, 1861–1865, Consisting of All Documents in the *War of the Rebellion: A Compilation of the Official Records of the Union and Confederate Armies* Which Relate to Louisiana." Typescript, n.d. Special Collections, Northwestern State University Library, Natchitoches, La.

Lewis, Berkeley R. *Notes on Ammunition of the American Civil War, 1861–1865.* Washington, D.C.: American Ordinance Association, 1959.

Lindsley, Philip, comp. *A History of Greater Dallas and Vicinity.* 2 vols. Chicago: Lewis Publishing, 1909.

Lubbock, Francis R. *Six Decades in Texas: Memoirs of Francis Richard Lubbock.* Edited by C. W. Raines. Austin, Tex.: Ben C. Jones, 1900.

Marchbank, B. F., comp. "Sacred Record: Special Orders Issued by Colonel W. H. Parsons, Commanding, Parsons' Cavalry Brigade, Texas, Confederate Army. Placed in my care by . . . W. H. Getzendaner." Nicholas P. Sims Library, Waxahachie, Tex.

Meiners, Fredericka. "Hamilton P. Bee in the Red River Campaign of 1864." *Southwestern Historical Quarterly* 78 (1974): 21–44.

Memorial and Biographical History of Dallas County, Texas. Chicago: Lewis Publishing, 1892.

Morris, A. B. Personal interview, March 17, 1974.

Morris, Annie Nance. Interview by Jackie Morris Warmsley, n.d. Photocopy. Original in the possession of Jimmy Lawson, Boston, Mass.

Morris, Don H. "D. C. Nance—Some Things I Remember about My Grandfather." Original typescript in the possession of the author, November 25, 1969.

———. Personal interview, November 9, 1973.

Muncy, Raymond L. *A Frontier Town Grows Up in America.* Searcy, Ark.: Harding Press, 1976.

Muster Roll RP 739315, Company E, Twelfth Regiment, Texas Cavalry (copy). Military Service Records (NNCC), National Archives (GSA), Washington, D.C. (copied from original records by W. H. Getzendaner and presented to B. F. Marchbank of Waxahachie, Tex.). Nicholas P. Sims Library, Waxahachie, Tex.

Nance, David Carey. Company E roster and personal account book. In the possession of Jimmy Lawson, Boston, Mass.

———. Miscellaneous papers. Essays, poems, and sermons. Originals in the possession of Jimmy Lawson, Boston, Mass.

———. Recollections of "Personal History." Labeled "For Annie," July 23, 1912. Original in the possession of Jimmy Lawson, Boston, Mass.

———. Soldier's Application for a Confederate Pension with Affidavits of Witnesses, filed June 16, 1925. Archives Division, Texas State Library.

———. Theological treatise with autobiographical sketch. Chapter 2, "Early Life: Military," January 1924. Original in the possession of Jimmy Lawson, Boston, Mass.

Nance, George W., comp. *The Nance Memorial: A History of the Nance Family in General.* Bloomington, Ill.: J. E. Burke, 1904.

New York Times, July 21, 1862.

Nichols, James L. *The Confederate Quartermaster in the Trans-Mississippi.* Austin, Tex.: University of Texas Press, 1964.

Noll, Arthur Howard. *General Kirby-Smith.* Sewanee, Tenn.: University Press at the University of the South, 1907.

Norman, N. Phillip. "The Red River of the South: Historical Aspects Pertaining to the Navigation of This River with a Tabulated List of Steamboats, Steamboat Masters, and Way Landings." *Louisiana Historical Quarterly* 25 (1942): 397–535.

North, Thomas. *Five Years in Texas; or, What You Did Not Hear during the War from January 1861 to January 1866.* Cincinnati: Elm Street Printing, 1871.

Oates, Stephen B. *Confederate Cavalry West of the River.* Austin, Tex.: University of Texas Press, 1961.

Olmsted, Frederick Law. *A Journey Through Texas.* New York: Dix, Edwards, 1857.

Parks, Joseph H. *General Edmund Kirby Smith, C.S.A.* Baton Rouge, La.: Louisiana State University Press, 1954.

Parsons, W. H. *Condensed History of Parsons' Texas Cavalry Brigade, 1861–1865, Together with Inside History and Heretofore Unwritten Chapters of the Red River Campaign of 1864.* Corsicana, Tex.: Parsons' Brigade Association, 1903.

———. *Inside History and Heretofore Unwritten Chapters of the Red River Campaign of 1864 and the Participation Therein of Parsons' Texas Cavalry Brigade: The Policy and Motives of the Then Proposed Federal Invasion of the Line of Red River.* Washington, D.C.: published by the author (?), n.d.

Parsons' Texas Cavalry Brigade Association. *A Brief and Condensed History of Parsons' Texas Cavalry Brigade Composed of Twelfth, Nineteenth, Twenty-First, Morgan's Battalion, and Pratt's Battery of Artillery of the Confederate States.* Waxahachie, Tex.: J. M. Flemister, 1892. Facsimile reprint. Waco, Tex.: W. M. Morrison, 1962.

Plummer, Alonzo H. *Confederate Victory at Mansfield.* Mansfield, La.: United Daughters of the Confederacy, 1969.

Potts, Charles S. "Railroad Transportation in Texas." *Bulletin of the University of Texas,* No. 119. Humanistic Series, No. 7, March 1, 1909.

Ray, Johnette Highsmith, ed. "Civil War Letters from Parsons' Texas Cavalry Brigade." *Southwestern Historical Quarterly* 69 (1965): 210–23.

Red River Journal (Alexandria, La.), March 6–August 6, 1975.

Richardson, Albert D. *Beyond the Mississippi.* Hartford, Conn.: American Publishing, 1867.

Richardson, Rupert N. *The Frontier of Northwest Texas, 1846 to 1876: Advance and Defense by the Pioneer Settlers of the Cross Timbers and Prairies.* Glendale, Cal.: Arthur H. Clark, 1963.

Richmond Sentinel, June 11, 1864.

Roberts, Bobby L. "General T. C. Hindman and the Trans-Mississippi District." *Arkansas Historical Quarterly* 32 (1973): 297–311.

Roberts, O. M. "Texas." In *Confederate Military History*, Vol. XI. Edited by Clement A. Evans. Atlanta, Ga.: Confederate Publishing, 1899. Facsimile reprint. Secaucus, N.J.: Blue and Gray Press, 1974.

Roland, Charles P. *Albert Sidney Johnston: Soldier of Three Republics.* Austin, Tex.: University of Texas Press, 1964.

Roster and Record Book of the Thirty-Fifth Annual Reunion of Parsons' Brigade and the United Confederate Veterans, Midlothian, Texas, August 4–5, 1915. Uncataloged materials in the Nicholas P. Sims Library, Waxahachie, Tex.

Sawyer, William E., and Neal A. Baker, Jr., eds. "A Texan in the Civil War." *Texas Military History* 2 (1962): 275–78.

Sibley, Marilyn McAdams. *The Port of Houston: A History.* Austin, Tex.: University of Texas Press, 1968.

Smith, E. Kirby. "Red River Campaign, March 10 to May 22, 1864." In *The Confederate Soldier in the Civil War, 1861–1865*. Edited by Ben LaBree. Louisville, Ky.: Courier-Journal Job Printing, 1895.

Smith, Rebecca W., and Marion Mullins, eds. "Diary of H. C. Medford, Confederate Soldier, 1864." *Southwestern Historical Quarterly* 34 (1930): 106–40, 203–30.

Spindler, Frank M. "The History of Hempstead and the Formation of Waller County, Texas." *Southwestern Historical Quarterly* 63 (1960): 404–27.

Spurlin, Charles, ed. *West of the Mississippi with Waller's Thirteenth Texas Cavalry Battalion, CSA.* Hillsboro, Tex.: Hill Junior College Press, 1971.

Squires, Charles W. "My Artillery Fire Was Very Destructive." *Civil War Times Illustrated* 14 (June 1975): 18–28.

Taylor, Richard. *Destruction and Reconstruction.* Reprint. Edited by Charles P. Roland. Waltham, Mass.: Blaisdell, 1968.

Thomas, David Y. *Arkansas in War and Reconstruction, 1861–1874.* Little Rock: Arkansas Division, United Daughters of the Confederacy, 1926.

Tri-Weekly Telegraph (Houston), November 7, 1861–July 21, 1862.

United States Navy Department. *Official Records of the Union and Confederate Navies in the War of the Rebellion.* 30 vols. Washington, D.C.: Government Printing Office, 1911.

United States War Department. *The War of the Rebellion: A Compilation of the Official Records of the Union and Confederate Armies.* 70 vols. in 128. Washington, D.C.: Government Printing Office, 1880–1901.

Wallace, Ernest. *Texas in Turmoil.* Austin, Tex.: Steck-Vaughn, 1965.

Walton, Buck. *An Epitome of My Life: Civil War Reminiscences.* Austin, Tex.: Waterloo Press, 1965.

Waxahachie Daily Light. June 28, 1932; April 12–June 10, 1936; August 29, 1957; April 17, 1973; and miscellaneous, undated, uncataloged clippings believed to have been collected during the late nineteenth or early twentieth centuries. Nicholas P. Sims Library, Waxahachie, Tex.

Weddle, Robert S. *Plow-Horse Cavalry: The Caney Creek Boys of the Thirty-Fourth Texas.* Austin, Tex.: Madrona Press, 1974.

White, Frank E. "A History of the Territory That Now Constitutes Waller

County, Texas, from 1821 to 1884." Master's thesis, University of Texas, Austin, 1936.

White, William W. "The Texas Slave Insurrection of 1860." *Southwestern Historical Quarterly* 52 (1949): 259–85.

Wilmeth, James R., Reverend. Personal diary entitled "Thoughts and Things as They Occurred in Camp—A. D. 1864." Microfilm copy in the Abilene Christian University Library, Abilene, Tex.

Winsor, Bill. *Texas in the Confederacy: Military Installations, Economy, and People.* Hillsboro, Tex.: Hill Junior College Press, 1978.

Winters, John D. *The Civil War in Louisiana.* Baton Rouge, La.: Louisiana State University Press, 1963.

Wise, Joe R., ed. "The Letters of Lieutenant Flavius W. Perry, Seventeenth Texas Cavalry, 1862–1863," *Military History of Texas and the Southwest* 13.2 (1976): 11–15.

Wooster, Ralph A., and Robert Wooster. "'Rarin' for a Fight': Texans in the Confederate Army" *Southwestern Historical Quarterly* 84 (1981): 387–426.

Wooten, Dudley G., ed. *A Comprehensive History of Texas.* 2 vols. Dallas: William G. Scarff, 1898.

Wright, Marcus J., comp. *Texas in the War, 1861–1865.* Reprint. Edited by Harold B. Simpson. Hillsboro, Tex.: Hill Junior College Press, 1965.

Yeary, Mamie, comp. *Reminiscences of the Boys in Gray, 1861–1865.* Dallas: published for the compiler by Smith and Lamar Publishing, 1912.

Zuber, William P. *My Eighty Years in Texas.* Edited by Janis Boyle Mayfield. Austin, Tex.: University of Texas Press, 1971.

Index